Store choice, store location and market analysis

Store choice, store location and market analysis

Neil Wrigley

ROUTLEDGE
London and New York

First published in 1988 by
Routledge
11 New Fetter Lane, London EC4P 4EE

Published in the USA by
Routledge
in association with Routledge, Chapman & Hall Inc.
29 West 35th Street, New York, NY 10001

Set in 10/12pt Imprint
by Hope Services, Abingdon,
and printed in Great Britain
by T. J. Press (Padstow) Ltd,
Padstow, Cornwall.

Library of Congress Cataloging in Publication Data
Store choice, store location, and market analysis.
  Contributions made to the Workshop on Methods
of Retail Analysis and Forecasting held at the
University of Bristol in Feb. 1986 and sponsored
by the UK Economic and Social Research Council.
  Bibliography: p.
  Includes index.
  1. Retail trade—Congresses. 2. Retail trade—
Forecasting—Congresses. 3. Store location—
Congresses. 4. Consumers' preferences—Congresses.
I. Wrigley, Neil. II. Workshop on Methods of Retail
Analysis and Forecasting (1986 : University of Bristol)
III. Economic and Social Research Council (Great Britain)
HF5429.S76 1988 658.8'7 87–26304

British Library CIP Data also available
ISBN 0–415–00199–4

CONTENTS

TABLES

Tables ix

FIGURES

ACKNOWLEDGMENTS

The majority of the chapters in this volume are revised versions of contributions made to a Workshop on Methods of Retail Analysis and Forecasting held at the University of Bristol in 1986 and sponsored by the U.K. Economic and Social Research Council (ESRC). The Editor and Publishers wish to express their thanks to ESRC for its generous sponsorship of that Workshop.

The Editor and Publishers also wish to express their thanks to the following for permission to reproduce material from copyright works:

American marketing Association for Chapter 9 reprinted from *Journal of Marketing Research*, Vol. 21 (1984) p. 399–409.
Institute of British Geographers for Fig. 1.2 from Fig. 1, p. 149 (L. Sparks, 1986).
Dr G. Rowley for Fig. 1.1 from Fig. 1, p. 41 (G. Rowley, 1986).

THE EDITOR AND CONTRIBUTORS

Editor

Neil Wrigley is a Professor of Town Planning at the University of Wales Institute of Science and Technology, Cardiff; Britain's largest university urban planning school. He is also a Member of the Research Resources Advisory Group of the U.K. Economic and Social Research Council and Editor of *Transactions of the Institute of British Geographers*. At the time of the ESRC Workshop on Methods of Retail Analysis and Forecasting, at which the majority of papers in this volume were presented, he was Reader in Geography at the University of Bristol and had just completed a major ESRC-funded research programme concerned with the development and testing of a new generation of models of store choice and market analysis.

Contributors

John Bates is a freelance U.K. transport planning consultant
John Beaumont is ICL Professor of Applied Management Information Systems at the University of Stirling and was previously Joint Managing Director of Pinpoint Analysis Ltd, London
Michael Breheny is Lecturer in Geography at the University of Reading
David Broom is a Senior Retail Consultant at CACI Market Analysis, London
Richard Dunn is Lecturer in Geography at the University of Bristol

Andrew Ehrenberg is WCM Professor of Marketing and Com-
munication at the London Business School
Stewart Fotheringham is Associate Professor of Geography at the
University of Florida
Cliff Guy is Lecturer in Town Planning at the University of Wales
Institute of Science and Technology, Cardiff
Clive Humby is Chief Executive of CACI Market Analysis,
London
Kau A Keng is Senior Lecturer, School of Management, National
University of Singapore
Laurence Moore holds an ESRC CASS Award Research Student-
ship at the Department of Town Planning, University of Wales
Institute of Science and Technology and The MVA Consultancy,
London
Nick Penny is Head of the Tesco Stores Research Unit and an
Associate Director of Tesco PLC
Mark Uncles is a Research Fellow at the Centre of Marketing and
Communication, London Business School
Alan Wilson is Professor of Geography at the University of Leeds

Addresses

J. J. Bates: John Bates Services, The Old Coach House, Wyke,
Gillingham, Dorset, U.K.
J. R. Beaumont: Business School, University of Stirling,
Stirling, FK9 4LA, U.K.
M. J. Breheny: Department of Geography, University of
Reading, Reading, RG6 2AB, U.K.
D. Broom: CACI Market Analysis, 59/62 High Holborn,
London, WC1V 6DX, U.K.
R. Dunn: Department of Geography, University of Bristol,
Bristol, BS8 1SS, U.K.
A. S. C. Ehrenberg: London Business School, Sussex Place,
Regents Park, London, NW1 4SA, U.K.
A. S. Fotheringham: Department of Geography, University of
Florida, Gainesville, Florida, 32611, U.S.A.
C. M. Guy: Department of Town Planning, UWIST, Colum
Drive, Cardiff, CF1 3EU, U.K.
C. Humby: CACI Market Analysis, 59/62 High Holborn,
London, WC1V 6DX, U.K.

Kau A. Keng: School of Management, National University of Singapore, Singapore

L. A. R. Moore: Department of Town Planning, UWIST, Colum Drive, Cardiff, CF1 3EU, U.K.

N. J. Penny: Research Unit, Tesco PLC, Dairyglen House, P.O. Box 40, 116 Crossbrook Street, Cheshunt, Waltham Cross, Herts, U.K.

M. D. Uncles: Centre of Marketing and Communication, London Business School, Sussex Place, Regents Park, London, NW1 4SA, U.K.

A. G. Wilson: School of Geography, University of Leeds, Leeds, LS2 9JT, U.K.

N. Wrigley: Department of Town Planning, UWIST, Colum Drive, Cardiff, CF1 3EU, U.K.

PART 1 The Context

CHAPTER 1
Retail restructuring and retail analysis

Neil Wrigley

Introduction

This book presents, with just two exceptions, the contributions made to a workshop on 'Methods of retail analysis and forecasting' held at the University of Bristol, in February 1986, and sponsored by the UK Economic and Social Research Council. The purpose of the workshop was to bring together researchers from both academic institutions and commercial firms to discuss techniques of analysis and forecasting in the fields of store choice, store location, store performance assessment, and market analysis. Its rationale lay in the major restructuring of the UK retailing industry which has taken place over the past twenty years, and in the profound implications of that restructuring for the nature and organisation of the research which is necessary to understand, maintain or enhance corporate profitability. These concerns informed the wide-ranging discussion which took place at the workshop, and they provide a common, but often implicit, agenda for all the chapters in this book. To capture some of this common agenda, and to place the individual chapters into a wider context, this introduction will consider, first, the nature of the retail restructuring in the UK and, second, the research imperatives which this restructuring implies for the techniques of retail analysis and forecasting used in the commercial sector.

Retail restructuring in the UK

As many commentators on the collapse of the traditional manufacturing base of the UK economy have been at pains to point out, capitalism is a system which requires the continual restructuring of the accumulation process. There are few clearer examples of what Harvey (1985, p. 25) has referred to as the 'perpetual struggle in which capital builds a physical landscape appropriate to its own condition at a particular moment in time, only to have to destroy it . . . at a subsequent point in time' than the retailing industry. Indeed, as the British economy has shifted from an industrial to a post-industrial phase, and the service sector overall has expanded to employ more than 65 per cent of the workforce, so the British retailing industry has undergone a major organisational and spatial restructuring which has contributed significantly to the transformation of the urban landscape.

Some of the key elements of this restructuring process are best understood in the context of specific sections of the industry and, below, we take as examples grocery retailing and the DIY/home improvement trade. However, there are several recurrent themes which can be treated, at least initially, in general terms. Of these, four stand out.

The concentration of the capital

In the post-war period, the number of retail outlets in Britain has fallen by 40 per cent, from 583,000 in 1950 to just 342,000 in 1984, with most of this fall occurring since the late 1960s. Yet this decline has taken place against the background of an increase in the real volume of retail sales; from £40.6 billion in 1950 to £57.4 billion in 1982, when measured in constant 1980 prices (Institute of Fiscal Studies, 1984). There have been two major results of these trends: first, a significant rise in the average size of stores: and, second, a marked increase in the concentration of capital.

Large corporate chains (those operating ten or more branches) have more than doubled their share of total retail sales, from 22 per cent in 1950 to 56 per cent by 1982, and they have captured this trade at the expense of single-outlet retailers and smaller corporate chains. Within this large-chain category, it is the biggest firms which have grown most rapidly. Those retail groups with 100 or more outlets accounted for 37 per cent of a total GB retail turnover of £69,784 million in 1982, and the ten largest groups alone accounted for no less than £15,356 million or 22 per cent of turnover. Moreover, these overall figures mask even greater degrees of concentration, and more rapid increases in concentration over time, within particular sectors of the industry. A particularly good example of this is grocery retailing where, by 1982, out of a total retail food market worth about £25,000 million, the largest five trading groups alone accounted for almost 43 per cent of sales. This example will be discussed in more detail below. At this stage it is sufficient to note that the trend towards concentration has been exacerbated by the capital requirements of investment in new larger stores, often on new sites, and by the capital requirements associated with investment in technological change both within stores and within organisations.

The concentration of capital in the industry has resulted in the emergence of a group of what might be termed *retail corporations*, with profit levels, employment levels, and sheer market and political power sufficient to rival the traditional giants of UK manufacturing industry. Moreover, the relative importance of these retail corporations within the UK economy has increased progressively during the recession of 1979–83 and the slow recovery in employment since 1983; a period which has seen the decline or collapse of many traditional manufacturing corporations but has left the emerging retail corporations largely untouched. (A good example of this can be obtained by comparing the manufacturing corporation GKN, which employed 69,000 workers in 1979 but only 23,000 in 1986, with the retail corporation J. Sainsbury, which increased its workforce from 35,000 to 64,000 during the same period.)

Several of the retail corporations either did not exist or were just tiny organisations in the early 1960s. Some have grown by a process of takeover and merger (the Dee Corporation is a good example) but several have grown by a most remarkable and sustained rate of organic expansion. Classic examples in this latter category are Sainsbury, which, on a turnover of £3,575 million and a profit level of £208 million in the year to March 1986, had increased its profits by over 20 per cent per annum for each of the last seven years, and Kwik Save, which achieved an average annual pre-tax profits growth of 24 per cent in the ten years to 1986.

The emergence of these retail corporations has also led to a fundamental shift in the balance of power between retailers and their suppliers (manufacturing companies/producers) which has almost completely reversed the balance typical in the inter-war years and 1950s. The inter-war years in Britain saw the growth of large-scale manufacturers supplying the retail trade, together with a rapid increase in the practice of branding goods and developing trade-marks. This, in turn, led to a growth in the importance of the identity of the manufacturer of the product and, via resale price maintenance (RPM), manufacturers were able to control the final retail selling prices of many of their goods. Indeed, by 1938 the proportion of consumer spending on goods subject to RPM had risen to 38 per cent. This situation, which helped to sustain the single-outlet independents and the relative power of the manufacturers *vis-à-vis* the retailers, continued into the 1950s. However, in the late 1950s and early 1960s RPM came under increasing pressure and was ultimately abolished in 1965. This gave the larger retail firms the freedom to set their own prices for the goods they sold, and the ability to pass on their lower operating costs to the consumer. It coincided with, and was partly a mechanism within, the expansion on the market share of the large corporate chains and the decline of the single-outlet independents; together, these trends led to a fundamental shift in the balance of power in the industry *towards* the rapidly expanding retail corporations and *away from* the manufacturers. By the early 1980s many retail corporations were much larger and more profitable organisations than even their largest suppliers, and the shift in power had progressed so far that the typical debates concerning the power relationship between manufacturers and retailers centred upon such issues as: the 'discriminatory' discounts demanded from manufacturers by the large retail corporations; the intense pressure being placed upon manufacturer's second- and third-ranking brands by the growth of 'own-label' trading; the much smaller display space being given to branded products than to 'own-labels'; and the flexing of retailer muscle in the field of distribution from suppliers to stores (see Davies, Gilligan and Sutton, 1986; Sparks, 1986).

The intensification of production

Alongside the concentration of capital in UK retailing has come a marked increase in the productivity of labour. However, as Table 1.1. shows, this increase is masked if just total numbers employed in retailing are considered. The retailing industry employs a large number of part-time workers and, therefore, a more sensitive measure of labour input is obtained by converting total numbers to full-time equivalents (where a FTE is defined as 39 hours or more per week). FTEs show a significant decrease since 1950, paralleled by a marked and continuous increase in labour productivity.

Table 1.1 Employment and labour productivity in retailing in Great Britain

	Numbers engaged in retailing		Labour productivity (sales per FTE)
	Total (000s)	FTE (000s)	(£000s)
1950	2,392.2	n.a.	n.a.
1957	2,529.6	2,158.2	24.01
1961	2,484.6	2,158.8	25.78
1966	2,555.7	2,138.2	27.44
1971	2,541.4	1,995.4	31.36
1976	2,503.4	1,897.0	36.62
1977	2,441.7	n.a.	n.a.
1978	2,424.0	n.a.	n.a.
1979	2,429.0	n.a.	n.a.
1980	2,368.0	1,780.0	39.92
1982	2,202.0	1,680.0	40.66

Sources: Census of Distribution, Retailing Inquiries, IFS.
Note: Labour productivity measured by retail sales revalued by the Retail Prices Index to 1982 prices and divided by FTEs (full-time equivalents).

Once again it is the biggest firms, the emerging retail corporations, that have achieved the highest levels and most marked increases in productivity. Moreover, there is little sign that such increases are levelling off. The 1980s have seen massive investment by the retail corporations in computerised stock, distribution, and financial control systems and this has already resulted in some corporations reporting their biggest gains in productivity for many years (e.g. in 1985–6 Sainsbury reported productivity at a record level and the best annual improvement for seven years). With the advent of advanced management information systems built upon the data supplied by EPOS (electronic point of sales) cash tills with scanners, further high-technology based labour-shedding by the corporations is inevitable.

Paralleling the increase in labour productivity, and as a direct consequence of the changing structure of the retailing industry and the nature of retail outlets, there has been a progressive de-skilling of the labour force. In the large self-service high-tech retail outlets of the 1980s, few staff are required to offer personal service to consumers or to have a specialised knowledge of the products they are selling. Instead a large proportion of retail labour is required for the relatively unskilled tasks of shelf-filling or till operation, and must be matched to periods of peak demand. The consequence has been a rapid increase in the proportion of retailing employees who are part-time, and a polarisation of the labour force into two very distinct skill-level groups.

The increase in the proportion of part-time workers is seen most clearly in the case of female employees. In 1957, 60 per cent of the workforce in retailing were female: 41 per cent full-time and 19 per cent part-time. By 1983, however, the part-time proportion had doubled and the 66 per cent of the workforce who were female, divided into 27 per cent full-time and 39 per cent part-time. Although changes in National Insurance, taxation, and employment legislation over this period have encouraged the use of part-time labour, the key to understanding this dramatic increase lies in the change in the nature of retail outlets, and the flexibility offered by part-time labour to meet fluctuations in demand over the week.

Increasingly, the retailing labour force has been polarised into two groups. The first group consists of a relatively small number of highly skilled and hierarchically-graded central and line managers, together with similarly skilled head office workers controlling such things as stock, distribution, finance, personnel, advertising, new store development and so on. The second group consists of a much larger number of single-grade, unskilled, and often part-time workers, who together account for almost 75 per cent of the workforce. The result is that employment statistics which relate to retailing as a whole are dominated by the second group and show that retail workers have lower general educational qualifications, lower expenditure per employee on in-service training, higher turnover, and earnings which are below the average for the economy as a whole.

The spatial switching of capital

Another trend which has accompanied the concentration of capital in UK retailing has been a significant, and in recent years increasingly rapid, switching of capital out of traditional central city shopping areas. In this respect, retailing is merely following an earlier movement of population and employment out of what Hall *et al.* (1973), Drewett *et al.* (1975; 1976) and Goddard and Champion (1983) refer to as the 'urban core' areas of Britain. As Table 1.2 shows, whereas the 1950s saw slight growth of population and employment in the urban cores, the 1960s witnessed a complete reversal, with large-scale decentralisation of almost 0.75 million people and 0.5 million jobs from the urban cores into the metropolitan rings and outer metropolitan rings. This decentralisation was even more pronounced in the seven largest cities. As Table 1.3 shows, the urban cores of these cities

Table 1.2 Population and employment change by urban zone 1951–61, 1961–71 and 1971–4

| | Population change 1951–61 | | 1961–71 | | 1971–4 | |
	Absolute (000s)	Relative %	Absolute (000s)	Relative %	Absolute (000s)	Relative %
Urban cores	+ 486	+ 1.9	− 729	− 2.8	− 459	− 1.8
Metropolitan rings	+ 1,721	+ 13.3	+ 2,512	+ 17.2	+ 442	+ 2.6
Outer metropolitan rings	+ 245	+ 3.1	+ 786	+ 9.8	+ 292	+ 3.2

| | Employment change 1951–61 | | 1961–71 | |
	Absolute (000s)	Relative %	Absolute (000s)	Relative %
Urban Cores	+ 902	+ 6.7	− 439	− 3.1
Metropolitan rings	+ 239	+ 6.6	+ 707	+ 15.0
Outer metropolitan rings	− 14	− 0.4	+ 130	+ 3.9

Adapted from Drewett *et al.* (1976) and Kennett and Spence (1979).

Table 1.3   Absolute and relative population and employment change, 1961–71, in the urban cores of the seven largest cities in Britain

| | Population change | | Employment change | |
	Absolute (000s)	Relative (%)	Absolute (000s)	Relative (%)
London	− 554	− 9.5	− 386	− 10.1
Birmingham	− 89	− 4.7	− 66	− 6.2
Manchester	− 165	− 11.9	− 110	− 14.0
Glasgow	− 161	− 12.4	− 97	− 15.3
Liverpool	− 140	− 13.7	− 69	− 13.2
Leeds	− 18	− 2.1	− 38	− 8.4
Newcastle	− 71	− 10.8	− 27	− 7.8

Adapted from Spence and Goddard (1976).

together lost almost 1.2 million people and 0.8 million jobs between 1961 and 1971, and evidence from the 1981 Census shows that the decentralisation continued throughout the 1970s. Moreover, the population decentralisation has not been uniform across social classes and age groups, but has resulted in a differential shift of the younger and more affluent to the metropolitan and outer metropolitan rings. For example, Pinch and Williams (1983) have estimated that, between 1961 and 1971, in the urban cores of the seven largest cities there was an 18.9 per cent decrease in professional and managerial socio-economic groups relative to the national average change for these groups. In contrast, in the outer rings of the largest cities there was a 15.9 per cent increase in these socio-economic groups relative to the same national average.

The implication of these absolute and differential population and employment losses has been a major loss of retail demand from the urban core areas, and the creation of large, relatively under-provided, concentrations of demand in the suburban, outer suburban, and urban fringe areas of Britain. Moreover, this outer-city demand has become increasingly mobile, as car owner-ship in Britain has risen from 2.25 million cars in 1950 to 15.25 million in 1981 and has been differentially concentrated into the outer areas. Retail capital has inevitably wished to shift outwards to meet this under-supplied demand and to exploit the opportunities presented for newer, larger, and more profitable forms of retail operation. However, until the mid-1970s, large-scale retail decentralisation in Britain was significantly retarded by planning authority regulation.

In the 1960s and early 1970s, planning policy offered protection to inner-city, particularly city-centre, retailing. The aims of such policy, although never clearly formulated, appear to have been threefold: first, to avoid the worst features of the retail decline in central cities experienced in North America; second, to encourage the renewal of the infrastructure of the city centres; and third, to protect the shopping opportunities of the 'transport poor' of the inner cities. Nevertheless, despite its lack of clarity, planning control of retail decentralisation was extremely effective. Whereas, between 1965 and 1977, major city-centre retail development schemes exceeding 50,000 ft^2 (4,650 metres^2) occurred in no less than 68 per cent of cities in England and Wales with central area sales of over £10 million in 1971, and in 88 per cent of cities with central area sales of over £25 million (Schiller and Lambert, 1977), the development of 'out-of-centre' superstores, hypermarkets or new larger-scale shopping centres was extremely limited. Indeed, by 1976 Britain lagged far behind Western Europe and North America in such development. At that time only one large-scale, 'free-standing' regional shopping centre had been developed (Brent Cross in North London opened in 1976) and there were only twenty-two 'out-of-centre' hypermarkets of more than 5,000 metres^2 in existence (URPI, 1982) perhaps only four of which met a stricter definition of hypermarket status proposed by Dawson and Kirby (1980). In contrast, in the same year, West Germany had 538 hypermarkets which met the stricter definition and France had 305.

Because the Department of the Environment had the power to call in for detailed consideration all proposals for new suburban retail developments in excess of 50,000 ft^2, a trend towards the building of slightly smaller 'superstores' (between 2,500 and 5,000 metres^2) and district shopping centres developed. However, as Figure 1.1 shows, taking both 'out-of-centre' food-based hypermarkets (greater than 5,000 metres^2) and superstores together, there were less than 100 in 1976. In addition, as shown in Table 1.4 (which uses 25,000 ft^2 or 2,325 metres^2 as the basis for defining superstores), there were approximately fifty electrical-goods-based superstores. Together, all these food-based and non-

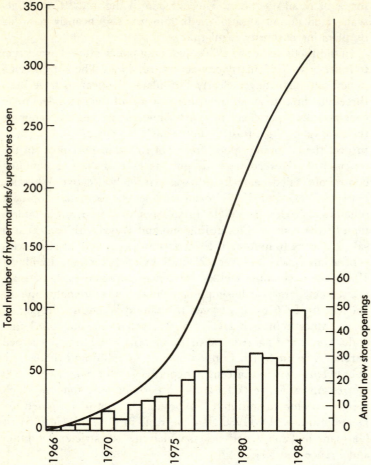

Figure 1.1 UK hypermarkets and superstores opening, 1966–84. (*Source*: Rowley, 1986)

food-based hypermarkets and superstores accounted for just 1.5–2 per cent of total retail sales.

In the late 1970s, however, there was a gradual softening of planning regulation *vis-à-vis* retail decentralisation, and the annual rate of new superstore openings rose significantly. There were a number of reasons for this softening of policy. First, the out-of-centre superstores which had been allowed to open in the early 1970s had been shown to have a less disastrous impact upon the existing retail structure, particularly central-city shopping areas, than had first been feared. Second, planners increasingly recognised that superstore-based district shopping-centre development could be exploited as a positive tool in urban infrastructure renewal. Third, as Britain moved into a period of severe recession in its manufacturing industry, the ability to attract new service-industry investment and employment became more and more important to metropolitan local authorities suffering from high rates of unemployment.

The trends of the late 1970s continued into the 1980s, and by the end of 1984 there were more than 300 out-of-centre food-based superstores and hypermarkets in Britain. In addition, as Table 1.4 demonstrates, there had been a truly remarkable increase in the number of out-of-centre non-food (electrical, DIY, furniture, etc.)-based superstores. As will be seen below, the late 1970s and early 1980s were the years of the great expansion of the out-of-centre DIY retail warehouses, and this rapid expansion of retail warehouses proved to be much more difficult to control using existing planning regulations (even in

Table 1.4   The growth of out-of-centre retail sales in superstores in Great Britain, 1975–95

Product category	1975 Stores	Sales (£m)	1984 Stores	Sales (£m)	1995* Stores	Sales (£m)
Food-based	100	400	350	3,000+	800	6,000
Electrical	50	50	150	300	250	600
DIY	—	—	520	800+	1,000	1,500
Furniture	—	—	250	550	400	1,000
Garden centres	—	—	170	170	200	200
Car parts	—	—	—	—	100	100
Toys	—	—	—	—	100	100
Other	—	—	—	—	250	500
Total	150	450	1,440	4,820	3,100	10,000
% of total retail sales	1.5%		6.7%		12.0%	

Adapted from Management Horizons, 1986.
* Estimates at 1984 prices.

those cities in which a real desire existed to do so) than had been the case with the hypermarket proposals of the early 1970s. By 1984, the total number of out-of-centre superstores/hypermarkets of all types had increased more than ten-fold since the mid-1970s and, together, they now accounted for 6.7 per cent of total retail sales. However, there still remained only one large-scale 'free-standing' regional shopping-centre development in the whole of Britain – that at Brent Cross.

As Figure 1.1 demonstrates, many commentators were by 1984 forecasting a further period of major growth in the number of out-of-centre retail developments in the mid- to late-1980s, and Table 1.4 suggests a further doubling of the number of superstores/hypermarkets to approximately 3,100 by 1995, and a virtual doubling of out-of-centre retail sales to 12 per cent. Early indications suggest that this forecast is likely to be borne out and, perhaps, exceeded. In fact Hillier Parker (1986) has recently shown that the amount of retail development in the pipeline, having remained fairly stable between 1980 and 1984, increased rapidly in 1985 and again in 1986. Compared to the 1980–4 annual average of about 19 million ft^2 of retail development under construction or with firm planning consent and 10–15 million ft^2 of proposed development, in March 1986 there was 31 million ft^2 under construction or with firm planning consent and 32 million ft^2 of proposed development. Of this, out-of-centre development accounted for almost 30 per cent (9 million ft^2) of that under construction or with firm planning consent, and 51 per cent (16 million ft^2) of that proposed. More remarkably still, between March and June 1986 a further 15 million ft^2 of retail development was proposed, of which no less than 80 per cent was for out-of-centre development. Although many of these proposal schemes may never be built, they nevertheless indicate an extremely rapid increase in market activity, give a broad indication of future construction levels, and confirm the market swing to out-of-centre retail development. Moreover, the Hillier Parker figures demonstrate that, after a ten-year gap, a new phase of North-American-style, large-scale, out-of-centre regional shopping developments will soon be added to the one at Brent Cross, the one existing example in the UK. In March 1986, two such centres with a combined floorspace of 2.1 million ft^2 were under construction, two more with a combined floorspace of 2.5 million ft^2 had firm planning permission, and a further thirteen regional centres which together would add more than 11.6 million ft^2 of retailing were proposed. The first of these centres to open will be the £110 million Metro Centre built in the Gateshead Enterprise Zone (south of the existing Newcastle-upon-Tyne central area) to allow the developer to take advantage of 100 per cent capital allowances.

Technological change

As noted above, significant increases in labour productivity have accompanied the concentration of capital in UK retailing. These increases have been achieved by an ever-quickening rate of technical change within the industry, demanding in its turn ever larger capital investment.

In the early 1950s the normal method of trading in British retailing was via 'counter sales' in which items were collected and wrapped for the customer by the shop assistant. Self-service was a virtually unknown trading method in many parts of the UK, and in grocery retailing for example there were just 600 retail outlets which could be classified as 'self-service' in the whole of the country, accounting for just 1.4 per cent of sales (Tounsey, 1964). From this base, the first major post-war period of technical change and investment in British retailing saw a rapid change in trading methods (from counter-service to self-service) but little increase in average store size. The change came first to grocery retailing but soon spread to most other types of retailing. The fastest period of switch-over occurred in the late 1950s and early 1960s. For example, by 1960 the number of retail grocery outlets which could be classified as self-service had grown more than ten-fold to 7,100, and by 1964 the number had doubled again to 15,680, accounting for approximately 35 per cent of sales. By 1969 the number of such outlets had almost doubled again to 28,062 (Institute of Fiscal Studies, 1984; *Institute of Grocery Distribution Food Statistics Digest*, 1984).

In the early to mid-1960s a second major period of technical change and investment began. This involved the development of larger stores able to take advantage of economies of scale and to continue the process of substitution of capital for labour begun in the 1950s. Again, grocery retailers, particularly the newly emerging corporations (Tesco, Asda, Sainsbury, etc.) led the way. Whereas in 1958 only 175 British grocery outlets were over 2,000 ft^2 in size, by 1971 this number had risen to 5,000. Reflecting this increase in average store size, average turnover per grocery outlet (measured in constant prices) rose by more than 50 per cent between 1961 and 1971, and labour productivity increased by more than 20 per cent. This trend towards larger average store size continued in the 1970s and 1980s and was particularly noticeable in the operations of the large retail corporations. For example, Figure 1.2 shows a continuous rise in the average size of Tesco stores from just over 4,000 ft^2 in 1972 to almost 17,000 ft^2 by 1985, and the ten-fold increase in the number of food-based and non-food based superstores of more than 25,000 ft^2 between 1975 and 1984 has already been discussed. The capital investment requirements of the large superstores which have been built in the late 1970s and 1980s are enormous. For example, in opening just fifteen new superstores with an average size of 27,000 ft^2 in 1985–6, Sainsbury's spent £187 million on site acquisition and store construction/development.

Overlaid on this trend towards increased store size, the 1980s have witnessed a third major phase of technical change and invest-

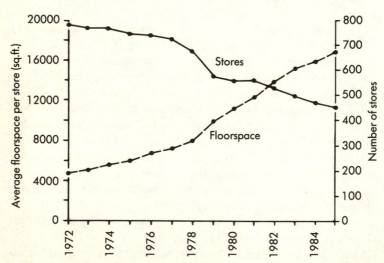

Figure 1.2 Changes in number of stores and average floorspace of Tesco stores, 1972–85. (*Source*: Sparks, 1986.)

ment in the industry. This has involved the introduction of computerised information technology in stock control, distribution management, and financial control systems. All these areas are critical to the profitability of retail firms, and together they offer the key to the increases in labour productivity which are being forecast or achieved in the mid-1980s.

As average store size increased and large retail corporations developed and expanded in the 1960s and 1970s, so the need for more sophisticated systems of stock control, both within individual stores and within parent organisations, became more critical. Once again, it was the new-style grocery retailers, dependent upon fast stock turnover on low margins to achieve high profits, who led the way. First, they experimented with new ways of using warehouse and sales space to its maximum efficiency. By moving over to mechanised handling, palletisation of stock, vertical stacking in warehouse areas and, sometimes, caging and pallets on the sales floor, firms such as Asda were able to reduce the ratio of warehouse-space to sales-space required, from 50:50 in 1974 to 20:80 in 1979 (Davies and Sparks, 1986). Second, several of the corporations began to restructure their distribution systems, replacing the old, direct manufacturer/supplier-to-store method with a centralised in-house distribution system. Tesco provides a very good example of this trend (see Sparks, 1986). From a distribution system in 1972 in which less than 20 per cent of goods sold at Tesco stores were supplied by their in-house delivery system, they had moved over by 1984 to a centrally controlled and operated system delivering almost 80 per cent of the needs of their stores. In so doing, Tesco moved from a system in which it was impossible to standardise delivery lead-times and impose service-level controls to a system which used common handling systems and could guarantee deliveries within a lead-time of a maximum of 48 hours (only 24 hours on many products). This further reduced the amount of stock which needed to be held at the store and the critical warehouse-space/sales-space ratio. Another example is the Dee Corporation which in 1986 reported that it had cut out 2 million miles of haulage by moving over to an integrated delivery system.

The centrally-controlled distribution networks and stock control systems now used by the retail corporations have provided fertile ground for the introduction of computer-based information technology. Initially, these computer systems were confined to particular areas of activity and did not attempt to link the sales, stock control/distribution and administration functions together into an integrated management information system. Good examples of these limited function systems are provided by Tesco's Dallas system which monitors stock levels and precise within-warehouse location of items, and which optimises stockholding and delivery patterns throughout the store network (Sparks, 1986), and by the automated invoice-matching/accounting system introduced by International Stores (Dee Corporation) which allowed the number of staff required for the function to be reduced from 300 to 120 between 1982 and 1985, despite increased volume (Norkett, 1985). However, there are now several indications that integrated management information systems may shortly be introduced by several of the major corporations. These systems (as Figure 1.3 shows) will be built upon EPOS laser-scanning/laser-wand cash tills reading bar-coded products. These tills will link to in-store or central computers creating a direct link between the sales area, the warehouse/distribution network and central administration. With a full EPOS system, as goods are purchased by the consumer, within-store stock levels are adjusted, orders for deliveries are made automatically, goods are made ready for despatch from automated warehouses, fresh supplies to the warehouses are requested, and invoices are matched and paid by an automated accounting system. Moreover, up-to-date sales information is available on-line to management, and sales can be analysed line by line, store by store, region by region, and informed decisions regarding shelf allocation, stocking policy, product promotion, new store location strategy, etc., can be taken. Indeed, very advanced management information systems can be built upon EPOS, and as some parts of existing administration systems become increasingly homeostatic, retailers will seek to achieve productivity rises by significant reductions in the numbers of junior administrative staff.

How far away the era of such EPOS-based, integrated information systems is in British retailing is as yet uncertain. However, most of the major retail corporations are now spending large sums on EPOS equipment (e.g. Sainsbury's recently placed a £20 million order with ICL – see Bird, 1985) and ICL estimate that the number of EPOS terminals used in British retailing will

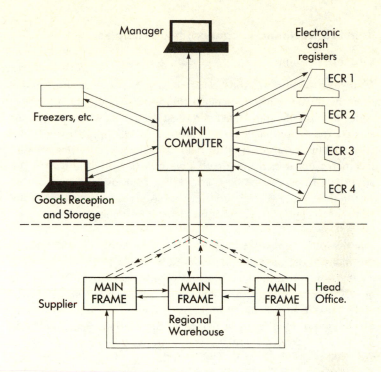

Figure 1.3 An EPOS management information system. (*Source*: Guy, this volume.)

have risen from 21,000 in 1984 to 244,000 by 1990. Moreover, the confidence of retailers in such systems has increased following the introduction of a successful prototype linking the 800 stores of Victoria Wine Company in 1984 (see *Retail and Distribution Management*, 1984), and the Tradanet system which allows electronic exchange of information between manufacturers, distributors and retailers, thus cutting out large quantities of paperwork (*Retail and Distribution Management*, 1985a). EFTPOS (electronic funds transfer at point of sale)-based systems appear to be much further away (see Guy, this volume) but potentially such systems offer retailers major opportunities to improve their working capital cycle still further.

Retail restructuring in context: two examples

Grocery retailing

It is this section of the industry which provides the classic example of many of the general themes discussed above: where concentration of capital has been most dramatic; where power has shifted most obviously from manufacturer/supplier to retailer; where labour productivity has been transformed; where store size has increased most dramatically; which is leading the way in the adoption of new technology; and so on. Moreover, it is from this sector that many of the retail corporations which now rival the status of the largest UK manufacturing companies have emerged.

The rise of the large corporations   From a situation in 1950 where the many thousands of independent single-outlet grocers, small chains, and consumer cooperatives together took over 78 per cent of UK grocery sales, grocery retailing has been transformed. By 1984 these traditionally dominant elements accounted for only 30 per cent of sales and just five retail corporations (listed in Table 1.5) which barely existed in 1950 took over 43 per cent of total grocery sales. By early 1987, following Dee Corporation's acquisition of Fine Fare, and Argyll Group's acquisition of Safeway, the top five corporations had captured a remarkable 52.3 per cent of grocery sales, and they now flex their corporate muscle to enormous effect in the UK economy.

What these emerging corporations have all done, to a greater or lesser effect, has been to understand the key principle in grocery retailing – that profits result from volume rather than margins, and that huge profits and positive net cash flows result from high volume and fast stock turnover on low margins. As Table 1.6 indicates, median stock turnover for the industry has fallen consistently, e.g. from 29.2 days in 1979 to 26.6 days in 1983. However, the most efficient corporations (in the upper quartile) can turn over their stocks much more quickly – every 18 days in 1983 compared to 37 days for retailers in the lower quartile. As a result, with an average credit period of around 40 days from their suppliers, and with cash sales, this gives the most efficient corporations a negative working capital cycle of up to 22 days (see Norkett, 1985). By understanding the management of working

Table 1.5   Sales and profits of the top five grocery retailing corporations in 1986

	Total sales† (£ million)	Pre-tax profits (£ million)	Approx. grocery market share (%)	Net margin (%)
Sainsbury	3,414	195	12.3	5.71
Tesco	3,355	131	12.0	3.91
Dee Corporation*	4,008	127	11.8	3.16
Argyll Group**	1,819	65	9.0	3.55
Asda***	1,933	103	7.2	5.33

Sources: company reports.
† Exclusive of VAT
   * Dee Corporation sales and profits include those of the Fine Fare Stores chain acquired in the summer of 1986.
   ** Argyll Group's sales and profits for 1986 do *not* take account of the Safeway chain acquired early in 1987.
*** Asda results refer just to Asda Stores, the grocery retailing part of the Asda/MFI group.
Behind these five large corporations come Kwik Save with approximately 2.7 per cent of the market (sales of £783 million and profits of £42 million in 1986), Waitrose with 2.3 per cent of the market, Bejam with 1.8 per cent, Morrison with 1.4 per cent, and Hillard with 1 per cent.

capital, and by the use of efficient management systems (the integrated financial control, distribution/stock control systems discussed above), several of these corporations have been able to turn this advantage into a position where they pay very little interest in relation to their profits. Coupled with their huge positive net cash flows, this then enables them to invest very large sums in their store expansion programmes, building large,

Table 1.6   Stock turnover and net margins in UK food retailing

	Quartile	1979	1981	1983
Stock turnover (days)	Upper	21.1	18.5	17.6
	Median	29.2	29.0	26.6
	Lower	39.7	39.2	37.2
Net margin %	Upper	3.8	3.2	3.1
	Median	2.0	1.4	1.8
	Lower	0.8	0.4	0.5

Source: Norkett, 1985.

highly-efficient superstores, which use the latest technology, on freehold sites. In its turn, this investment and the increased efficiency/labour-productivity which accompanies it allows them to raise their net margins above the level for the industry as a whole (e.g. compare Sainsbury's 5 per cent plus margin in 1985–6 with the industry median of only 1.8 per cent in 1983). Very soon the virtuous cycle becomes self reinforcing, and it is this which is the key to understanding the rapid rise to power of the large corporations.

The store expansion programme is a vital component within this virtuous cycle. In particular, the substantial *annual* increases in turnover and profit which the Stock Market has come to expect from the major grocery corporations are heavily dependent upon the expansion programmes. For example, of the 13.8 per cent increase in turnover reported by Kwik Save in the half year to March 1986, 2.3 per cent was attributable to inflation but no less than 7.8 per cent (i.e. 68 per cent of the net increase) was attributable to the new stores opened within the previous twelve months. In contrast, Asda only managed to open four new superstores in the full year to May 1986, and so the growth in Asda's turnover slowed significantly to only 11.4 per cent over the year, pre-tax profits rose by only £8.2 million (5.2 per cent), and the Stock Market began to express doubts about the performance of the corporation.

It is for these reasons that site acquisition and store location research have, in the 1980s, became such vital ingredients in the enhancement of corporate profitability (see next section on pages 30–3), and that the costs of site acquisition have soared. Moreover, the increase in these latter costs has been compounded by the intense competition which has developed between the major corporations for key sites. The reasons for this competition are two-fold. First, the areas of expansion of the major corporations have increasingly intermeshed as they have moved outwards from their traditional core areas. For example, Asda has expanded southwards from its core in the northern metropolitan areas (it was completely unrepresented in the South East, South West, London and East Anglia until the late 1970s), whilst, at the same time, Sainsbury has expanded northwards and westwards from its core in the South East. Second, because in the 1970s some of the corporations adopted the out-of-centre superstore/hypermarket format more quickly than others, a marked regional differential in the density of grocery superstores had emerged by the early 1980s. As Table 1.7 indicates, London and the South East were relatively underprovided with food-based superstores, yet these are the prosperous boom areas of recession-hit Britain, the very areas where the potential rewards to the grocery corporations are at their greatest, and where general competition from other commercial, industrial, and residential developers is at its most intense, further fuelling the rise in site acquisition costs. The result is that individual key sites can fetch extraordinary sums (e.g. Asda paid £20 million, between £2 million and £3 million per acre, for one site in Watford in 1985), the £150–200 million annual site acquisition and store development budgets of corporations such as Sainsbury, Tesco and Asda in 1985–6 do not go very far, and new store location decisions become critical.

Table 1.7   Regional differences in the density of food-based superstores in 1985

Region	Food-based superstores per 1 million population
West Yorkshire	13.6
Greater Manchester	8.8
South East	2.9
Greater London	2.8

Sources: Management Horizons, 1986; Collins and Mughal, 1985.

Capital concentration in the small-store sector   Despite the dominance of the large corporations, current trends in the restructuring of the grocery retailing industry are not to be understood entirely in terms of the top five or ten corporations. The emergence of out-of-centre superstore/hypermarket trading has been largely at the expense of the intermediate-size 'high street' supermarkets developed in the 1960s and early 1970s rather than the small convenience store and, therefore, restructuring has tended to polarise activity into the two ends of the size spectrum (Kirby, 1986). Small stores have increasingly seen a window of opportunity open to them, in which they can trade upon their convenience (nearness, long opening hours, etc.) and can make a profit based upon serving the 'top-up' and/or specialised grocery requirements of consumers. However, because the fortunes of the largest grocery corporations have increasingly been identified with their out-of-centre superstore expansion programmes, they have ignored this section of the market and an opportunity has arisen for the growth of a new type of corporate power in grocery retailing based upon the small/convenience-store sector.

In this respect, Britain is following similar trends in the USA, where the Southland Corporation's '7-Eleven' franchise, and similarly structured competitors, became an important force in the late 1960s and 1970s and had captured over 10 per cent of food sales in states such as Florida, Arizona and Texas by the end of the 1970s (Dawson and Kirby, 1980). In Britain, the same format is being used by the new convenience-store chains such as Sperrings which, by 1985, had forty-eight company-owned outlets (mainly in southern England) plus eleven franchised outlets, and total sales in the region of £40 million. The average size of these stores is 2,500 ft^2 and typically they require a catchment of at least 5,000 homes (within ten minutes walk in suburban areas, or within similar driving distance in more rural areas). Unlike the small independent grocer, these new-style convenience stores employ relatively large numbers; usually about twenty to twenty-four people (most of whom work four-hour shifts). A typical store offers about 4,000 lines, and draws 40 per cent of its sales from confectionery, newspapers and tobacco products, 25 per cent from packaged food, 5 per cent from fast food, 3 per cent from fruit and vegetables, and 15 per cent from other non-food items (Wood Mackenzie, 1985).

Two alternative concepts of the new-style grocery convenience store are: first, one targetted at the more specialised requirements of the 'time-buying' affluent consumer of the high-income neighbourhood; and, second, one based around a petrol filling station. A good example of the first type is the reorganised Cullens group which, in 1986, had just twenty newly remodelled stores of average size 1,400 ft^2 in the most affluent areas of South East England, but plans to expand to 300 stores. Examples of the second type are now being opened by several of the major oil companies, or are actively being researched.

It appears, therefore, that the small-store sector of British grocery retailing is on the verge of a major concentration of capital. This concentration will differ fundamentally from that associated with the growth of contractual chains (e.g. the Spar and VG groups) in the 1960s and 1970s. Those chains were composed of independent retailers who, for certain operational functions (bulk purchasing, etc.), had entered into cooperation with other independents. In contrast, the new convenience store chains are potentially mini-corporations in their own right, or off-shoots of giant multinational oil corporations, operating in a niche of the market which has been passed over by the now-established large grocery corporations.

DIY/home improvement retailing

The restructuring which has taken place in grocery retailing since 1950 has involved the transformation of a level of demand which has risen very little in real terms (increased affluence has been accompanied by a reduced proportion of the average family's budget being spent on food, e.g. 31 per cent in 1962 but only 21 per cent in 1982). In contrast, restructuring in DIY retailing has taken place in a sector of the industry which virtually did not exist in its own right until the 1960s, i.e. restructuring has taken place simultaneously with the creation of demand.

DIY retailing in the UK grew out of the traditional hardware and builders' merchants trades, in response to increased home ownership, an ageing housing stock, the rising cost of professional labour, the creation of new markets through product innovation (e.g. self-assembly furniture, power tools, adhesives and sealants, etc.) and the general 'demystification' of many home improvement and repair tasks. Over the past twenty-five years a consistently increasing proportion of the average family's budget has been spent on DIY items, and by 1985 DIY sales amounted to over £2,500 million, or 3 per cent of total British retail sales. The most important firms operating in the market in the mid-1980s are shown in Table 1.8, and a consideration of the methods of operation, and changing ownership, of these firms soon reveals the key features of the rapid restructuring which has transformed the DIY sector over the past ten years.

From a position in the early 1970s where the concentration of

Table 1.8 The most important firms in the DIY sector in 1984–5

Firm	No. of Stores	Selling Area (000s ft²)	Sales (£ million)	Profit (£ million)	Net margin (%)	Parent company
B & Q	153	4,500	301	28.6	9.5	Woolworth
Texas	125	2,600	183	10.8	5.9	Home Charm (acquired by Ladbroke Group 1986)
Payless	59	1,100	91	7.4	8.1	Marley (acquired by Ward White Group 1986)
Do It All	54	1,600	76	4.2	5.6	W. H. Smith
Great Mills	37	1,000	45	n.a.	n.a.	RMC
Homebase	24	1,000	64	n.a.	n.a.	Sainsbury
Wickes	20	450	60	n.a.	n.a.	—
Sandfords	9	320	15	n.a.	n.a.	Sharpe & Fisher

Sources: company reports; Wood Mackenzie, 1985

capital in DIY retailing was low, and sales were spread across hundreds of small chains and thousands of single-outlet independents, concentration increased rapidly to a point where, by the mid-1980s, the top seven firms accounted for approximately 30 per cent of total sales. Of these seven firms, some by origin were small chains which had grown and prospered in the 1970s and 1980s but had lost their independence and had become merely parts (often extremely profitable parts) of larger retailing and non-retailing corporations by the mid-1980s. Others (e.g. Do It All and Homebase) were by origin subsidiary components of larger retail corporations created specifically to take advantage of the growing and highly rewarding DIY sector where annual profit increases in excess of 35 per cent have so far been possible throughout the 1980s.

Typical of the first type of DIY firms are B & Q and Texas, the market leaders, and a brief review of the recent histories of these chains will serve to illustrate many of the most important trends in capital concentration in the sector. Both firms have origins in the late 1960s and were created in the first phase of capital-shifting in the sector, a phase in which investment in small traditional 'high street' home improvement outlets was replaced by investment in larger, often out-of-centre, outlets of around 15,000–17,000 ft^2. By 1980 both chains had grown considerably. Texas (the principal subsidiary of the Home Charm Group) had almost seventy stores and just over 1 million ft^2 of floorspace, whilst B & Q had thirty-three stores and just over half a million ft^2. In that year, B & Q was aquired by F. W. Woolworth, a traditional and major high street retailer wishing to diversify. In its turn, F. W. Woolworth (UK) was bought in 1982 by a city consortium (Paternoster) from its US parent. As the consortium struggled to restructure and revamp the Woolworth high-street branch network (150 sites were disposed of over the next four years), investment was switched into the B & Q chain which soon became the cornerstore of the group's profits. Indeed by 1985, following a five-fold increase in the number of B & Q outlets to 153 and a nine-fold increase in floorspace to 4.5 million ft^2, B & Q's profit of £28.6 million represented no less than 75 per cent of total Woolworth group profits. During the same period, as Table 1.9 shows, the Texas chain grew more slowly to 125 stores, 2.6 million ft^2, and profits of £10.8 million by the beginning of

Table 1.9   The growth of the B & Q and Texas chains

		Years*			
		1981–2	*1983–4*	*1984–5*	*1985–6*
Sales (£ million)	Texas	74	106	137	183
	B & Q	45	139	197	301
Number of stores	Texas	71	99	101	125
	B & Q	53	100	112	153
Sales area (000s ft²)	Texas	1,077	1,840	1,932	2,612
	B & Q	980	2,670	3,200	4,500
Profit (£ million)	Texas	2.8	3.2	7.0	10.8
	B & Q	2.5	9.1	19.3	28.6
Net margin (%)	Texas	3.8	3.0	5.1	5.9
	B & Q	5.6	6.5	9.8	9.5

Sources: company reports; Wood Mackenzie, 1985.
* Texas (Home Charm) figures for year ending 31 December, B & Q figures for year ending 31 January: therefore years written as 1981–2, etc., to indicate comparable Texas and B & Q figures.

1985, and to 3.3 million ft² and profits of £14 million by the beginning of 1986.

In 1986 the parent companies of both DIY chains were the targets of takeover bids. Home Charm, having been courted by Harris Queensway, a furniture and carpets retailer specialising in similar out-of-centre warehouses but keen to diversify and with larger profits and floorspace (£37 million and 6.3 million ft²), was eventually acquired by the Ladbroke Group. Ladbroke was a large corporation, with interests in gambling, entertainment and property investment, which in 1985 produced a profit of £75 million on a turnover of £1,300 million. Along with similar groups such as Rank and Granada it was seeking to diversify its investment to ensure a wider capital base. It recognised in the 35+ per cent annual profits increases being achieved in DIY retailing in the mid-1980s, and with superstore penetration of the market not forecast to reach the 60–70 per cent level until the early 1990s, a dynamic sector for capital investment. Similar potential was also recognised by Dixons, the electrical retailer, who in 1986 made a bid of £1,800 million for F. W. Woolworth. Dixons' bid, which was ultimately unsuccessful, was a complex one, involving the transfer of underperforming Woolworth high-street floorspace. Nevertheless, B & Q represented a major prize of the bid, and would have become part of a large non-food retail corporation consisting of many different chains selling to specific niches in the market (similar groups such as the Burton and Storehouse groups had already been created). In part, therefore, the bid can be represented as yet another attempt by a retailer, constrained by high-street capital investment, to move into the most dynamic sector of out-of-centre retailing.

Alongside the concentration of capital in DIY retailing has come both a marked spatial shifting of capital and a significant level of technological change. The shifting of capital in DIY retailing from traditional high-street locations to out-of-centre warehouse operations has been commented upon several times above and, as Table 1.4 shows, it was one of the major engines powering the out-of-centre shift of over 5 per cent of total British retail sales in the period 1975–84. This role is set to continue (see final part of Table 1.4); in fact some forecasters (e.g. Wood Mackenzie, 1985) suggest an even faster rate of growth, with perhaps 1,240 out-of-centre DIY superstores by 1990. In this outward shift, the size of DIY outlets has increased considerably (e.g. consider the size trends in B & Q and Texas stores revealed in Table 1.9), such that the average store size in this sector may reach 30,000 ft^2 by 1990. The new concept in the DIY sector in the mid-1980s is the integrated out-of-centre non-food retail park, such as the one opened in early 1986 by B & Q at Cribbs Causeway outside Bristol. This includes a 70,000 ft^2 B & Q DIY store, a 35,000 ft^2 B & Q Autocentre, a 50,000 ft^2 B & Q Homecentre, and parking for more than 500 cars. Once again, as in the case of grocery retailing, there are only a limited number of sites in the UK which will support this scale of development, and store location research is becoming increasingly important to the DIY chains.

Within the larger out-of-centre DIY superstores, new technology has recently been taken up enthusiastically. For example, B & Q has embarked upon a £40-million EPOS programme scheduled for completion in 1988. Overall, from a position in 1984 when the penetration of EPOS systems in DIY retailing was only 2.5 per cent, by the end of 1985 it had risen to 12 per cent, and by the end of 1990 it is estimated it will have reached 80 per cent. Such programmes will help to improve the already high levels of labour productivity in the sector, and to maintain the highly favourable net margins which (on such high and growing volume) are the key to understanding the attraction of this sector of retailing to larger corporations both within and outside retailing.

Retail analysis, locational analysis and the new retail environment

The concentration of capital in British retailing, and the critical nature of store expansion programmes and niche marketing in maintaining the rates of profit growth which the capital markets have come to expect, has ushered in a new 'golden age' for store location and market analysis. Never before have the skills of locational analysis, developed and practised by geographers and planners, been so closely identified with the commercial imperatives of retailers. In response have come two developments which are of great importance to the nature of British retailing research.

First, there has been the growth of specialist market analysis firms such as CACI, Pinpoint, MPSI, Management Horizons, etc., offering services which complement those provided by the more general market research companies such as AGB and Nielsen. The market analysis firms offer a wide range of consultancy services to the retail sector, particularly market potential and store location assessment, catchment area profiles, market share modelling, store turnover forecasting, and store performance assessment. In addition, they (together with firms like URPI) provide basic retail census statistics, and retail expenditure estimates for small areas. Frequently, the services provided by the market analysis firms are based upon large geographically-organised (spatially addressable) computerised databases, of which the UK Population Census Small Area Statistics licensed for commercial exploitation under a special agency agreement with the Office of Population Censuses and Surveys (OPCS) usually form the key element. The databases are then manipulated to provide the range of retail consultancy services described above, together with target marketing and, sometimes, area-based credit rating.

CACI Market Analysis provides a good example of such firms. CACI in the UK is one part of a New York Stock Exchange quoted international consultancy founded in 1962 which now employs over 1,500 people in eight countries. The UK operation began in 1978 with just two employees and was the first market analysis firm to sign the crucial agency agreement with OPCS. Initially, it was concerned with selling a classification of British residential neighbourhoods (ACORN) based upon the small-area (enumeration district) statistics from the 1971 Census, and with matching postcoded customer addresses to small-area census data. Since then it has expanded from this base to offer the wide range of retail planning, market analysis, target marketing/direct mail services described above, and now employs over sixty consultants in London and Edinburgh. A new version of ACORN based upon the 1981 Census data, which classifies every address in Britain into one of thirty-eight types, was developed by 1983 and is now regularly updated to reflect population changes since 1981. ACORN forms a core element in many CACI retail analysis products, e.g. the SITE system which provides a standard package for retail location assessment, and which can be merged with information on retail employment, consumer expenditure, and the size and mix of shopping centres.

Second, there has been the development of in-house 'store location research units' by a number of the major UK grocery retailing corporations responding, as the *Financial Times* on 17 April 1985 put it, to the fact that the 'battle lines in the latest round of the grocery war are being drawn not around the price wars of the 1970s, but around the frantic grab for the best superstore sites left in the UK'. The most well-developed example of these in-house units is that of Tesco, which has grown from three staff in 1981 to twenty-four staff in 1985, and has plans to expand still further. The Tesco unit (see Penny and Broom, this volume) has three basic tasks. First, to direct the search process for new sites. Second, to screen the sites uncovered by this search process and to identify those which are worth more detailed consideration. Third, to provide detailed and accurate sales forecasts for each of these promising sites, forecasts which are then used as part of a capital investment appraisal which goes to the acquisitions committee of Tesco's main board. To meet these objectives, the Tesco unit has developed a relatively sophisticated locational modelling system which has at its heart a sales forecasting model of classical spatial interaction form. This forecasting model is then calibrated on a high-quality, specially designed, and continuously updated geographical database. The database contains some particularly important, and commercially sensitive, information, e.g. on the shopping behaviour of existing Tesco customers, on the store characteristics and sales performance history of all existing Tesco branches, and on the extent and quality of competitive activity at each location. In addition, it contains small-area 1981 Census data, Family Expenditure Survey data, etc., and can be interfaced with a digitised road network which allows the computation of travel time between any two locations. Given the low net profit margins characteristic of grocery retailing, the sales forecasts produced by this model must be particularly accurate, and projected average weekly sales figures for each in-store department during the first three years of trading must meet strict target levels of accuracy. Moreover, these forecasts must be produced within the space of just a few working days to allow Tesco to respond quickly to the development opportunities which are so critical to each of the major grocery retailing corporations. Finally, the sales forecasting model must be sufficiently flexible to allow the consideration of various development options (i.e. alternative store sizes, product ranges, store formats, etc.) at particular sites, and to facilitate a director-level assessment of the vulnerability of the location/investment decision. In this way, the sales forecasts are usually extended to provide a wider business analysis which considers both the potential new store and the existing network of stores in an area.

It should be clear from the preceding descriptions that the store location research and market analysis which has developed so rapidly in the UK commercial sector over recent years is typically conducted under intense pressures both of time and/or the need to create new business. Such pressures, and the need for a relatively 'fail safe' product, are not conducive to the development of new approaches to retail analysis and forecasting, and the danger is that the locational analysis methods being adopted by the industry may fossilise and, therefore, perhaps ultimately disappoint. It is in this context that the retail research groups in British universities/polytechnics and the UK Economic and

Social Research Council (ESRC) have a critical role to play. Given relatively limited financial support from both the ESRC and commercial sector firms, such research groups have the skills, computing resources and research time to develop and test new methods of retail analysis and forecasting – methods which, ideally, will be sensitive to, and informed by, an understanding of the dynamic nature of retail change and restructuring discussed in this chapter. However, as Penny and Broom (this volume) point out, whilst 'the culture of retail decision making is especially receptive to answers and advice, it does not appreciate esoteric analytical problems which invariably surface in any detailed research and modelling approach'. As a result, there is a vital need to translate the results of current and future academic research on methods of retail analysis and forecasting into a form which will be understandable and utilisable by commercial companies. In this context, both the market analysis firms and the Economic and Social Research Council have critical roles to play: the market analysis firms because they are in many senses natural intermediaries between academic research groups and the end-users of the retail industry, and are therefore likely to play a pivotal role in the translation of academic research into commercially acceptable systems of analysis; the ESRC because of its ability to bring together academic and commercial sector groups, and its often repeated objective to transfer the results of commercially useful social science research into British industry and commerce.

This volume, together with the workshop on which it was based, represents an attempt by the editor and the ESRC to fill this role. Its objective is to foster dialogue between those academic and commercial research groups who are developing or using techniques of analysis and forecasting in the fields of store-location/store-performance assessment, store-choice modelling, and market analysis. To this end, it contains four types of chapters. First, a group which summarise the current state of commercial development of store location and market analysis research in the UK. Second, a group which suggest the adoption of techniques which are new to the field of retail analysis and forecasting but which have been widely tested and commercially exploited in other fields. Third, a group which provide wider and/or international perspectives on retail analysis and forecasting. Fourth, papers which report pure, abstract, and perhaps relatively esoteric, academic research – the kind of creative endeavour which is vital if the long-term vitality of research, both academic and commercial, in this field of retail analysis is to be maintained.

PART 2   Models of store location and techniques of market analysis

This section of the book begins with two overviews of the methods of store location analysis currently available to assess both the performance of existing stores and the viability of potential new store developments. The stress in these chapters is upon *practical* methods which are accurate and robust, and which are sensitive to the constraints imposed by the type and quality of the data typically available for retail analysis and forecasting purposes.

The themes developed by Breheney and Beaumont in Chapters 2 and 3 are then illustrated in Chapter 4 by the experience of the Store Location Research Unit of Tesco PLC, one of Britain's largest retail corporations. Penny and Broom demonstrate that the store location modelling system used by the Tesco Unit plays a key role in the annual £150 million new store development programme of the corporation, and the Unit provides an excellent example of the increased awareness of the commercial potential of store location analysis by British retailers.

The contribution from the Tesco Unit is then complemented in Chapter 5 by Fotheringham, who examines the use of similar store location modelling/market share analysis techniques in the United States, and extended in Chapter 6 by Wilson into the realms of dynamic models of the evolution of retail systems. Although the more sophisticated models described by Wilson are not yet used in commercial practice, they nevertheless offer important insights into the development of retail systems and retail competition over time, and they explore techniques which have the capacity to enrich the structure of the current generation of commercial store location modelling systems.

Finally this section of the book concludes with a consideration of stated preference techniques. In Chapters 7 and 8 Bates and Moore suggest that these techniques, which are new to the field of retail analysis and forecasting but which are widely used and commercially exploited in fields such as transport planning, provide a methodology which can enrich the current range of methods used to forecast the patronage/sales levels and viability of new stores.

CHAPTER 2
Practical methods of retail location analysis: a review

Michael J. Breheny

Introduction

Anyone writing a review of the use of analytical techniques in retailing ten or even five years ago would have concentrated almost exclusively on the methods developed and used by the public sector; that is, by local authority planning departments. Some reference might have been made to impact techniques used by both planners and retailers' consultants at public inquiries, but apart from this it is unlikely that any reference would have been made to private sector, that is retailer, use of rigorous techniques.

Remarkably, writing now, such a review will concentrate almost exclusively on the development of techniques in the private sector. This is because the last five years or so have seen a revolutionary change in the approaches adopted by retailers in making decisions about the locations of their stores. Before this, the large majority of the large multiple retailers in Britain made their locational decisions – for example on where to locate new stores, where to close stores, how much to bid in tendering for sites, and how to judge the performance of branches – on the basis of intuitive judgment and experience. Only a handful of companies used any kind of systematic analysis in making such judgments. This increased interest in the use of systematic methods in the private sector has occurred at a time when the use of such methods has declined in the public sector. Putting it in a broader context, as interest in strategic planning, and hence in decision-making techniques, seems to have increased in private corporations, so it has almost disappeared in the public sector generally and certainly in local government.

Many retail companies now recognise the crucial importance of location to their success and acknowledge the need to make locational decisions in a much more rigorous fashion than in the past. As a result of this, many companies are now adopting a range of analytical and forecasting techniques as part of their decision-making procedures. In some cases companies have established internal research units to carry out this work on a continuous basis, recognising that the cost of such units can quickly be recouped in the improved trading resulting from their efforts. Other companies rely on consultants to carry out research for them. In consequence a number of consultancies have specialised in carrying out this kind of research and in providing the necessary data. In turn academic geographers have found themselves with the opportunity to offer their advice, particularly on the appropriate use of techniques.

Such has been the speed of this revolution in retail location decision-making that very little effort has been made – by retailers, consultants or academics – to take stock of the appropriateness of the methods being offered and used to the nature of the problems faced by the retailers. It is inevitable in this situation that some poor advice will be offered, inappropriate methods used, and, in consequence, some bad decisions made.

The aim here is to contribute to a stocktaking exercise by providing an overview of the locational problems faced by retailers and relating to these problems the range of techniques available. The initial result of this is a rather formal classification of problems and techniques in an attempt to map out a framework of problems and methods. The chapter will argue, however, that whilst this framework is important in helping to understand problems and in relating techniques to these problems, it should be used as a way of helping to understand peculiar problems and deciding on which techniques or combination of techniques or parts of techniques is appropriate. It would be unwise to use it as a kind of checklist from which a given technique is chosen to resolve a given problem. Many practical retail problems will be peculiar to the retailer concerned and will require specific analytical and technical responses.

The changing nature of retail location problems

Why has this revolution occurred, at this time and in this form? Bowlby, Breheny and Foot (1984a) suggest four major reasons for the increased interest in more rigorous decision-making.

'The "easy" sites go first' A number of major retailers, particularly those involved in out-of-centre food store developments, found themselves in the late 1970s and early 1980s in a situation in which each decision on a new store opening became more difficult than the last. Most of the 'easy' sites, on which the advantages of trading were so obvious that no rigorous analysis was required in making the decision to proceed, had been developed. Further expansion would obviously require decisions on sites whose market, competition and cost characteristics were not so evidently favourable. The response of a small number of the major food retailers was to invest in more rigorous location decision-making methods. The fact that the market leader, Sainsbury's, had been doing this for some years added to the urgency. The dramatic change in attitudes is best illustrated by the response of Tesco at this time; from having no location analysts in 1981, by 1986 they had a highly profesional research unit of some twenty-five staff (Penny and Broom, this volume).

The problem felt by the large food retailers five or so years ago has been appreciated more recently by other out-of-centre retailers. The DIY store operators, for example, now find themselves in a mature market where each new location decision requires very careful consideration. Likewise, they have responded by using analytical techniques to make such decisions.

'Experience becomes a less reliable guide' Whilst retailing progresses slowly and steadily, experience will always be a useful guide to current decisions. Many major companies have developed on the basis of this experience alone. However, as the pace of change has increased in recent years, with increased competitiveness and the rapid introduction of new forms and locations for retailing, such experience has become a much less reliable guide. These changes arise from both the retailers themselves – the preference for out-of-centre sites, the move to larger stores, the use of new technology, for instance – and the changing nature

of demand – arising, for instance, from a population which is rapidly decentralising from our cities and which includes many more single-person households, more owner-occupiers and more women workers. All of these changes make the past experiences of retailers less and less useful, and rigorous analytical techniques more useful, in making location decisions.

'The cost of mistakes' As average store size grows and as the competition for the remaining good sites increases, so each individual investment by retailers becomes greater. As each investment becomes greater so does the risk attached to each location decision. In this situation it is imperative that the retailer is confident in making the decision either to proceed with a site or to leave it to others to agonise over. Again, a rigorous research-based approach is more likely to give such confidence than simple trading experience.

'The pressure to invest in new outlets increases' The intensification of competition between a few large retail companies has resulted in a drive for further expansion and for the most effective employment of their growing financial resources. Companies are conscious that shareholders expect tangible evidence of expansion and growth, while the accelerating pace of change puts further pressures on companies to expand and innovate. While there are many alternative types of investment in organisation and equipment that successful companies must and do make, geographical expansion and the battle for territory continues to be an important ingredient in the competitive strategies of most large retail companies. Failure to use resources as effectively as the competition and to respond to the locational strategies of rival companies may spell disaster, but so also may the adoption of an over-ambitious or poorly-conceived pattern of geographical expansion. Again, all the more reason to develop a strong research capability.

According to Bowlby, Breheny and Foot (1984a), these, then, are the major reasons, all of them mutually reinforcing of course, which have led the major retailers in the UK to adopt more rigorous methods of location decision-making. These imperatives were first felt by the large food retailers, but many other companies, incuding those operating mainly in high-street locations, have subsequently followed their example in moving towards more rigorous location decision-making. Now, as consultants are only too willing to point out the folly of not adopting this approach, companies relying solely on their experience in making such decisions are probably in the minority. However, this 'bandwagon' effect, with retailers anxious not to miss out on the fashion for more rigorous location analysis, increases the possibility of problems being misunderstood and inappropriate techniques used. This chapter aims to present a framework that will facilitate much more thorough consideration of these issues.

The nature of retail location problems

The response of many consultants and academics to practical retail location problems is often to rationalise what may be a vague description of the problem by the retailer into a form that will permit use of a readily available or 'pet' technique or data set. Occasionally this may fit the bill and the retailer will be happy with the results. It is also possible, however, that the advice offered may be inappropriate; that the problem was not understood, or that it was manipulated to suit the analyst, or that the form of technique used was not suited to the problem. This is not to imply sharp practice on the part of such consultants and academics, but to suggest that to date the tendency has been for solutions to seek problems rather than the other way around. This situation might be improved if more thought were first given to the nature of the range of retail location problems likely to arise. It may then be easier to respond with the most appropriate analysis. In the approach that tends to prevail now, the response is often to offer a particular, single technique to be applied in full. It is suggested here that if the nature of problems is given more thought at the outset, responses may involve more use of hybrid techniques and even of simple non-technical analysis; in short, customised responses.

A classification of retail location problems

In attempting to develop some means by which we can assess the nature of retail location problems, we might start with the framework put forward by Breheny (1983b) for what he called the 'large store planning process'. This framework attempts to characterise the stages in the development of a large out-of-centre store in the UK that involve location decisions. The framework also takes into account the responses of the planning authority. The framework was devised in order to identify clearly those stages of this process where analytical techniques might be of use to both retailers and planners. Four such stages were identified.

(a) Where retailers might be involved in a general *search* for areas, but not at this stage specific sites, where trading might be profitable.

(b) Where retailers (and just possibly planners), having decided on an area with potential, wish to assess the *viability* of a store on a particular site within this area.

(c) Where retailers and planners wish to assess the likely *impact* of a proposed store on nearby existing retail facilities. This situation is most likely to occur when a retailer and the planners are in dispute over a proposed development.

(d) Where retailers wish to *evaluate* the performance of their existing stores.

Breheny (1983b) pointed out that up to that time most effort had been put, by both planners and consultants acting for retailers, into the development of impact assessment techniques, largely because of the lengthy series of superstore and hypermarket inquiries. He argued that this effort had diverted retailers' attention from potentially valuable work on systematic search, viability and evaluation methods, and that such work would be necessary in an increasingly competitive market.

Bowlby, Breheny and Foot (1984a; 1984b; 1985a; 1985b) have elaborated on Breheny's (1983a) framework, extending the viability issue in particular. They subdivide this category further into three stages: trade area considerations, which are concerned with the catchment areas of stores; micro-site factors which may be important in determining store performance; and in-store issues, which are affecting performance more and more as the fashion for expensively designed refits continues. The purpose in making this sub-division of the viability category is to distinguish factors that require separate consideration in assessing likely store performance.

If we put these two classifications of retail location problems together, we have a more detailed basis for a framework within which to consider the availability and appropriateness of techniques. Figure 2.1 shows the combined classification.

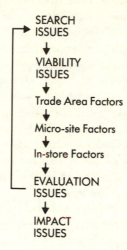

SEARCH
ISSUES

↓

VIABILITY
ISSUES

↓

Trade Area Factors

↓

Micro-site Factors

↓

In-store Factors

↓

EVALUATION
ISSUES

↓

IMPACT
ISSUES

Figure 2.1 An initial classification of retail location problems into a location research strategy.

The types of retail location problem are shown in Figure 2.1 in the temporal sequence in which they ought to be considered by a retailer as part of a 'location research strategy'. Such a strategy should begin with searches for appropriate areas in which to consider specific sites. Given specific sites to assess, a viability analysis might firstly consider the trade or catchment area characteristics of each site in order to determine their likely effect on the performance of new stores. A first estimate of store performance might then be refined by consideration of micro-site factors and intended in-store factors.

For a company with existing outlets, a crucial part of a research strategy would be constant evaluation or monitoring of the performance of these outlets. This is in fact necessary for satisfactory viability assessments, as will be explained below, but is also an important part of a research strategy in its own right. Many retail companies are particularly weak at evaluating the performance of their existing stores. Given the enormous investment tied up in such stores, this is surprising. An important part of the evaluation exercise will, of course, eventually involve the monitoring of work at the viability stage; that is, of store turnover forecasts relative to actual store performance. Again, many retailers have been reluctant to monitor the accuracy of their turnover forecasts. One suspects the exercise would often be painful, but it is necessary if forecasting is to be improved.

In an ideal ongoing research strategy these types of location problem – from search through to evaluation – would be being addressed on a continuous, cyclical basis, with the feedback of information constantly improving the quality of the whole exercise. Unfortunately, many retailers still regard location research as an occasional necessity and will usually only tackle the core, viability element of our framework. For a serious research effort, however, the search and evaluation elements must be included in a continuous programme.

Impact assessments are included in our framework for the sake of completeness, but they would not figure as part of a retailer's location research strategy. Retailers will regard the use of impact assessments as a necessary evil imposed upon them by the planning system. However, a retailer with a strong research capability will find that it is relatively easy to develop such impact assessments, given the expertise built up from other work. Those retailers with research units will now be quite capable of presenting their own technical evidence at inquiries, whereas until recently they would have had to employ consultants.

Although originally developed in relation to large out-of-centre stores, this framework of types of location problems, serving also as a location research strategy, is equally relevant to all forms of retailing. High-street specialist retailers, for example, should be just as concerned with search, viability and evaluation issues as the out-of-centre operators. Of the elements of the framework, it is only the impact issue that is likely to be the peculiar concern of the large out-of-centre retailers.

Before attempting to relate techniques to the retail location problems in our classification, we can usefully add another dimension to that classification to account for the fact that different types of retailing will involve very different factors when considering search, trade area, evaluation issues and so on. For example, the factors to be considered in a general search for areas of potential by, say, a chain of supermarkets and a quality jeweller will differ considerably. In trying to reflect these differences in our framework, a simple but useful distinction is between those types of retailing relying heavily upon the size and proximity of a local population around an outlet, such as newsagents and supermarkets, and those relying upon the quality and speciality of the products sold. This is the geographer's classic distinction between 'low'- and 'high'-order goods. The distinction, of course, is between ends of a spectrum of types of retailing rather than discrete categories. We might call these ends of the spectrum 'outlet-dominated' and 'product-dominated' markets.

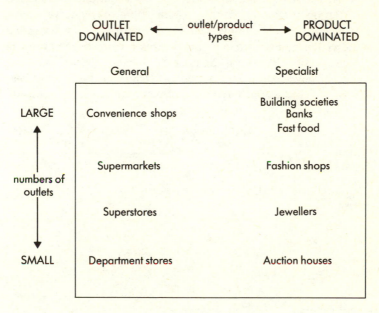

Figure 2.2 A classification of types of retailing.

Figure 2.2 gives examples of types of retail outlet that fall at different points on this spectrum, adding the extra dimension of the number of outlets. Thus, we see that newsagents and hypermarkets fall at the outlet-dominated end, but that there are large numbers of the former but few of the latter. At the more specialist end of the spectrum, some types of outlets, such as building societies and banks, exist in large numbers, but are not convenience stores in the same way as newsagents, for example. Their performance will depend as much on the nature of the product as on the location of outlets. Those specialist retailers selling very high-order goods, such as high-quality jewellers, will rely heavily for their performance on the nature of the product they sell rather than on the particular location of their outlets. At the extreme of the product-dominated part of the spectrum we could place those retailing operations, such as mail order, where there are literally no retailing outlets and where company performance is not affected at all by outlet location characteristics.

We can complete our attempt to provide a framework of location problems by combining this outlet-product-dominated markets distinction with the classification of retail problems presented earlier. The result is shown in Figure 2.3. Doubtless, we could elaborate even further, but in this form the framework is sufficiently detailed to suit the purpose in hand; that is, to have a comprehensive picture of types of retail location problems, against which the appropriateness of techniques can be assessed.

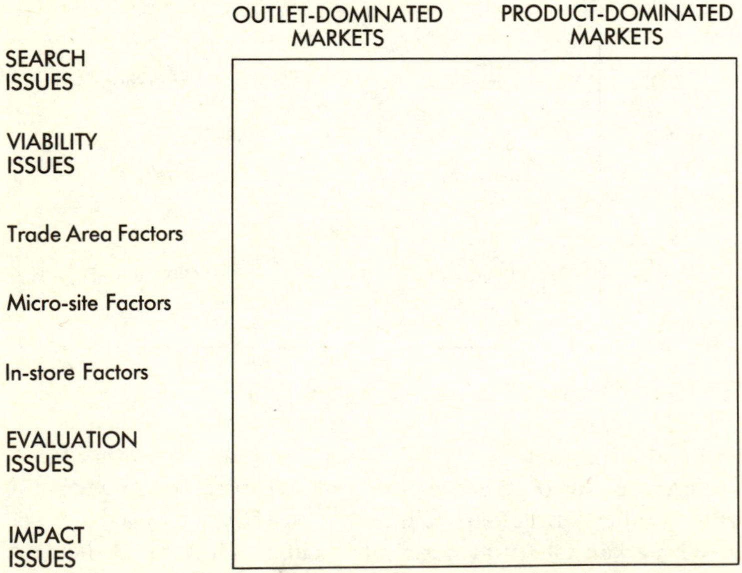

	OUTLET-DOMINATED MARKETS	PRODUCT-DOMINATED MARKETS
SEARCH ISSUES		
VIABILITY ISSUES		
Trade Area Factors		
Micro-site Factors		
In-store Factors		
EVALUATION ISSUES		
IMPACT ISSUES		

Figure 2.3 A classification of retail location problems.

Relating retail location problems and techniques

This classification of retail location problems will be useful as a device for helping to determine appropriate techniques; however, it is also intended as a device for encouraging retailers to think in terms of the full range of potential applications of analytical approaches. Even now, as retailers and their analysts show a keen interest in such approaches, they have tended to concentrate on viability issues, and in particular on turnover forecasting techniques. Thus, search and evaluation issues, which might be equally important, tend to be ignored. By broadening the range of considerations to include these, the classification suggests ways in which more comprehensive location-research strategies can be developed. Thus, instead of techniques being used just to help with particular location problems, they can aid the development of a broad research strategy. This is the way that the larger in-house retail research units are developing their work.

The classification developed above is intended to counter the rather myopic way in which techniques are currently matched to location problems, by showing the full range of problems that need to be addressed and by relating them together. We get some idea of the extent of this myopia if we begin to relate the techniques commonly offered to and used by retailers to the classification of problems. Bowlby, Breheny and Foot (1984b) suggest that only two main types of techniques have been adopted, *store-turnover* forecasting techniques and *spatial marketing* techniques.

Store-turnover forecasting techniques are intended to forecast store performance from knowledge of existing stores in the same retail chain. Such techniques, which have their origins in academic geography, usually include various forms of what are called 'analogue' techniques, in which an analogy is drawn between the performance of existing stores and a proposed store. Multiple regression analysis has been used to extend this analogue principle. Retail gravity models have also been used for turnover forecasting. All of these techniques treat distance or travel time explicitly.

What we might term 'spatial marketing techniques' have rather different origins to the turnover forecasting techniques. Although they do have an academic pedigree, they are best understood as deriving from the product-marketing field. These techniques have their roots in large-scale data processing and classification systems. The best known work is the statistical analysis which classifies geographical areas according to their dominant socio-economic characteristics. Given these area typologies, it is possible to determine, at a national level, the purchasing characteristics of each typology for a range of goods and services. Having identified potential purchasers in this way it is then possible to target those purchasers by, for example, direct mail or localised advertising. The best known national typologies are ACORN, PiN, and Super Profiles, developed by CACI, Pinpoint and McIntyres respectively.

The same companies offer a range of services based on speedy and thorough analysis of large data sets, in particular the national census. By relating different data sets together, they can produce information of value to retailers. For example, they can produce profiles of the population, or estimates of the retail expenditure available, within any given geographical area.

In recent years, the role of these two sets of techniques in helping to solve particular retail problems has become confused. In particular, many retailers looking for methods to help forecast store performance have turned to the spatial marketing consultants. The result must occasionally have been inappropriate advice. For example, potential locations for new stores might have been identified by using area typologies or profiles to determine areas with a large number of people of the socio-economic groups which most frequent the stores of the retailer concerned. In certain cases this would be valuable information, but for many retailers the socio-economic composition of the local population is trivial as a determinant of performance relative to, say, the size of the population, its density around the store, and the location of competitors. In short, where the issue is store turnover, and local locational factors are important to performance, then store-turnover forecasting techniques are more appropriate than spatial marketing techniques. The spatial marketing consultants now appreciate this and offer a full range of techniques, often on a more customised basis than in the past.

Before attempting to relate these two major groups of techniques to our classification of problems, there may be some merit in considering them first against just the outlet-product-dominated markets dimension of this classification. This will help us to gain a simple idea of the types of retailing to which the two types of techniques are generally appropriate.

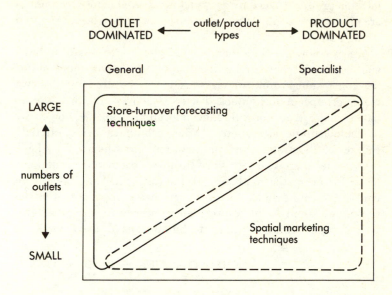

Figure 2.4 Matching major techniques and types of retailing.

Figure 2.4 relates together this spectrum of types of retailing and the two main types of location technique currently being used. Store-turnover forecasting techniques will be most useful where retail performance is a function of the location of outlets; where the market is outlet dominated. They may also be useful in a relatively specialised sector of retailing where there is a large number of outlets, as in the case of building societies. Spatial marketing techniques will be most useful where the performance of an outlet is more dependent on being in the right general location, with the right socio-economic structure, than on local catchment area characteristics. For example, a high-quality women's fashion retailer might find it profitable to locate in spa towns, but not be too concerned about finding a site with a high population density, low competition, etc.

A simple matching of types of retailing and major groups of techniques of this kind might have avoided the problem mentioned above where spatial marketing techniques have been used by retailers in outlet-dominated markets. The point demonstrates clearly the message that careful consideration of the nature of the location problems faced by a retailer is essential before techniques are chosen and applied. Such care has not always been exercised in the past.

We can now conclude our general attempt to relate problem and technique types in retail location by asking how much of our two-dimensional problem classification is covered by the two major groups of techniques discussed above. In other words, having mapped out the full range of location problems, how many of these can be addressed by the techniques being offered? Figure 2.5 illustrates those problem areas to which efforts have been made to apply either store-turnover forecasting techniques (STFTs) or spatial marketing techniques (SMTs). Upper-case entries indicate problem areas to which the applications of the techniques seem to be appropriate; lower-case entries suggest where applications of these techniques have been weak or

	OUTLET-DOMINATED MARKETS	PRODUCT-DOMINATED MARKETS
SEARCH ISSUES	smts ?	SMTs
VIABILITY ISSUES		
Trade Area Factors	STFTs	smts ?
Micro-site Factors	?	?
In-store Factors	?	?
EVALUATION ISSUES	STFTs	?
IMPACT ISSUES	STFTs	?

Figure 2.5 A framework of retail location problems. STFTs = store-turnover forecasting techniques; SMTs = spatial marketing techniques.

questionable. Question marks indicate areas where it is considered that virtually no effort has been made to develop and apply techniques.

The obvious feature of Figure 2.5 is that when we do relate existing techniques being used in retail location analysis to the full range of possible problem areas, quite a number of these areas are either not catered for or have had inappropriate techniques applied. Search techniques for outlet-dominated retailing are poorly developed in practice, the whole of the micro/in-store field has not really been addressed at all, and evaluation has not been seriously considered.

The rest of this paper will review each of the problem areas in Figure 2.5, with the exception of impact issues which do not fit neatly into a location research strategy (see Guy, C. M. 1981), Breheny, Green and Roberts (1981) and Breheny (1983a) for a discussion of impact assessment), considering the nature of the techniques that have been developed and used, and briefly assessing prospects in those areas where techniques have not been developed. This review ought to demonstrate that the availability of a classification of problems, prior to consideration of techniques, makes the adoption of the appropriate techniques or combination of techniques much easier.

Search problems and techniques

Whilst retailers have been keen to develop methods to assess the likely viability of a store on a particular site, they have to date done little to search systematically for such sites in the first place. The sites which are tested are often those found by the company's property division. Such sites will usually come to the attention of the property section in a random fashion, using their own intelligence information about land sales, property transactions and so on.

Whilst this approach has obviously stood many companies in good stead in the past, there is no guarantee in this approach that the best sites are being considered or that opportunities elsewhere are not being ignored and lost to competitors. It should be possible, as part of a location research strategy, to improve upon this 'sub-optimal' approach.

The techniques most readily available for search purposes are those offered under our 'spatial marketing techniques' heading. These techniques have, however, not usually been presented to retailers as having this limited role, but as having a general-purpose store location role. As explained earlier, the range of data analyses and applications of statistical techniques offered by the spatial marketing consultants is very broad.

Search exercises could be based, for example, on simple profiles of the catchment areas of shopping centres, giving, say, the number of people in a target demographic group. Alternatively, expenditure profiles are available for any given area, calculated from knowledge of the national relationship between socio-economic structure and expenditure patterns, which may indicate to a retailer areas with trading potential. Such expenditure profiles are now a standard product offered by many consultants; Pinpoint Analysis, for example, offer their Retail Potential Reports. CACI offer another service which may be of use in a general search exercise; this classifies retail centres in Britain (CORA – a Classification of Retail Centres, see Whitehead (1983)) into typologies using similar methods to that which produces ACORN. A retailer with a successful store in one town might use this to identify other towns with similar characteristics and, hopefully, similar trading potential.

If information is available, from surveys or customer records, about the customers of a retail chain, then more sophisticated analyses can be carried out. It may be possible to determine patterns of expenditure between different social or age groups. If certain groups are likely to be good customers, then areas with a predominance of such groups might be identified as potential locations for a new outlet. Target groups of this kind might be identified directly according to demographic characteristics or by relating sales information to typologies of the kind mentioned earlier. In the latter case, having determined that good customers tend to come from particular types, areas with a high proportion of their population in these typologies might be identified for further consideration. Such an exercise might produce more specific indices of trading potential if an expenditure rate can be applied to, say, per head of population in the right typologies.

The possible permutations of data sets and forms of analysis mean that the range of possible uses of this spatial marketing approach in search procedures is considerable. Humby (1984) and Sleight (1983) give a much better idea of this range than is possible here. A feature of this work, however, is that it aims to identify general areas with trading potential. It does not, however as some retailers might have interpreted it, suggest that a retailer will inevitably trade well from any site within identified areas.

This point is best understood by reference back to our outlet-product-dominated markets notion. Retailers in product-dominated markets, whose performance is not heavily dependent upon local catchment-area characteristics, but upon having access to particular socio-economic groups and trading in an area with the right image, might find that search procedures of this kind are sufficient in identifying appropriate locations. For such retailers, the precise siting of a new outlet may be a relatively trivial issue once the right general location has been found. The decision on an actual site might miss out the trade-area considerations discussed below, and crucial to many retailers, and rely on getting micro-site factors correct.

For retailers at the outlet-dominated end of our spectrum, the spatial marketing approach to searching for areas of trading potential may not be entirely appropriate. Such retailers, and particularly the increasing number operating in large out-of-centre stores, will be less concerned with socio-economic structure than with population densities, the distance of such population from any site, and the level and proximity of competition. Although certain socio-economic groups, or area types, might be more loyal to such retailers than other groups, their role in determining store performance is likely to be small compared to these catchment area issues. Thus, whilst spatial marketing techniques may be of some use to outlet-dominated retailers, they will not be as valuable as they are to the product-dominated operators. The greater applicability of spatial marketing techniques to this group of retailers is illustrated in Figures 2.4 and 2.5.

As Figure 2.5 demonstrates, search techniques have not been developed specifically for outlet-dominated retailing. This is probably a function of both the slowness of consultants and academics to realise the possibilities, and of the limited perceptions of the retailers, who still do not think in terms of research strategies and tend to focus their efforts on viability assessment.

What techniques are available, then, that might be adopted and probably adapted to help outlet-dominated retailers search for areas of trading potential? One general source of analytical approaches that may help retailers in searching for areas of potential is the field of geographical optimisation. What is meant by optimisation is the systematic search for broad locations that will prove to be the best, either for a single retailer or for retailers generally, or, indeed, for a planning authority looking to plan positively for retail development. For a retailer the aim might be to find, say, two or three areas in a region that will provide high levels of turnover, given the distribution of population, consumer expenditure and competitors. A company might adopt such a search at a broad regional level in the hope of identifying areas that are likely to suit their requirements. Having identified such areas, more detailed work, possibly using 'viability' techniques of the kind discussed below, might be used to identify specific sites.

From the planners' point of view, search techniques might be used to identify systematically areas where the development of a store or stores might best serve the interests of the community. The large majority of local authorities have, in the last ten years or so, chosen to oppose the development of large out-of-centre stores and hence have not needed to consider this optimisation problem. However, more recently planners have tended to accept the inevitability of such stores and have begun to plan for them. Positive planning of this kind is regarded as preferable to the development of a pattern of stores that results from a series of individual permissions gained on appeal. As part of this positive approach, optimising methods designed, say, to minimise travel distance to a number of stores may be appropriate.

The field of spatial optimising models is diverse and hence difficult to comprehend. This problem of comprehension for practical purposes is exacerbated by the heavy mathematics often involved in the literature. This situation may be helped by some attempt to classify the major characteristics of the various models. In this way it will be easier to focus on the types of models likely to be of use in practical search exercises. Generally the area of work we are interested in is covered by the term 'location-allocation' models; that is, models concerned with the location of facilities and the allocation of consumers, population or trips to those facilities.

A major distinction must be made at the outset between models developed for the private sector and those developed for the public sector. Whilst much early work was concerned with the private sector, following the industrial location problems posed by geographers early this century, by far the major effort in recent years has been into problems of public-facility location (see reviews by Hodgart (1978) and Leonardi (1982)). In the private-sector work the concern has been with industrial location issues, often dealt with by academics as warehouse location problems, in which the focus of attention has been the minimisation of transport costs and the discrete division of space into efficient units. Some work has been done on retailing (Huff (1966), Wilson (1976), Coelho and Wilson (1976)), but it has been of little practical value.

Another major distinction concerns the way models seek to partition space in the allocation process, either into deterministic, discrete units or probabilistic, overlapping units. Many of the public-sector models are concerned with the allocation of a population to the nearest centre, subject possibly to capacity constraints, and in this way divide space discretely. An example of this would be in the definition of hospital catchment areas, where it is assumed that allocation to the nearest hospital will suffice. In the private sector, warehousing problems would be dealt with in this way.

Other models are based on notions of spatial interaction and gravitation in which allocations of, say, consumers will be on a probabilistic basis, reflecting the distance-decay effect away from centres, caused by the preferences of shoppers for different centres. Thus, for example, shoppers are less likely to visit a centre the further they live from it, but may also frequent centres other than the nearest one. This might also be true in certain public-sector allocation problems – with general practitioners or dentists, for example. It is probably best to regard this deterministic/probabilistic issue as a continuum of possibilities, rather than as comprising distinct categories.

Taylor (1977) identifies three types of solution methods for these location-allocation problems; simple allocation methods, mathematical programming techniques and heuristic search algorithms. In Taylor's classification the size of the problem is important in determining the appropriate method of solution. Thus relatively small problems are dealt with by the simple allocation methods. Large complex problems may warrant heuristic search procedures.

Under the 'simple allocation' method Taylor (1977) suggests a number of approaches; geometric Theissen polygons to produce exact catchment areas and a series of map overlay procedures. Such approaches are suitable for problems which are quite tractable by complete comparison of all options. For example, Taylor quotes the problem of finding two new sites for a facility from five possible sites, with the aim of minimising travel time. This involves twenty assessments.

One very practical approach that can be added under the 'simple' heading is the use of 'potential' measures of the type originally proposed by Hansen (1959). Smith (1974) reviews this type of work. This approach produces spatial surfaces, or zone scores, reflecting the potential of a site relative to chosen characteristics of other locations around it. Thus, for example, zones could be scored according to the number of potential retail customers around each zone, disaggregated by type if required. Such models would normally involve a gravity element, reflecting the distance-decay effects. A variant of this model for use in retailing has been suggested by Arrowsmith (Distributive Trades EDC, 1970). A related area of work, but one in which the gravity element is omitted, is that of 'spatial opportunity' measures of accessibility (Breheny, 1978). These could, for example, measure the number of customers available to all sites within given travel times.

Taylor's (1977) second category of solution methods concerns mathematical programming, or specifically linear programming. This is a strict optimisation technique in which an objective function is maximised or minimised. The spatial version of this approach deals with the 'transportation' or allocation problem. Again, most applications of linear programming have been in the public sector (see ReVelle et al. (1970) and Leonardi (1982) for reviews). In the private-sector work, much of the effort in recent years has been with linear-programming versions of spatial interaction models. In some of this work the concern has been with the allocation process only; that is, minimising travel, given fixed locations. Clearly, this tends to give trivial solutions, in which allocations are to the nearest zones. More realistic, but mathematically complex, approaches have been concerned with optimum locations of retail facilities from the consumer's point of view, in which the trade-off between size of facilities as a benefit and travel time as a cost has been modelled (Wilson (1976), Coelho and Wilson (1976), Bertuglia and Leonardi (1981)). Much of this work, however, is of little practical value at present.

Taylor's (1977) third category of solution methods concerns 'heuristic search' procedures. These deal with complex location-allocation situations in which the number of possible permutations of locations and allocations is very high and in which the above methods cannot be used. The heuristic search methods are not strictly optimising, in that they are based on the assumption that it is not feasible to consider all possible permutations. A heuristic algorithm is a set of rules that guides the search procedure and allows a convergence on the (near) optimum solution, using various short cuts along the way. Something akin to the optimum is likely to be found, but is not guaranteed.

Examples of the development and use of heuristic search methods come almost exclusively from the public-sector literature (see Massam (1975) and Hodgart (1978)). Much of this kind of work originates in Sweden, but examples of British applications are available (see Robertson (1976)). Usually, such methods are concerned with deterministic solutions, giving discrete spatial divisions, rather than probabilistic ones, but there seems to be no reason in principle why the approach should not be based on the latter, concentrating on location (say of shopping centres or stores) rather than location and allocation.

There is one notable application of heuristic search methods to large-store retailing. Newman (1980) suggests that gravity models are inappropriate when considering superstores and hypermarkets, and uses instead a search algorithm to define catchment areas for four hypermarkets and to locate three additional ones in the West Midlands.

Given these major characteristics of the optimisation models reported in the literature, what conclusions can we draw about their practical value for retailers and planners? Generally speaking, as it stands, much of the literature is of little help. Many of the models reported have been developed for the academic purpose of testing mathematical formulations. Often the application to, say, retailing is a trivial extension of the formulation; the concern is with the mathematics, not with retailing. This is shown in the unrealistic manner in which the retail system is characterised. It is usually too simplistic, or occasionally too complex, for the purpose at hand. Abstract models attempting to maximise retailers' profits, maximise consumer welfare, minimise travel times and maximise developers' profits all in one go are unlikely to be of much practical help.

It seems that no attempt has been made to develop an optimising model specifically to suit the practical requirements of retailers or planners. In many cases the requirement may be relatively simple. Planners seeking sites within, say, a county will only be concerned with a small number of possibilities to be assessed against existing facilities. In Taylor's (1977) terms this is a simple problem. Hodgart (1978) considers the possible aims of a local authority in optimising: it might be concerned with equity of service and hence may wish to find solutions minimising the distance travelled by the least accessible customer; it might be concerned with the simple distance or time minimisation solution; it might wish to achieve a given standard of, say, having no customer more than so many minutes from a superstore or hypermarket (the 'covering problem').

Retailers may also only be interested in a number of general locations and permutations of these. Again simpler methods may suffice. Even where a large number of locations is being considered, the criteria to be satisfied are likely to be limited. Usually the aim will be to identify locations where turnover or the number of customers visiting a store is maximised. Spatial interaction models, with their probabilistic treatment of allocations, form the most obvious basis for retail optimising models. The linear programming version of Coelho and Wilson's (1976) model could possibly be made more practicable. Given a small number of possible locations for stores it may suffice to run a retail gravity model a number of times. If the possible permutations are more numerous, there seems to be no reason why an heuristic search could not be run on spatial interaction principles.

For both retailers and planners, some simple approaches may be a useful first step in developing some sort of search procedure. Initially, search procedures can be carried out which simply aim to find areas with straightforward characteristics. For example, a retailer selling children's clothes might identify, say, local authority districts with a high absolute number of people under the age of ten. Such a simple measure could be improved by developing an index for each district which divides this number by the number of competing branches in each district. Such measures can be developed with very little effort or resources. To academics such measures may seem trivial, but many retailers will not have considered any form of systematic search, never mind having reached this degree of sophistication.

Simple measures of this kind fail, of course, to take into account factors (population, competition, etc.) beyond each area or zone for which the measure is taken. Other simple measures can be developed which do this. For example, following our simple suggestion above, the measures for each zone might take the population and competition within a given distance of the centre of each zone, regardless of whether this distance includes areas beyond the zone in question or not. Thus, distance bands are likely to overlap.

Adding a further degree of sophistication still, we might measure distance allowing for some decay effect, as in gravity models. For example, we might have a measure of the following form:

$$\text{Potential at zone } i \;=\; \sum_j \text{Population at zone } j / \text{Distance from } i - j^{\alpha}$$

Here each zone i will have a higher measure of potential the larger the population in nearby zones j. Conversely, the measure will be low if there is little population nearby. The parameter α on the distance measure builds in a distance-decay effect. This simple form of measure can be made more realistic by making the population measure specific to the retail problem. For example, it could be persons under the age of ten rather than population in total.

This form of measure is referred to as a 'potential measure'. It can take on various forms to suit the problem in hand. For example, we might wish to incorporate some measure of competition into the above formulation. We might do this as follows:

$$\text{Potential at zone } i \;=\; \sum \left(\sum_k \frac{\text{Populaton at zone } j / \text{Distance from } i - j^{\alpha}}{\text{Competition in zone } k / \text{Distance from } j - k^{\beta}} \right)$$

Here, the measure of potential at each zone takes into account the number of customers around that zone, but also accounts for the choice of stores – the competition – faced by each potential customer at the home. The index of potential for each zone is thus based on a realistic assessment of factors increasing potential (high numbers of potential customers) and those reducing potential (high numbers of competitors).

Given the appropriate data and a simple computer program to make these calculations, potential measures of this type could be taken for each of a large number of zones across a whole region. The result would be a surface of values, with high values representing areas of the greatest business potential. Specific sites could then be identified within such areas and a viability assessment carried out. Within an ongoing location-research strategy, such surfaces could be produced regularly to see how population changes, new roads and changing competition affect the surfaces. Indeed, hypothetical changes in these values could be tested to see how robust are the areas of highest potential to changing trading conditions.

Few retailers appear to use systematic search procedures, preferring to commence analytical work at the viability stage. This seems to be shortsighted because whilst a viability assessment may suggest that a site will trade well, the retailer will have no idea if there is a better site elsewhere – a site that may be being taken by a competitor. This failure to develop search procedures is all the more surprising because any retailer carrying out systematic viability work will have all of the information required to carry out search procedures of the kind suggested here.

Viability problems and techniques

The issue of viability is the one that has been most directly addressed by retailers and for which most technical development has taken place, at least as far as trade-area problems are concerned. Viability problems here refer to doubts that retailers have over the likely performance of a new store on a particular site. Clearly, this is a crucial issue. If the retailer has some confidence in making a judgment about likely performance, then decisions to proceed or not with land acquisition and store development will be much easier. As explained earlier, more complex trading conditions now make such judgments more and more difficult; hence the need for some rigorous methods of forecasting likely store performance.

Various factors will affect store performance. For many retailers, the crucial factors will be those relating to the nature of the trade or catchment area: whether it has a sufficiently high population; whether this population can gain easy access to the store; whether strong competitors are present; and so on. This will be the case particularly for those retailers operating in our outlet-dominated markets. For many retailers, the very localised trading conditions – the micro-site factors such as pedestrian flows, public transport facilities, proximity to other key traders, etc. – will affect the performance of their stores. Taking our analysis to even finer levels, clearly the relative performance of stores in a retail chain will depend on the internal characteristics of each store. Some may have had recent stylish refits and others not.

Ideally, in assessing store viability all of these three levels of analysis should be undertaken. The possibilities for systematic analysis at these three levels will be considered below, but, as will be obvious, the latter two levels have been neglected relative to trade-area issues.

Trade-area problems and techniques

The techniques developed to deal with trade-area viability problems have their origins clearly in the 'store-turnover forecasting' group identified earlier. Much of the early practical work in the field was developed in the United States, much of it inspired by William Applebaum. Various categorisations of these techniques are available, but here the distinctions will be made between a group of simple methods we might call 'univariate' techniques, a group of 'analogue' techniques, forms of 'regression analysis' which extend the analogue concept, and a group of 'spatial interaction' models of which the retail gravity model is the best known.

Univariate techniques   Before going on to look at the techniques likely to be considered as part of a serious location research strategy, mention should be made briefly of a group of simple techniques, labelled 'univariate techniques' by Jones and Mock (1984), which may be of use either to a retailer with extremely limited resources or as a preliminary to a more substantial approach.

Under this heading, we might include various rules of thumb that retailers sometimes use in making judgments. For example, a retailer might be happy to trade in an area if it has a minimum population level, or a minimum population level in a particular age or social group. Alternatively, it may be assumed that a given size of market can be split equally between competing retailers, thus assuming, rightly or wrongly, that they will all have the same turnover per ft^2.

Simple rules might be established through the calculation of ratios taken from readily-available information about existing stores in a retail chain. For example, a plot of turnover against catchment-area population levels will give the retailer some idea of required market sizes. Comparing a plot of this kind against another showing turnover against competition, measured as say total floorspace, could be quite revealing.

We might also place under the univariate heading a set of simple map-based assessments methods. For example, simple plotting of stores in a chain, along with competitors, might give a retailer a clearer idea of how the market is divided spatially and how the presence or absence of competitors affects performance. This might, in turn, help to identify 'ideal market areas' (Jones and Mock, 1984, p. 339) and hence gaps in the existing spatial market.

The value of simple approaches to understanding the spatial structure of a retail operation should not be underestimated. Even when more sophisticated approaches are to be used, it is a good idea to carry out simple analyses at the outset. For example, as part of a multiple regression exercise, it is useful to assess initially simple two-dimensional plots of the most important independent variables against the dependent variable. It may well be at this initial stage of assessment that the peculiar nature of a particular retail location problem is appreciated.

Analogue techniques   The use of analogues to help forecast store performance is more a basic approach than a specific technique. Consequently, there are numerous variations on the basic theme. The idea is very straightforward, involving the systematic comparison of the characteristics of a proposed store with those of a number of existing stores in the same chain for which information is available. The characteristics will fall into two groups: those concerned with the stores themselves; and those concerned with the catchment areas and customers. The approach thus relies heavily on case histories of similar stores. Obviously, the aim is to deduce the likely performance of the proposed store from knowledge of the 'analogue' stores. Drummey (1984) provides a recent description of the method.

The approach usually involves the calculation of market penetration rates at different distances from each of the analogue stores. In the simplest applications of the method the average of such rates might be applied to the available expenditure at the appropriate distances from the new store to give an assessment of likely expenditure in the new store. The sum of such expenditures will then give store turnover. Most applications, however, go further than this. Usually a sub-group of the stores surveyed will be chosen carefully − as the 'analogue group' − on the basis of similarity with the proposed store's internal and catchment characteristics. The variation in the observed penetration rates around each analogue group store might be related to differences in, say, competition and socio-economic structure of the population. Thus, zones (say grid squares) can be classified according to these characteristics and a certain penetration rate. Zones around the proposed store will then be classified and the appropriate penetration rate applied to give expenditure forecasts. Thus an approach can be developed that is sensitive to local circumstances.

An important point stressed by the proponents of this approach, and particularly by its initiator, Applebaum (1968), is that the results of this type of exercise must be regarded as a forecast 'benchmark' against which the analyst's experience and judgment will be applied. Only after careful consideration will a forecast level of turnover be put forward.

This analogue approach, used carefully and rigorously, has considerable merit. However, it has a number of shortcomings. An obvious one is that it is difficult to separate out the effects of each of a number of variables on penetration rates in this manual approach. Thus, for example, it is difficult to determine the effect that social structure and competition each have on expenditure flowing from a zone. Rogers and Green (1979) point out that the ability of the analyst to keep track of data and complex relationships must decline as the size of the problem increases. They also suggest that the approach is often very idiosyncratic, with the results likely to differ considerably with different analysts. In short, the problem with these analogue approaches is that the interdependence of variables that is inevitable in forecasting store turnover is difficult to handle intuitively, even when done as systematically as possible.

Multiple regression analysis The use of multiple regression models to assess store turnover is an obvious progression from analogue models used for this purpose. Multiple regression models can be used in the same basic way as the analogue model; that is, to generate a relationship between store turnover and a range of store, population and competitor characteristics. Again, the observations will come from surveys of analogue stores, although, as will be seen below, the different forms of regression model proposed have very different data requirements.

The advantage of multiple regression analysis is that the relationship between turnover, as the dependent variable, and a range of independent variables can be assessed more systematically. Analogue approaches tend to deal only with pairs of variables at a time; multiple regression analysis, by definition, allows more complex relationships to be investigated. Also, because the regression analysis will be computerised, the approach facilitates speedier and more flexible analysis; numerous variables and even forms of model can be adopted and tested very quickly.

The multiple regression equation will take the following form:

$$Y = a + bX_1 + bX_2 \ldots bX_n + bX_{n+1} \ldots bX_m$$

	Constant	Store characteristics	Catchment area characteristics
Dependent variable		Independent variables	

where Y is the dependent variable (store turnover, or money flowing to a store from a zone) and the Xs are independent variables, split in this case into those concerned with the characteristics of each store (typically store size, car parking facilities, etc.) in the analogue group and those concerned with the characteristics of the catchment area (population and competition, for example).

Given the data on the dependent and independent variables for all of the analogue stores involved, the multiple regression program will determine which particular form of the independent variables best explains the variation in the dependent variable between the analogue stores. It will produce an equation accordingly. This can then be used in forecasting turnover for a proposed store simply by putting values for the independent variables into the equation to produce the predicted value of the dependent variable.

Various forms of regression model for predicting turnover are possible. Very few applications to retailing have been reported, but those that have (see for example Rogers and Green (1979) and Fenwick (1978)) do reflect different possibilities. However, these reported applications have not been explained in relation to the total range of possibilities. A typology of multiple regression models for store-turnover forecasting is put forward here.

It is suggested that three basic types of store viability model can be developed from multiple regression analysis.

(a) *Model 1*, with store turnover as the dependent variable, regressed against the aggregate characteristics of the defined catchment area of each store in the analogue group. This model produces one equation.

(b) *Model 2*, with expenditure flowing from each defined zone to the store as the dependent variable. This model will also produce a single equation to be applied to each zone within the catchment area of a proposed store.

(c) *Model 3*, again with expenditure flowing from each zone as the dependent variable, but an equation developed for each of a number of typologies of zones. Typologies will reflect distinct differences in customer behaviour towards the stores in question. There will be as many equations as there are typologies.

Figure 2.6 attempts to illustrate the differences between the three models.

As will be seen below, these types of model are not necessarily

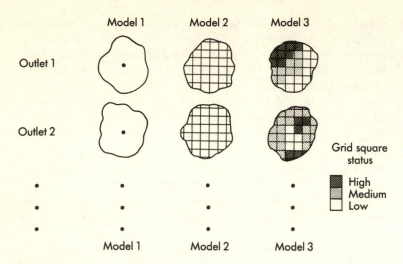

Figure 2.6 Three forms of multiple regression model.
Model 1: Each observation is an outlet trade area. The single regression equation estimates turnover for a new trade area.
Model 2: Each observation is a grid square. The single regression equation estimates turnover for grid squares within a new trade area.
Model 3: Each observation is a grid square, but grid squares are grouped into different types. A regression equation is calculated for each type of grid square, and turnover is estimated for each grid square using the appropriate regression equation.

discrete. Hybrids between them, and indeed between these and analogue approaches, can be developed and may be appropriate in certain circumstances. The three models will be discussed in turn.

Model 1: single equation, catchment area model   This is the simplest model and is likely to be adopted both in its own right and on the way to using models 2 and 3. It is likely to be used on its own when detailed zonal data is unavailable. The aim of this model is to develop a single equation to describe the relationship between the variation in the turnover in the analogue group of stores and the range of variables describing store characteristics and aggregate catchment area characteristics of each of these stores. Given this, the aggregate variables for the catchment area of the proposed store are fed into the equation as independent variables. The independent variables used in this model can be almost as numerous and detailed as those used in models 2 and 3.

The obvious disadvantage of this model is that it fails to make use of the detailed variation in the relationship between consumer spending and population/competition characteristics shown up at the zonal level.

The dependent variable in model 1 will be turnover at the store, or possibly some measure closely related to this, such as turnover per ft^2. The independent variables can be the same as those for other models, except for those that are calculable only on a zonal basis; these will include most measures of competition. The values of the independent variables will usually be averages for the whole of the catchment area (for example, percentage of population of certain age group, percentage in specific social group). For each variable there will be one measure for each analogue store, and hence as many values as there are analogue stores. If, as is likely, population data are available at a zonal level when other data are not, a slight variation on the model is possible. Population by a number of distance bands around each store might be included as independent variables.

The model can be assessed by forecasting the turnover of an established store that is similar to those used in the analogue group and for which data are available. However, if the number of stores in the chain is small, and hence the analogue group small, it may not be possible to keep one store out of the analogue group for testing purposes. In this case there is no alternative to using one of the stores in the analogue group. In principle this is dangerous because the known data for that store will have influenced the regression equation. Clearly, the smaller the analogue group the greater this problem. In practice, if the results of the test are interpreted sensibly, this should not be too much of a problem.

One possible variation on model 1 is to develop equations not for the whole catchment area of stores, but for graded catchment areas, or 'primary, secondary or tertiary markets' as Applebaum (1968) calls them, giving, say, 60 per cent, 75 per cent and 90 per cent of turnover. Summing the results of forecasts for each area would give store turnover. This approach does, however, imply availability of more detailed information on the geographical origin of store turnover and on catchment-area characteristics generally. If such information exists, models 2 or 3 might be preferred.

Table 2.1 gives examples of the regression equations and residuals resulting from an actual application of model 1 to a small supermarket chain. In this case, the largest possible analogue group was eight stores, which ideally is too small, but was of necessity used. Although a range of store and catchment area independent variables was used, the regression program selected the simplest and more obvious ones of store size, population size within a given drive time, and competition. With the highest residual in the second run not exceeding 7 per cent, and the

Table 2.1   Example of two runs of multiple regression model 1

Run 1

Turnover = 24,940 + 7.26 (Store size) − 0.38 (Competition within 5 mins) + 0.35 (Population within 5 min)

$R^2 = 0.9515$		Actual (£)	Forecast (£)	Difference (%)
	Store 1	195,400	187,300	− 4.1
	Store 2	94,950	101,300	+ 6.6
	Store 3	108,700	98,100	− 6.8
	Store 4	140,900	151,800	+ 7.7
	Store 5	102,900	100,500	− 2.3
	Store 6	172,800	165,700	− 4.1
	Store 7	169,000	172,900	+ 2.3
	Store 8	135,600	142,700	+ 5.2

Run 2

Turnover = 42,094 + 6.74 (Store size) + 0.023 (Population within 5 min) − 0.963 (Competition within 2 min)

$R^2 = 0.9706$		Actual (£)	Forecast (£)	Difference (%)
	Store 1	195,400	193,100	− 1.1
	Store 2	94,950	98,340	+ 3.5
	Store 3	108,700	106,400	− 2.1
	Store 4	140,900	150,400	+ 6.7
	Store 5	102,900	101,000	− 1.8
	Store 6	172,800	162,000	− 6.1
	Store 7	169,000	175,600	+ 3.9
	Store 8	135,600	133,200	− 1.7

selected variables and their signs making intuitive sense, this result was quite useful and the model used to make forecasts for new stores. In this case forecasts directly from the model were treated with some caution and considered alongside all other information and knowledge that could be brought to bear upon the issue.

This use of model results as a starting point for discussion about the likely turnover of a proposed store, rather than as the answer, is a sensible approach, even in those cases where the analogue group and the data available to the model are considerably better than in this example.

Model 2: single equation, zonal characteristics model   This model assumes the availability of detailed data at a zonal level within catchment areas. Preferably these zones should be uniform, such as grid squares, so that the observations going into the equation are directly comparable. If data are not available in this form, irregular shaped zones should be defined that are as near equal in size as possible.

The model requires that observations for both the dependent and independent variables are available for each analogue store. For the *dependent variable* this means that survey work to ascertain the flow of expenditure from each catchment-area zone to the store, for each analogue group store, is necessary. If this information is gathered from a questionnaire survey, information on the socio-economic characteristics of customers might be useful. The need to carry out a substantial amount of survey work for the development of model 2 means that the use of this version of the regression model implies a much greater financial commitment than model 1.

The dependent variable in this model can be expressed either in absolute terms, as the amount of money flowing from each zone to the store in a given period, or in percentage terms as the share of available expenditure in the zone drawn to the store. In the former case the forecast values will be summed to give store turnover; in the latter case the summing will take place after the percentage figures have been multiplied by an estimated zonal retail expenditure figure. Care must be taken in the precise definition of dependent and independent variables to ensure that statistical rules of combining various definitions are not breached.

Independent variable observations on store characteristics will be the same for each zone in model 2. The types of information used in model 1 apply equally to model 2.

The collection of zonal data for the independent *catchment-area variables* may also involve a heavy resource commitment. If only total population counts are required, it should be possible to obtain the data without too much effort or cost. If more detailed information giving the socio-economic characteristics of the zonal population is required, then it may be necessary to pay a bureau to extract the data in the appropriate form. Information on competitors, located by zone, should be easier for the analyst to gather, although again this can be obtained from specialist bureaux.

The assumption behind model 2, and one that should be rigorously tested, is that the spending and socio-economic characteristics of the surveyed customers reflect the consistent behaviour of all residents of that zone to the store in question. This is important because surveyed information on flows of expenditure will be related back to the total population; for example, the surveyed money spent by socio-economic group X from a particular zone might be calculated as a proportion of the estimated total available retail expenditure of that socio-economic group in that zone. In using the model for forecasting, we would then need estimates of available retail expenditure by socio-economic group by zones around the proposed store.

In addition to data on customer and zonal characteristics, details of competitors in the area of each analogue store are required. Zonal measures of competition are likely to be very useful, but difficult to define. Simple measures, such as the total number of competitors within so many kilometres, may be used, or more sophisticated measures devised. Model 2 improves considerably on model 1 in offering the possibility of much more sensitive measures of competition. The consumer will obviously view the merits of competing stores from home. Thus any competition measure which is calculated by residence, in this case by zone, will be preferred.

Model 2 differs from model 1 in that it develops an equation based on the detailed zonal variation in the relationship between money spent in the store and zonal characteristics, rather than an aggregate relationship. Nevertheless, model 2 in its basic form, produces just one equation again, in this case used to forecast expenditure at the proposed store coming from each zone.

Reported applications of regression models of type 2 are rare, although it has certainly been used in practice. Rogers and Green (1979) do explain one application, in this case using percentage of available expenditure as the dependent variable.

In the basic version of model 2, as described above, a single equation will be produced for the analogue grouping. In setting up and experimenting with the model it may be found that the best result is for a reduced catchment area. For instance, the model may forecast better for a 20-minute catchment area, taking in, say, 80 per cent of turnover, than with a 30-minute catchment, taking 95 per cent of turnover. This could arise for a number of reasons, such as the relatively random behaviour of shoppers at the margin of the catchment area. In this situation it may be preferable to use the 20-minute equation and add on the unexplained turnover on a simple ratio basis. This will only be determined by experimentation.

Clearly, a major independent variable in this form of model 2 will be the distance of a zone from the store. An important variant on model 2, which in fact takes it towards model 3, removes distance from the equation. This variant, which we might call model 2A, takes a number of distance- or time-bands around the store (say 2.5 or 5.0 minutes) and develops a regression equation for each. The equation is developed in the same way as in the basic form of model 2, except that distance is excluded as an independent variable and there will be as many equations as distance-bands used. The advantage of this version of model 2 is that in the basic form distance is so dominant as a variable that it tends to disguise the possibly important role of other independent variables. Model 2A treats distance explicitly by using time-bands, but outside the equations.

In developing model 2A the time-bands should be drawn sufficiently tightly that time or distance within each band is not significant. This leads to an obvious statistical problem, however; with narrow bands, and hence a small number of zones in each band, the number of observations in the analogue grouping may be too few. A general rule must be that model 2A, used with tight bands, should only be used if a relatively large number of stores is included in the analogue grouping.

One likely problem with any form of model 2 concerns zones that on the basis of survey data contribute little or no expenditure to the store. A large number of such values, which are more likely to occur in zones some distance from the store, will have too strong an influence on the regression line. It may be appropriate to exclude some zones with zero or low expenditure to overcome this problem. However, not all such zones can be excluded because the model must have the capacity to predict those zones from which only a limited amount of expenditure is drawn.

Initially models 2 and 2A can be tested according to the values of R^2 gained for each equation. A considerable amount of experimentation may be necessary before satisfactory results are obtained; for example, different independent variables may be tried, measured as absolute or percentage values. Different analogue groupings should also be tried. Ultimately, the real test of the models must be store-turnover predictions, preferably against existing stores not included in the analogue group.

Model 3: typology equations, zonal characteristics model This model is, in principle, the most sophisticated of the three in that it aims to make the best use of the variability in the data available. The approach is similar to model 2A described above, except that the grouping of zones is done more systematically according to their socio-economic characteristics. The idea behind the model is that certain groups in the population can be identified, each of which has distinct patterns of shopping behaviour in relation to the store chain in question. Regression equations developed for such groupings, or typologies, should then be more informative than general equations.

There are various ways in which such typologies of zones could be produced. Standard area classifications could be used. For example, the ACORN system of classification (CACI, 1981) gives, at the most detailed level, thirty-nine socio-economic classifications in to which any small area (enumeration district, grid square, etc.) can be allocated. If such classifications are considered relevant, then each zone in the catchment area of each store in the analogue group can be allocated to a typology. Regression equations can then be developed, as in model 2 but for each typology.

If the use of national classifications for local purposes is considered too crude, then it is possible to develop a classification specifically for the task in hand through the use of multivariate techniques such as cluster analysis. Having developed a local typology in this way, it could be used in exactly the same way as described above.

A further alternative approach might be to develop a classification more directly related to knowledge of the socio-economic characteristics of customers of a chain store. From survey information of the type gathered for analogue stores in model 2, it should be possible to trace consistent characteristics of customers. Classifications of customers who use the stores to differing degrees can then be used to classify zones in the catchment areas of analogue stores. Such a procedure might be based on the principle characteristics of types of customer, avoiding the complication of multivariate analysis.

Having defined typologies in one of these ways, the development of model 3 would be the same as that for model 2A above. There will be as many equations as typologies. The *dependent variable* could be absolute flows of expenditure to a store or proportion of available expenditure in each zone. The independent variables representing *store characteristics* will again be identical for each zone and for each typology. The *catchment-*area independent variables will be of the type discussed under model 2, but in this case socio-economic variables, which are reflected here in the typologies, will not be included.

In using the model for forecasting, each zone around the proposed store will be allocated to a typology and will then have the appropriate equation applied to it. Again, zonal values will be summed to give forecast store turnover.

Producing analogue groups   One important issue that is common to both the analogue and multiple regression techniques is the choice of an analogue group or groups. In both cases, it is the information gathered for the stores in these groups that will determine the quality of the resultant model. It is likely for both types of models that specific groupings of observed stores will yield better analogies for a proposed store than will the complete set of stores. In deciding upon which stores to group together, and in some cases to survey, the most important criterion must be the type of store to be built in the future. The larger the number of stores in an analogue group the better for statistical reasons; very small groupings must be avoided. The appropriate number to use in regression analysis will also depend on the type of model to be adopted. Model 2 can be developed with a smaller analogue group than model 1 because the number of observations is the number of zones in all analogue stores, rather than the number of stores.

In the testing of a regression model it may be necessary to produce analogue groupings that are likely to be useful for forecasting in advance of knowledge of specific proposed store sites. In this case, some criterion for grouping stores would be useful. One relatively sophisticated way of doing this would be to look systematically for similarities between stores through the use of, say, factor analysis. Davies (1977b) has carried out an exercise of this kind in producing a classification of the branches of a durables retailer. Other, less systematic methods for grouping might be adopted; for example, Rogers and Green (1979) rely largely upon regional groups.

Spatial interaction models   For British academics, a remarkable feature of very recent developments in store-turnover forecasting work has been the re-emergence of spatial interaction models, and the gravity model in particular, as proposed techniques. As recently as 1983, Breheny (1983a and b), in reviewing the use of techniques in large-store location planning, did not refer to gravity models except in relation to impact studies. In Britain practical applications of such models was limited in the 1960s and 1970s to the public sector, particular to strategic planning, and work on the practical use of such models virtually ceased in the late 1970s. This was a result of both disenchantment with the models themselves and a government warning that use of such models for impact assessment in large-store public inquiries was not appropriate. It was the possibility of using such models for impact assessment that had been the major impetus to their practical development up to that time.

Throughout this period, some practical development of gravity models was taking place in the United States, but as much for private-sector use as for public planning. Rogers (1984) reviews the form of model developed and used at this time. Some of the interest in using the gravity model again in Britain is a direct result of Rogers' marketing of his American model.

One peculiar feature of this work was that, of necessity, the models were developed to deal with flows of customers and money to particular kinds of stores, not shopping centres. Certainly in Britain, retail gravity-models had always dealt with trips to shopping centres. One advantage of this was that all retail expenditure was accounted for. This meant there was no need to decide on what proportion of the total was being modelled, and that the competition was all other retailing. In the form of model now being proposed, specific choices have to be made on these issues and more detailed information required for calibration purposes.

One interesting feature of this resurrection of the gravity model in practical retail work will be the response of academics, who have continued to work on the technical development of this form of model, despite its unpopularity amongst practitioners. They may welcome the opportunity to try out their new formulations in an applied context. However, there may be a conflict of interest if they respond in this way. The model formulations being adopted for practical retailing may have some peculiar features, such as the modelling of home-to-store trips, but they are essentially very simple. Rogers' (1984) work, for example, involves the use of a very basic gravity model, and reflects the principle adopted in much practical research work; if in doubt, keep it simple. A lot of academic modellers, of course, work according to the very opposite principle. To be fair, a very small number have combined academic development and practical applications of models (see, Fotheringham, this volume). Nevertheless, it will be interesting to see how this particular sub-field of retail location work develops.

Micro-site and in-store problems and techniques

Whilst the issue of viability is the location problem addressed most directly by retailers, and the one for which most technical work has been developed, this work has focused very heavily on what are termed here 'trade-area' issues. Clearly for many retailers, store performance will be heavily determined by these issues; population levels, proximity of population to the store, location and size of competitors, etc. However, it may well be that a proportion of performance cannot be accounted for by these factors and that more site-specific issues – what are called here micro-site factors – need to be considered.

The problem is, how to consider them systematically? Certainly, there is very little guidance available because neither retailers, consultants or academics appear to have given the matter much thought. Bowlby, Breheny and Foot (1985b) attempt to make some progress by suggesting that the task is to:

(a) identify which micro-level factors will be important to particular retail businesses; and

(b) estimate the effect of these factors on store turnover.

The schema introduced above in Figure 2.3 to identify types of retailing provides a basis for considering which micro-site factors may be important to which types of retailing. Bowlby, Breheny and Foot (1985b) present a simplified version of this schema against which they relate the micro-site factors that seem most likely to affect store performance in each different type of retailing. Figure 2.7 shows the result. The micro-site factors may seem rather obvious; however the intention of the schema is not to provide an exhaustive list, but to demonstrate that careful thinking about micro-site factors is a necessary prelude to any attempt to measure their effects.

Having identified potentially relevant micro-site factors, one initial way of trying to assess their importance is to carry out small-scale surveys of customers at existing stores to check whether particular site features are in fact significant in explaining customers' shopping behaviour or images of the stores. Such surveys could examine the other shops, car parks or public transport terminals used by customers as well as their images of, and attitudes towards, the retailer's existing stores and sites. Larger surveys might attempt to survey people who do not use a store, in order to determine their reasons for not doing so. There is considerable experience amongst academic researchers of such investigations of consumers' behaviour and preferences (see, for example, Shepherd and Thomas (1980) and Guy (1975)). There has been a variety of studies of the 'images' consumers hold of different types of shopping environment and the degree to which trips to one type of store are linked to trips to complementary or

(a)

	Convenience	Specialist
Large number of outlets	Newsagents Supermarkets Laundrettes	Building societies Banks Fashion multiples
Small number of outlets	Superstores Hypermarkets DIY Stores	Jewellers Quality fashion Auction houses

(b)

	Convenience	Specialist
Large number of outlets	Public transport Pedestrian flows Car parking	Presence of other retailers Public transport Pedestrian flows 'Image'
Small number of outlets	Car parking Other services (e.g. filling stations, restaurants)	Presence of other quality competitors Presence of other complementary quality stores Exterior design 'Image'

Figure 2.7 A simple schema for identifying micro-site factors. (a) A classification of retail activities. (b) Micro-site factors important to each of these groups of activities. (*Source*: Bowlby, Breheny and Foot, 1985b.)

competing stores. Perhaps this work could be more directly geared to the relationship between store performance and these factors.

Just as surveys of consumers might help to reveal the relative significance of different micro-site factors, so might surveys of retailers. In particular, store managers, whilst they may not have an appreciation of the more strategic factors affecting the performance of their stores, will probably have a sound appreciation of the significance of the more localised factors. Some way of synthesising their views might reveal consistencies in the importance of particular micro-scale factors. Timmermans (1986) reports on the use of a 'decompositional multi-attribute preference model' to glean from a survey of varied retailers their preferences for particular site characteristics. It would be interesting to carry out a similar exercise on a survey of store managers from a single retail chain.

Clearly, when a retailer has some idea of which micro-site factors affect the performance of stores, these can then be related to turnover in an attempt to account for their individual contribution. The most positive factors can then be planned for at new stores. The obvious problem in trying to relate micro-site factors to turnover is to distinguish what proportion of turnover is accounted for by these factors relative to trade area characteristics such as population, distance and competition. It was suggested above that the performance of stores in outlet-dominated markets is more likely to result from trade-area characteristics, and hence could be assessed using store-turnover forecasting techniques. It was also suggested that for the more specialised retailers in product-dominated markets, micro-site factors, and hence assessment methods, could be particularly important. In the former case, a technique advocated for the forecasting of turnover was multiple regression analysis, based on trade-area characteristics. It was not suggested that micro-site factors be included as independent variables. However, the differences shown by the analysis between actual and forecast store turnover for each store in the analogue group may indicate the influence of micro-site features on turnover. The size of these 'residuals' can be assessed against known micro-site factors. Thus, for example, stores that perform better than predicted may be found to have particular local characteristics. In some cases, where examination of residuals suggests that only one micro-site feature, such as, say, the level of car parking, is responsible for the divergence between actual and predicted, this variable could be included directly into the regression. More commonly, however, a variety of different combinations of micro-site features will be responsible and hence a study of the residuals will simply suggest micro-site factors which should be examined on new sites. Assessment of residuals can therefore be useful, but care must be taken because their size may be influenced by errors of measurement in the variables as well as by micro-site and other 'real' factors.

For product-dominated markets it was suggested above that regression analysis of trade-area characteristics was not likely to be a useful turnover forecasting technique. However, regression analysis might be useful for specialist stores when looking at micro-site issues. Thus, for those specialist retailers with a reasonably large number of analogue stores, we might attempt to predict turnover in relation to a set of micro-site measures. For example, if we were to analyse the outlets of a multiple fashion chain, we might take measures at each store of pedestrian flows, distance to bus stops, number of other fashion shops within a given distance, and so on. We could measure less tangible features such as design quality of each store by use of a scale measure reflecting the retailer's judgment of this quality.

The outcome of this use of regression will be an equation that can be used to forecast the turnover of a store as a function of micro-site factors. Just as it was suggested above that certain important micro-site factors might be included in trade-area regression models, so for micro-site regressions some trade-area features might be included if they improve the performance of the model. Again, residuals from a micro-site model may give some clue as to the importance of trade-area characteristics.

For specialist retailers with very few outlets, regression analysis may not be possible because of the problem of providing a large enough analogue group. For such retailers, a commonsense but systematic analysis of micro-site factors likely to affect turnover should still yield useful information for helping to choose new sites.

If, in principle, we continue to focus on more and more detailed factors likely to influence store performance, we inevitably move from exterior micro-site factors to in-store issues. Traditionally, of course, store location assessments have not considered such issues. There is no intention here of drastically changing this tradition, other than to point out the fact that increasingly the performance of individual stores in a retail chain may depend as much on where they feature in the design strategy of the company as on trade-area or micro-site factors. It has become very fashionable in recent years for retailers to undertake major, expensive refurbishments of their stores, adopting completely new images. These have, in some cases, had a dramatic effect on performance. For example it was reported that the turnover of a branch of Marks and Spencer rose 40 per cent immediately after such a refit. The trade-area and micro-site factors did not change. The problem for modelling the performance of stores undergoing such changes is obvious. In principle, the answer is simple; newly refurbished stores must form a separate analogue group for analytical purposes. The problem in practice, however, may be one of time; even in the largest retail chains it may take some years before sufficient stores with the same image have settled down to trading. The problem may be exacerbated if a part of the refurbishment strategy is to create diversity across the range of branches, with each store having peculiar characteristics.

The aim here is not to suggest ways of resolving this problem – it is not essentially a technical issue – but to point out the importance of extending a location research strategy to account as far as possible for all factors that affect store performance.

Evaluation problems and techniques

Remarkably, given the massive financial commitment involved on the part of all major retailers, it is in the area of existing store evaluation that the least modelling work appears to have been done. On the face of it little effort is made to determine why particular stores in a chain perform better or worse than might be expected; indeed, it may be that there is no clear idea of what is expected. Other, more specific questions often go unasked, never mind answered. For example, what are the socio-economic characteristics of the company's customers? Do these differ from those of competitors? If so, why? Do a company's stores perform consistently well or badly in the presence of particular competitors? Do they perform better against them in specific replicable circumstances? Does the presence of non-food sales increase food sales? How does store size affect sales? How do refits affect performance? How will changing demographic structures affect sales?

There are, then, many important aspects of retail performance that are not evaluated. The implication is clear; lessons are not learned, mistakes are repeated and money is lost. The issue is obviously important for all retailers, but increasingly so as programmes of store openings are matched by closures and as major refits are undertaken. Stores should only be closed if their potential trade is inadequate; this potential needs to be assessed systematically before decisions are made. An expensive programme of refitting stores should also be based on careful assessment of their potential; there is no point in carrying out such a refit if a store is already trading to its maximum potential.

It is easy to point out the problems that might arise from not carrying out careful evaluation of existing store performance, but what might be done to facilitate such evaluation? In Britain, the only substantial reported work on this has been carried out by Davies in a series of reports (1973; 1977b).

In the first of these studies (Davies (1973)), in which the seventy-two stores of a national durable retailer were being evaluated, three objectives were set.

(a) 'To identify underlying regularities in the characteristics of all stores and assess the relative strengths or weakness of each store in relation to those common dimensions.' For this purpose principal-components analysis and factor analysis were used.

(b) 'To classify the stores according to degrees of similarity among their characteristics and provide a framework for comparing average statistics of retail attributes and performance.' This involved the use of cluster analysis.

(c) 'To distinguish certain more important diagnostic variables which accounted for most of the variation in sales performance among stores and construct models to compare theoretical levels of attainment with those sales actually achieved.' This was accomplished through the use of multiple regression analysis.

Each of these multivariate techniques used a common data set which gave details for each store across a range of variables dealing with catchment and store characteristics. In relation to objective (a) above, the techniques were used to identify major 'factors', relating to particular sets of variables, which explain differences in store performance. For example, two of Davies's (1973) factors related to 'trade potential' and 'selling efficiency'. Each store can then be related to each factor to see whether it performs positively or negatively. Davies (1977b) reports on the application of this method to grocery retailing.

The cluster analysis used to meet objective (b) produced groupings of stores in which the similarities within the groups were maximised and the similarity between groups minimised. The performance of stores in particular groupings can then be assessed against average figures. In this way, consistencies in performance amongst groups with particular characteristics can be determined. The use of multiple regression analysis to achieve Davies's (1977b) objective (c) is similar to the use of the technique for forecasting store turnover as discussed in the section on viability above. A regression equation was generated to relate the turnover of existing stores to a range of independent variables. This, in effect, produces an 'average' explanation of the determinants of store turnover. If the equation is then used to forecast the turnover of each store individually, the difference between this forecast and the actual turnover – that is, the residual – shows the deviation of each store from the average. The idea is that the reasons for this deviation can then be assessed systematically, often by reference back to the raw data (Davies, 1977b). Fenwick (1978) also discusses the use of multiple regression analysis in this way in his work on building-society branch performance.

One obvious additional benefit, then, from the use of multiple regression as a viability assessment technique is that it automatically gives information that is of use in evaluating existing stores. As a general rule, store-turnover forecasting work should give valuable assistance in store evaluation, either directly, as in the case of multiple regression, or indirectly. However, the best use will only be made of this information if it is seen as part of a proper evaluation exercise.

The work reviewed earlier under our spatial marketing approaches to store viability forecasting are valuable in store evaluation. Any work that assesses the potential sales of a good or goods in an area, such as CACI offer for their Local Expenditure Zones, or Pinpoint in their Retail Potential Reports, will provide a useful datum against which retailers can assess the share taken by their stores. Penetration-rate assessments of this kind also feature as part of McIntyre's Statsfile.

Although the amount of literature and evidence relating directly to store evaluation, particularly as part of a comprehensive programme, is sparse, it is reasonably clear that methods are available and can be developed to aid existing store evaluation. Obviously retailers do consider the relative performances of their stores, but there does seem to be a need for more explicit and rigorous evaluation programmes. Again, rigour does not necessarily imply the use of complex techniques; a lot can and should be achieved by careful consideration of carefully gathered information on each store.

Conclusions

This chapter has described a revolution – in the approaches adopted by retailers in making their location decisions. But, like all revolutionary change, one suspects, its very speed makes it less effective than it might have been. In this instance, dramatic changes have taken place in the practices adopted by retailers without them having a clear collective, and in most cases individual, grasp of the opportunities afforded by more systematic locational analysis. Consultants and academics have been so eager to be party to the exciting changes that they have done little to clarify these opportunities, or to point out the pitfalls of poorly-conceived retail-location analysis.

What is needed is a stocktaking exercise, in which present practices are assessed against a considered view of the possibilities for thorough, but practical, retail-location research. This chapter has attempted to contribute to such an exercise by sketching out a classification of retail location problems, both as a means for encouraging a broader understanding of these problems and as a basis for considering the appropriateness of a range of techniques for addressing these.

Although this review of retail location problems and methods has been lengthy and in places rather convoluted, the basic messages it intends to convey are simple. Lest the detailed classifications developed in the first half of the paper and the discussion of techniques in the second obscure these, they will be stated baldly here.

(a) A necessary preliminary to any work on the development and application of retail location methods is an understanding of the range of location problems retailers are likely to face or – because these problems are often also opportunities – should face. The classification of problems presented here is intended to focus attention on this full range.

(b) The appropriate use of retail location techniques and data is likely to be much clearer when they are related to a fuller understanding of location problems.

(c) Many practical retail problems will be peculiar to the retailer concerned and will require specific analytical and technical responses. These responses will often not involve the neat use of readily available techniques, but hybrid types of analysis, possibly using established techniques in a particular way and often in combination with sensible use of simple step-by-step procedures rather than statistical or modelling techniques as such.

(d) Substantial progress in location research can be made by using relatively simple methods of analysis.

(e) If more sophisticated analysis is required, there is a range of techniques that can be developed and which, if used thoughtfully, can be of considerable help in making location decisions.

(f) Retailers should consider search and evaluation issues as well as the more obvious store viability problems.

(g) Above all, location issues are so important to retailers that 'location research strategies', that will link together search, viability and evaluation considerations, should be developed and used on a continuous basis. A basic procedure for such a strategy has been outlined here.

CHAPTER 3
Store location analysis: problems and progress

John R. Beaumont

Introduction

Background

Retailing is now changing more rapidly than for a very long time. Opportunities and risks associated with store locations are heightened by a retail business environment of rapidly evolving technological developments, .changing competitive positions, altered consumer behaviour and expectations, and modified regulatory situations.

Store location analyses are required both to assess and improve the sales performance of existing stores and to examine the viability of potential new stores. Opening new stores and extending or closing existing stores are such fundamental investment decisions that it is crucial to evaluate a store's or a set of stores' market potential and competitive position.

Store location analysis, particularly with the increased availability of computer-based techniques, can provide invaluable information to assist retail management with their decision-making at an extremely small fraction of the cost of the aggregate investment.

As a basis for this discussion, three different, albeit interrelated, components of store location analysis can be identified:
(a) management needs;
(b) data availability and quality;
(c) methodological requirements.
The success and relevance of store location analyses are dependent primarily on communication between technical analysts, who produce the studies, and management, who use the results.

Failures to provide meaningful and actionable analyses are often more attributable to poor lines of communication between the analysts and management than to any technical shortcomings *per se*. Management must comprehend the limitation of the results, the data inputs and the underlying assumptions. The isolation of research is currently a fundamental constraint.

It is appropriate to quote from Lodish and Reibstein's (1986, p. 180) recent examination of the changing practice of marketing research.

> Persons with expertise in marketing science, employed either as full time staff or as external consultants, can improve decision making when they serve as liaison between the manager and the new technology.
>
> The liaison people have two very important skills. They understand the business and the strategic problems that management faces. They also understand enough about data analysis, statistical analysis and modelling to make sure that appropriate checks and questions have been asked when a recommendation based on computer analysis is made. These people should report directly to top and middle management as part of staff groups. That way, they will control the quality of the analysis being done. We cannot emphasise enough the importance of having someone who understands data analysis review management's decisions on strategy.

Recognition of this situation is demonstrated by the positive support for the ESRC Workshop on which this volume is based from both the academic and commercial sectors. That workshop represented an important and much-needed first step, providing the platform both for academics to be involved in the entire model-building process from purpose to evaluation and for retailers to be made aware of the latest operational methods of retail analysis (see also Beaumont (1986a)). However, the situation of academic researchers linked with research units in retailers is unlikely to be sufficient. Technical analysts in the commercial sector are often isolated from the decision-making process, acting at best as a responsive, rather than proactive, service function. (For real progress, management must be involved directly in applying methods of retail analysis and forecasting.)

In addition to management involvement to satisfy their needs, it is essential to consider both data availability and quality and methodological requirements. As a general tenet, further enhancements to many of the available techniques cannot be justified until the quality of available data is improved. The proliferation of computer hardware and software does little to facilitate the sound application of techniques in store location analysis; the key determinants are availability of necessary input data and experienced staff.

Contents

In this discussion, store location analysis is viewed as transforming data into relevant and useful information to assist retail management's decision-making. The emphasis must be on applied problem-solving, rather than fitting a problem to a method! Ultimately, effectiveness is not dependent on methodological criteria or sophistication, but on an ability to provide useful and meaningful insights for retail management on the impacts of alternative plans. Obviously, this topic is broad, and, while this discussion is necessarily selective, a number of general issues are considered. No detailed description of different techniques is presented (there are a plethora of suitable methodological textbooks available!).

As background, in the next section, an outline specification of the store location problem is presented. Given the earlier comments, data availability and quality is discussed in the third section, and special reference is given to geographic information systems, the analysis of company data, the availability of secondary data and the power of linking data sets to create new information. In the fourth section the methodological discussion focuses on the applications of both categorical data analysis and gravity-based spatial interaction models, two approaches that offer enormous practical potential for store location analysis in the future. (For more detailed discussion, see the chapters in this volume by Fotheringham, Wilson and Wrigley.) In the final section, some concluding comments are made in relation to the future outlook.

Outline specification of the store location problem

Discussion

Briefly, store location analysis can be viewed as matching demand and supply interrelationships over space. There is a demand for goods and services from different household types with various needs that can be supplied by competing stores. Three general problems can be distinguished:

(a) 'Free location problem' – planning the location of a network of stores from their inception.
(b) 'Incremental location problem' – given the existing network of stores, in a growth programme, what are the best stores to expand/sites for new stores?
(c) 'Reorganisation location problem' – given the existing network of stores, in a rationalisation programme, which stores should be removed to generate the best network?

Store location analysis should not be interpreted narrowly as selecting sites for new stores/closing existing stores; merchandising, advertising and so on, leading to development through greater sales, have direct locational ramifications for both existing and new stores. For many retailers, analysis focuses on appropriate product mix rather than location *per se*. The basic premise underlying this discussion is that store location analysis should be an integral component of the formulation, implementation and evaluation of any marketing strategy plan in relation to:

(a) identifying target customer groups;
(b) assessing alternative store locations;
(c) establishing realistic market and sales targets;
(d) monitoring performance and tracking the impacts of advertising and promotion.

Retail management need to pay explicit attention to the best available store location not only because of the direct influence of the consumers' behaviour patterns and the competitive situation on the magnitude of sales and hence profit, but also because of the implications of service provision in terms of both organisation and selling techniques. Store location analyses must incorporate a consideration of development and operational costs in order to be able to assess profitability and consistency with an overall marketing strategy – a relatively high-cost location may have a disproportionately greater sales and profit potential.

Sales forecasting and performance evaluation are integral components of store location analysis. It should be possible to set realistic targets to permit comparisons of the performance of different stores in a network; consistent and operational benchmarks – performance indicators – are necessary because some stores possess a 'locational advantage' and others a 'locational disadvantage'.

Simply stated, any store location strategy must be an integral part of an overall marketing strategy, involving management policy on store size, market coverage, merchandising, distribution, advertising and so on.

Data availability and quality

Background

In the so-called IT age, it should not be underestimated how information gives a company competitive advantage (see, for instance, Porter and Miller (1985)). Advances in methods of data collection, such as split-cable technology and uniform-product-code (UPC) scanners, offer enormous scope for market-driven store location analysis. Moreover, computers have meant that accessibility to data has grown exponentially; the computer is not only a tool for completing mathematical and statistical analyses, but also a medium for transforming raw data into usable information.

Emphasis, however, is usually given solely to the potential to assist management's decision-making, often neglecting the dangers that data overload can actually hinder sound decision-making. The sheer volume and complexity of data – official statistics, market surveys and internal company data – can be a problem. For instance, the future growth of EPOS, particularly the resulting direct availability of sales data, will provide enormous opportunities for store location analysis only if the data are collected and stored in a suitably structured and flexible format.

A number of primary and secondary data sources are available to assist retail management. For store location analyses in the United Kingdom, in comparison with North America, there is a general lack of marketing statistics disaggregated by location. For decision-making, retail management rely on secondary published data sources complemented by individually-commissioned market research and internal company data.

In this section attention is given to the potential to analyse primary data sources and the need to re-examine the availability of pertinent secondary data sources for retail management; the power of linking different data sets is also mentioned. First, however, for reference, some basic characteristics of Geographic Information Systems are noted because of the new opportunities being opened by digital mapping and analysis.

Geographic information systems

The essence of handling geographic information in store location analysis is the linkage of different data sets. The fundamental problem today arises from constraints on cross-referencing and aggregating data sets because they are based on different spatial units; for example, in many studies, it is necessary to link socio-economic and demographic household data based on census enumeration districts with customer data referenced by postal geography. Additional difficulties arise when trying to build up consistent historical series of data.

For store location analysis, significant features of any data source are the need for consistency over time and disaggregation over space. Conceptually, it would be possible to develop a spatial referencing system to overcome such problems, and other problems that are unavoidable, such as the 'modifiable areal unit problem' (Openshaw and Taylor, 1981), could be quantified in a meaningful way.

The power of using digital Ordnance Survey 1:1,250 maps demonstrates the enormous potential for flexible data integration in decision support systems for interactive store location analysis. However, today, there is a lack of national coverage of geographic information in a similar form, and, moreover, the current Ordnance Survey timescale to complete this task, beyond the turn of the century, makes this path impractical to follow in the short-term. For the future it is important that the existing technology is proven, and, therefore, the issues are of a practical and developmental, rather than research, orientation. Development coordination is a basic prerequisite because of the multidisciplinary and scattered interests involved in handling geographic data.

Primary data sources

It is not an understatement to say that the majority of companies need to enhance their ability to generate, process and interpret available market information. A most relevant place to start is with internal company databases; many companies have developed their own management information systems that offer enormous potential for marketing purposes (although they are often used exclusively to satisfy an accounting function). For instance, postcoded customer files can be analysed to derive appropriate market segmentation.

The usefulness and power of 'geodemographic' discriminators, such as ACORN (A Classification of Residential Neighbourhoods) and PiN (Pinpoint Identified Neighbourhoods), to describe and identify markets have been recognised, and they are likely to become more important with greater specialisation in retailing. Applications include not only targeting potential customers but also cross-referencing *ad hoc* market research surveys and monitoring store performance with a meaningful and consistent base.

While general-purpose discriminators, such as ACORN and PiN, provide an off-the-shelf ready-made market segmentation, there is no such thing as a single classification either for a particular data set or for all problems (see also Charlton *et al.* (1984)). With available customer data and trends of greater specialisation, there will be an increased incidence of customised discriminators developed in the future. Such bespoke solutions are more powerful discriminators than general-purpose ones because their derivation is driven by the important socio-economic and demographic household characteristics of the specific problem of interest.

Secondary data sources

Given the cancellation or suggested cancellation of official data both on the demand side (such as customer demographics in a mid-term 10 per cent sample census) and on the supply side (such as the Census of Distribution and the Annual Commercial and Industrial Floorspace Statistics), much reliance must be now placed on the decennial Census of Population. For information on customer expenditure patterns, the annual Family Expenditure Survey and General Household Survey are useful sample-based data sets, although they do not provide detailed local area data; the latter is nationally based and the former is disaggregated by region. The sole government data source exclusively for the retail sector is the sample survey of VAT-registered businesses and shops in the biannual Retail Inquiry, which, unfortunately, is only available at a national level. Explicitly locational data of direct relevance from commercial companies include property surveys providing floorspace, rental and other statistics (see for instance, the computerised databases available from Hillier Parker, Newman, A. C. Nielsen and Media Audits).

This current situation regarding secondary data sources raises two important issues:

(a) the general availability of official statistics in the public domain;

(b) the need to update 1981 census statistics.

In the 1984 Data Protection Act attention focuses on data that identify individuals. However, with the availability of digital data, a cogent argument can be made for re-examination of data confidentiality and security under the 1947 Statistics of Trade Act. Two extreme paths could make more data available that would be beneficial for store location analysis. At one extreme, following the US example, more data in the public domain could be made available and readily accessible. For example, without breaking obvious confidentiality constraints, VAT returns could be used to provide invaluable information for retailers. (Note also the suggested purchase of a sample of micro-census data by ESRC, which would have important benefits for many modelling exercises.) Alternatively, if more data are not available in the public domain, commercial firms may develop their own data sets that 'clone' other ones.

Data issues are not only their availability and flexible storage, but also their updating. For instance, a fundamental input in store location analysis is the 1981 UK Census of Population, and, as the decade progresses, it begs the question as to the extent to which this data are outdated at a local level. Attention must be given to population forecasting, and, while OPCS mid-year estimates and population forecasts are available, they lack the necessary detailed spatial dissaggregation.

More fundamentally, however, as store location analyses are often founded on data about household composition, such as the 'geodemographic' discriminators ACORN and PiN, population updates disaggregated by age, sex and location are often insufficient. Clearly, for many applications, it would be both invalid and misleading to assume a constant household structure and to simply scale the base using updated estimates.

Briefly, to model the dynamics of household structure, it must be appreciated that a range of complex and interdependent processes exist that cause household composition to change. Moreover, a change in a state often acts as the trigger for further alterations that directly affect household structures. For example, such unfortunately common events as loss of job and divorce are not purely demographic processes, but they do have direct repercussions on the form or even disintegration of households. Micro-level simulation models have been developed in which household dynamics are represented formally as a set of coupled differential equations (see, for example, Clarke (1986), Clarke and Williams (1988) and Orcutt *et al.* (1976)). In the present context, such models relate to conventional forecasting approaches, generating estimates of households with different characteristics. However, the approach has potential applications in other fields of locational marketing analysis and decision support systems.

Linkage of data sets

While it is necessary to consider future secondary data availability, for completeness, it is important to reference some of the ways in which different data sets have been linked ingeniously together (although differences in variable definitions and spatial scale across available data sets create problems that require careful manipulation). Computers have facilitated the linkage of different data sets to produce new, actionable information – the product is greater than the sum of the individual data sets. For example, the computer-based linkage of census data and market research data, such as the National Readership Survey and the Target Group Index, has proved a most useful means of creating information about spatial variations in market potential. Although approached differently, local area estimates of consumer spending potential on different goods and services at various store types are available as self-contained products from Pinpoint Analysis/DSR Marketing and from the Unit for Retail Planning Information.

This data linkage approach to store location analysis can be enormously helpful, at least as a first stage in an evaluation. For the future, the consistent power of data manipulations should be assessed in practice; in addition, from a theoretical perspective, the associated technical difficulties of classifying households and making inferences from both individual and aggregate data – 'ecological fallacy' – should be examined further (see, for instance, Openshaw (1984)).

However, in terms of the store location problem, the data linkage approach remains lacking, particularly as changes in consumers' behaviour and retailing organisation have broadened catchment areas. The sales potential of specific stores is also dependent on consumers' store choice patterns and the incidence of competing stores, two features that are often not examined explicitly. Will the customers choose our store or one of our competitors? Towards a more complete answer, the linkage between data and model-based analyses provides a further opportunity to transform and extend data on relative market potential into useful information on the implications of alternative store location strategies.

Methods of retail analysis and forecasting in practice

Background

As emphasised earlier, in practice the type and quality of available data constrains the form of analyses that are possible. This fundamental consideration underpins the following, necessarily selective, discussion (a coverage of introductory methods for store location and store assessment research is provided in Davies and Rogers (1984)). Interestingly, in a recent survey of forecasting, Mahmoud (1984) found that even simple quantitative methods performed better than the unstructured intuitive assessments of experienced management (and that the use of subjective judgment to adjust values from quantitative forecasts often reduced accuracy).

From the basis of data availability, two important methods of retail analysis and forecasting are considered:

(a) categorical data analysis;

(b) gravity-based spatial interaction modelling.

Attention focuses on their benefits for retail management, rather than methodological issues *per se*. Much of the promise of recent theoretical developments in these areas remains unrealised, although their applicability has been developed.

Categorical data analysis

Most introductory statistics courses include a discussion of bivariate/multivariate linear regression; that is, a causal relationship is expressed to explain variations in a dependent/response variable by a set of independent/explanatory variables. For example, variations in store turnover are explained by different factors, such as store size, merchandise mix, real prices/income, competitive situations, and relative accessibility.

An important and attractive feature of regression modelling is that the chosen models fit and test relationships against data; that is, using economic theory and statistical inference as an analytic foundation and historical data as the information base, it establishes a relationship between the variable to be forecast and the explanatory variables. If this relationship can be assumed to continue to exist and if it is possible to obtain some view about future changes in the explanatory variables, an ability to forecast the variable of interest exists. A fundamental advantage of this regression approach is that it is founded upon an attempt to understand how a system operates. If a comprehensive understanding can be achieved, there is a greater likelihood of developing a properly integrated store location analysis and also a knowledge for management of its limitations and potential pitfalls.

Without dismissing conventional problems of regression, such as multicollinearity (which can be overcome by using principal components analysis to summarise the correlations between the raw variables) and heteroscedasticity, with the recent development of very large out-of-town superstores, in practice it is often questionable whether the sample of stores from which data are collected can be defined as a single representative sample in terms of the range of store types. Even with very careful sample design, sample size may prove restrictively small.

More fundamentally, much of the available data are of low-order categorical type and, when methods are needed to analyse them, non-parametric statistics are employed conventionally. However, in the early 1970s, categorical data analysis advanced, providing a closer linkage with econometrics and using the integrated structure offered by the general linear model (see Wrigley (1985) for an excellent comprehensive discussion of the state of art). For store location analyses, early applications in this field have included clothing retailers' location in Boston, shopping behaviour in Manchester, and shopping trip destination and travel mode choice in Eindhoven.

In categorical data analysis a family of statistical models can be recognised that are differentiated by whether the response variable is continuous or categorical and by whether the explanatory variables are continuous, mixed or categorical. Traditional regression models can accommodate problems with a continuous response variable; for a categorical response variable, logistic, linear logit and log-linear models are required. Fortunately, computer packages, such as GLIM, are available to undertake the necessary analyses.

In comparison with gravity-based spatial interaction models, such models of shop choice are only beginning to be applied in the commercial sector. For the future this modelling approach represents a major area for applied research in the retailing sector, particularly as appropriate data become more readily available.

Gravity based spatial interaction modelling

Spatial interaction shopping models of varying degrees of sophistication have been employed widely to describe observed patterns of consumers' behaviour; such descriptions provide the basis to undertake impact analyses of store developments and performance monitoring. In this sub-section, brief attention is given to different operational issues for applications, rather than to the implications of alternative theoretical bases, such as entropy maximisation and random utility theory, and of model specifications (for a discussion of such issues see Fotheringham (1983a), Wilson (1971), Wilson and Bennett (1985) and Wilson *et al.* (1981)). Reference is given to both data availability and modelling approaches.

Without discussing the practical difficulties of defining and measuring the variable for the relative attractiveness of stores (by, say, linear footage), to date the fundamental constraint on applications has been the general unavailability of trip-pattern data that is required to calibrate the models. In the so-called 'bogus calibration' problem, for example, without suitable data, a trivial solution is generated where predicted store sales are a simple function of the attractiveness variable and are unaffected by a distance deterrent factor.

In terms of data for calibrating gravity-based spatial interaction models, the recent availability of shoppers' trip-patterns from the Lupin Database Company provides a unique opportunity. For store location analysis, accurate data on catchment areas and on the characteristics of the types of shoppers patronising different competitive store locations is essential. The data resources necessary for thorough analysis are very considerable, although individual market research surveys are undertaken for specific existing/proposed stores. To help rectify this situation, an original and nationally comprehensive database, based on 100,000 telephone interviews, is available from Lupin covering shopping trips and consumers' usage of named food stores, such as ASDA, Sainsbury and Tesco, and individual shopping centres. This description of the observed micro patterns of shopping behaviour throughout Britain not only is a most useful input for modelling but also provides a relevant description of both individual food shops and shopping centres in terms of:

(a) the actual geographical configuration of their catchment areas (rather than hypothetical catchment areas based on travel time or mileage bands);

(b) the relative importance and market share of particular stores and shopping centres from the proportion of customers attracted to them.

Moreover, as this survey will be repeated on an annual basis, an important historical data series will develop to provide an empirical basis for many types of impact analysis.

In terms of modelling and assuming calibration has been completed correctly, two approaches can usefully employ spatial interaction shopping models:

(a) simulation;
(b) optimisation.

For retail management, comparing and contrasting the results of various 'what if' simulations would provide a comprehension of the implications of alternative actions. Disaggregate data on consumer expenditure patterns, together with data on the number, size and location of competing stores, would provide the basis for assessing the potential impacts of future alterations to the product mix and space allocation within existing stores or of the potential rationalisation or expansion of the number of stores in a network. What will be the 'cannibalisation' effects on existing stores of new store development? Recent work by Clarke and Wilson has demonstrated how this simulation approach can be operationalised to powerful effect for retail management.

In another context, simulation models can be of immense pedagogic value as business games (see for example Beaumont and Beaumont (1987) for a successful international application in telecoms management training). To be successful, realistic strategy-formulation and decision-making would have to be highlighted in a realistic retailing business environment. The computer-based model would be merely a tool, although it could provide another way of demonstrating to retail management the power of method-based store location analyses.

Alternatively, spatial interaction shopping models can be incorporated into mathematical programming models to allow for the optimisation of an objective function, such as profit maximisation, subject to specified constraints (see, for example, Beaumont (1982) and Wilson *et al.* (1981)). The basic problem is to determine the optimum location and size of stores (see, for example, Coehlo and Wilson (1976)), and it can be approached in a variety of ways.

A particular type of mathematical programming formulation is a location-allocation model which jointly optimises the location of stores and the spatial allocation of customers to them (see

Beaumont (1981, 1986b)). An attractive characteristic of location-allocation modelling is its minimal data requirements (the distribution of potential customers, existing stores and competitors) importantly, there are no difficulties in implementing the approach with existing data. Store location analyses can be examined using different location-allocation models, and it is stressed that the various results from different formulations will provide retail management with additional information for decision-making. Different objectives are appropriate in different situations, particularly with regard to the type of store and the services provided. For instance, in terms of competition, maximising access to a target market would be generally pertinent. However, in relation to some services, the criterion of minimising the aggregate distance is consistent with the neighbourhood concept. An alternative objective, which relates to the individual customer level, would be the minimisation of the maximum travel distance (or time) to patronise a store in the network. For specified objectives, the results of the models are not only the optimum locations and sizes; insights into trade-offs and conflicts between alternative aims are generated, and the implications of selecting 'sub-optimal' locations for other reasons are known – for example, what is the current efficiency of our actual network of stores in terms of an optimal one?

In connection with the general store-location problem, additional issues relate to the product range, and the size and the number of stores in the network. For a variety of reasons, for example, it may be appropriate to constrain the problem so that all stores have the same capacity, because a company has a network of nearly identical branches offering similar services. Alternatively, the number of stores at any point in time may be specified by a strategic plan, and therefore the locational analysis is concerned with sequencing development. Moreover, analyses can be undertaken for groups of stores, which may be pertinent not only to the regional organisation structure of a company but also to potential mergers between companies.

Finally, for the assessment both of the performance of existing stores and of the viability of potential store developments, it is important to be able to present results not only in marketing terms but also for financial appraisal and budgeting. Consequently, a cogent argument can be made for integration of existing spatial-interaction modelling-based store location analyses with financial modelling (for a broad overview of financial modelling see Sherwood (1983)).

Many financial-modelling computer packages, such as Empire, FCS-EPS and Wizard, are available and could be incorporated at the end of existing modelling exercises. Store location analysis, for example, should include investment appraisal, a special type of forecasting involving estimating future cash flows and using an appropriate discounting procedure to estimate the likely financial return to be achieved by both existing and new stores.

Computer-based financial modelling makes it practicable to complete a range of forecasts using optimistic and pessimistic assumptions. Information of potential opportunities and risks can be comprehended readily by retail management and interpreted in terms of their required levels of performance and profitability; costs and benefits of alternatives are indicated, and competing priorities can be ordered. It is insufficient to provide the 'best' point forecast for sales; management requires an understanding of the asymmetry of the possible risks and benefits. It should be appreciated that an assumption underlying the majority of methods is that current relationships will be maintained in the future. In this context, recent methodological comprehension of structural change, such as shifts from neighbourhood corner shops to out-of-town supermarkets, is especially pertinent (for an overview of dynamic systems analysis, see Wilson (1981a and b), and, for applications of Q-analysis and elementary catastrophe theory, see Beaumont (1984) and Wilson and Oulton (1983), respectively). While many applications in this field remain confined to numerical experiments and the data requirements for empirical studies would be daunting, this perspective is likely to become very important. How resilient or stable is a specific store in the face of new competition? For example, it would be very helpful for retail management to know that their most profitable branch could also be their most vulnerable!

Future outlook

Some personal reflections

For the majority of us, many of the available methods of store location analysis are daunting, filled with uncertainty and obfuscating jargon. A knowledge of the experience of others is a prerequisite for a successful introduction, and, therefore, the interactions between the academic and commercial sectors is important. While there could be a natural tendency to try to progress too quickly because of excessive enthusiasm, excitement and expectations, carefully applied techniques can be a powerful form of assistance for retail management, and therefore should be encouraged. Fortunately, there is a range of relevant methods of retail analysis and forecasting, from simple data manipulation to sophisticated mathematical and statistical modelling.

It would be incorrect and dangerous to believe that the increased accessibility of computer power and range of application software means that the more sophisticated techniques are appropriate for everybody in all situations. In many respects, unfortunately, such developments only mean that wrong or misleading results are obtained more quickly (the 'garbage in, garbage out', black-box approach)! The provision of 'user-friendly' packages for unqualified personnel is not a practical solution; the mere mechanical use of statistical and mathematical techniques can be dangerous. (Note the vast investment to develop an expert system for regression analysis has not been completed.) A detailed appreciation of statistical theory and mathematical methods and a broad experience in the application of alternative techniques are necessary qualifications for successful store location analysis to provide management with both an explanation of the factors affecting market potential and the generation of sound impact assessments. Would greater interactions between the academic and commercial sectors provide the foundation to complement further the range of available analytic skills with a commercial orientation?

In the next few years a continued growth in the application of computer-based techniques in store location analysis will occur. There will be a growing need to be able to retrieve and manipulate data and to model more efficiently and effectively. Significant developments in location analysis will be not only the benefits of a continuing fall in the real cost of computer processing power, but also the increased opportunities for more widespread application with the growing availability of integrated (database management, modelling and analysis, graphics and mapping, and word-processing) and micro-based software. Opportunities and challenges will grow.

Thus, in terms of store development and performance evaluation, there is no longer a need for policy formulation and monitoring to lack the rigour that is commonplace for other investment decisions. It is important that retail management is provided with more useful and relevant information on the implications of alternative locational strategies. A continuous monitoring is required not only to assess existing operations, but also to provide the basis for business planning. Indeed, as the availability of prime locations for development diminish, this requirement becomes more significant.

Towards a research agenda

In conclusion, for store location analysis generally, progress has been in the development of a range of methods of retail analysis and forecasting by academics; the problems arise because of their lack of application in the commercial sector. An immense intellectual stimulation can be provided by tackling policy-related problems (although it is easier to hide behind the 'workings' of a few numerical simulations with a brief concluding paragraph alluding to potential future applications!).

At this stage it would be rather misguided to have a list of different methods for inclusion or exclusion in potential future applications; let the problems speak for themselves. However, with some modifications and extensions, existing models could be made more useful to end-users. For instance, for a retailer it would be appropriate to link a financial model, with a balance sheet, a profit and loss statement and cash-flow analyses, to shopping models for the evaluation of the viability of future stores. Packaging is also important, although not necessarily to deliver sensational results. For store location analysis, maps are a most apposite medium to present a message; they are much more comprehensible than hard-copy computer printout.

As a foundation it is pertinent to list some important management criteria for assessing the relevance of alternative methods of retail analysis and forecasting in specific situations:
(a) the required accuracy of any analysis;

(b) the time period (short- or medium-term) for which the forecast is needed;

(c) the data requirements of the techniques;

(d) the ease of comprehension;

(e) the cost of implementation and operation.

Moreover, there is the basic practical issue – can the analysis be completed in good time at an acceptable cost? Technique selection is highly dependent on the scale of investment planned and the size of company, rather than methodological considerations *per se*. Small companies, for example, do not have the resources to justify sophisticated modelling. In fact, in most cases, a combination of approaches would be sensible, if only to act as a cross-check on the results.

CHAPTER 4

The Tesco approach to store location

Nicholas J. Penny and David Broom

Introduction

Over recent years there has been a major increase in commercial awareness of the subject of store location analysis. A variety of articles have appeared in the press and a number of conferences and seminars have been organised to consider the topic. Davies and Rogers' recent publication (1984), however, provides the most comprehensive single source currently available to the store location analyst. Alternatively, the extensive literature on consumer behaviour research provides many helpful guidelines (e.g. Shepherd and Thomas, 1980).

There are many reasons for this renewed enthusiasm for a research area pioneered by William Applebaum in the early 1960s in North America. These conveniently provide a framework for the approach of Tesco PLC to be discussed in this chapter.

The chapter begins by introducing Tesco's needs and requirements for store location analysis. This is followed by an outline of the initial research response and details of the current locational modelling system. The chapter concludes with a consideration of the current decision-making processes operating within the company.

Why does Tesco need store location analysis?

Tesco PLC is one of Britain's largest multiple retailers, trading from over 360 stores, with annual sales over £3 billion and profit performance continuously improving. The company is committed to expansion both through entering new product markets and developing new stores that are fully equipped to sell these products. The hundredth Tesco superstore which opened in June 1985 at Brent Park, Neasden is a very different type of retail operation from the historical base of the company. Our core business is, and will continue to be, in the traditional high street; however our development plans seek commercially attractive sites throughout Britain.

Similarly, other supermarket companies are expanding, and the 1980s has witnessed, and will continue to witness, a change in the structure of food retailing. As all operators seek to expand we are currently becoming more selective regarding the sort of sites we develop. Many myths surround the development policies of the major store operators; we are all considering many different options in our determination to seek and trade from profitable locations. Such policies, however, must eventually lead to a saturation of the market. As that market is relatively static we must therefore be more competitive and, in order to expand, find the best store locations. This underlying trend has been visible to practitioners within the retail trade for many years.

Two statements from an article in the *Financial Times* of 17 April 1985 particularly summarise the position. As David Churchill points out, 'the battle lines in the latest round of the grocery war are being drawn up not around the price wars of the 1970s, but around the frantic grab for the best superstore sites left in the U.K. At stake in the present retail manoeuvres is the very structure of large store retailing in the 1990s'.

The Tesco position is emphasised by the company chairman, Ian MacLaurin: 'There are only a finite number of superstore sites available in the U.K. . . . It is my job to make sure that we get our share of the remaining sites.'

These considerations prompted Tesco into an increased awareness of hitherto unconsidered methods of site selection and evaluation during the early 1980s. The company obviously needs to evaluate a vast number of opportunities, not only to find the best (or optimum) location in the competitive market but also to secure a retail opportunity given the many uncertain constraints in store development. The planning process will not always help; what may be a highly profitable retail opportunity for Tesco will not always find favour with the planning system.

A less than satisfactory sales and profit performance of certain stores also focused attention on previous location decisions. The company's desire for improved profit performance, particularly highlighted by the achievements of our major competitors, provided an opportunity to concentrate on the process of site selection. This is just one of many areas of decision-making that have changed in Tesco over the last five years.

Tesco has also undergone a transformation towards more centralised control from head office, and an increased profession-alism amongst its retail management has seen the development of new head office departments. Store location analysis was therefore identified as an opportunity to supplement the vastly experienced intuition and entrepreneurial ability of senior directors in the company. Our approach was not to replace the previous method of decision-making but to provide a research analysis alongside the existing and somewhat colloquial 'gut-feel' of the retail directors.

The last five years have also seen major increases in the cost of developing a modern superstore. Land prices have escalated, with rumours of figures of around £2–3 million an acre for sites in South Oxford and Watford.

The consideration of company culture is tremendously impor-tant to the success of store location analysis in retail decision-making. The issues help provide the momentum for investment in the analysis system and faith in the corresponding results once established.

Many of these issues have contributed to the fact that site selection and store location now receive considerable attention. The store location analyst embarking on a development process today is faced by an abundance of advice from professional consultancies (e.g. CACI, Pinpoint, Management Horizons) and academics.

In 1980 when Tesco embarked upon a process of developing store location research, little experienced commercial advice was available in the U.K. Consequently, the background for the development of our research system was both the North American business literature and the experience of academic research into consumer behaviour and space preference.

Tesco's requirement for store location analysis

Against the cultural background of Tesco the development of a store location analysis system had to meet certain requirements of the company. These needs had to be met to ensure both the credibility of the ensuing research department and, more significantly, that the results were used. The culture of retail decision-making is especially receptive to answers and advice; however it does not appreciate esoteric analytical problems which invariably surface in any detailed research and modelling approach.

Professional guidance

Store location analysis in Tesco must provide a three-tier system of professional guidance. Firstly, the analysis has to provide suitable guidelines for our development strategy and direct the search process for new sites by our in-house property and development executives. Simply, techniques are needed to identify areas of the country that may offer sales or market potential for new stores. Secondly, a filter system, whereby sites are screened for further detailed evaluation, is necessary in order to minimise the work of the store location analyst and the property executive. Finally, a detailed system of forecasting potential sales for the new sites is needed. This latter stage is not simply a question of providing general guidance as to whether a site is a good opportunity or not, but of producing a detailed sales forecast that can be subsequently used for capital investment appraisal. This requirement is critical and truly determines the research method, tolerance levels, degree of expertise required and resulting cost of operating a research department.

The appraisal of capital investment through profit and loss calculations determines the need for projected average weekly sales figures by department for the first three trading years of the new store. Departmental sales are necessary to reflect different gross margins and consequently the acceptable tolerance levels for forecast error is minimal.

Undoubtedly sound advice as to the respective merits of a site, i.e. whether it represents a good or poor opportunity, would have been a much cheaper and easier objective to attain. However, the system would have then failed to meet the company's decision needs and inevitably its long-term use would have been jeopardised.

Inherent within this three-level approach are a number of additional requirements.

Accuracy   This is without question the primary issue. Profit margins are so fine that the sales forecasts must always meet their target level of accuracy (initially ±10 per cent). Similarly, the cost structures of the organisation are such that any error in the sales forecast is unacceptable, in that we may pay too much for the site or may lose a tender for a competitive bid and ultimately advise the company towards an unprofitable decision. All stores must be profitable; sales volume and market share is not sufficient justification for a new store development.

Timeliness   It is also essential for the company to make the decision as quickly as possible. Invariably the site is only available for a short period of time, given the pressures of the commercial property market. Other retailers may operate quicker decision systems than Tesco and respond immediately to a possible development opportunity. Consequently, a reasonably quick turnaround of an individual site evaluation is necessary and five working days are allocated for a single analyst to produce a sales forecast.

Volume capacity   This has to be met and although site screening techniques facilitate the decision-making, the Research Unit has to produce approximately 300 detailed sales forecasts a year (approximately 50 per cent of all sites offered to the property/ development executives) for evaluation.

The retailer's intuition   This does not always have to be met (and arguably the system exists to contradict that intuition) but it does have to be considered. This is manifest through the development of forecasting models with the benefit of broad retail concepts (for example, on the intuitive attractiveness of a store) and a thorough justification when differences of opinion are apparent. The resultant modelling approach must therefore be sufficiently objective and the methodology and variables intuitively correct.

Statistical relationships may be especially strong but spurious (and counter-intuitive) associations must be avoided.

A *monitoring process*   This allows the resultant sales forecasts to be measured against actual sales following the opening of a new store. The modelling technique must adapt to the subsequent test of their accuracy and be continuously updated and enhanced. Such requirements necessitate both considerable investment and in-house expertise. The current Tesco system is constantly improving with our experiences. Monitoring also enhances the credibility of the approach to store location analysis through honest communication of our success and failures to the company. The system demands a two-way process of confidence whereby the senior retail directors understand the forecasts and the researchers receive commitment from these individuals. Good communication is therefore both a necessity and a challenge in seeking suitable means of expressing often complex statistical problems.

Arguably such requirements produce a truly valid test for the accountability of research in a commercial organisation. Undoubtedly as researchers we sometimes find ourselves in a highly vulnerable and somewhat uncomfortable position from which we cannot hide. Nevertheless, it is this 'real world' interface between research techniques and commercial decision-making that is an intrinsic attraction of the issues discussed here.

Flexibility   This is essential in the sales-forecast model in order to consider varying development options. The sales-forecast system must be responsive to changes in the attractiveness of the store through variable size and product ranges. Similarly, the sales-forecast system needs to include a method of optimising the relative merits of the specific site in question against other hypothetical opportunities in the area; put simply, is the site the best location in the local area? This need for evaluating risk or vulnerability in the location decision is a sophisticated requirement of the system that reflects the most recent views of the senior directors in Tesco. Invariably, the sales forecast will be extended to provide a wider business analysis of the particular location problem. This may involve a profitability analysis of both existing trading and future store opportunities. These issues have arisen in response to the race for sites that is currently a feature of retail development in the UK and a requirement that supports the development of an expert in-house research department.

Finally, Tesco require the vast amount of information and knowledge produced by the research process to be readily available for wider applications in the company. Recent developments have seen the expansion of the company's requirements to adapt the sales forecast system for store and local market planning purposes. Alongside the current sales-forecasting responsibilities, the research unit considers ranging and store size issues, space allocation, the ideal store format and operational research considerations.

The development of locational analysis in Tesco

Early response

The current system of store location analysis operated by Tesco originated during mid-1981. Our initial objectives were met by a comprehensive literature review of the relevant techniques which highlighted the way forward.

The first location model developed by Tesco combined the analogue approach (see Kornblau, 1968) with multiple regression analysis to produce a simplistic forecasting model. This early attempt considered each analogue store in the data set as a single observation. A large number of acceptable stores were subsequently analysed to produce a regression equation expressing the relationship between store sales and a series of explanatory variables describing the site, store attraction, accessibility, the surrounding market population and competition. This original model not only prompted investment into the necessary computing facilities and data sets, but established a department within the organisation which subsequently has grown to a team of over twenty researchers. The application of suitable research techniques has continued and is manifest in the current locational modelling system.

The locational modelling system

The company's requirements of locational analysis were outlined in the previous section. Briefly, these were:

(a) to direct the search process for new sites;

(b) the screening of sites to identify those which merit detailed consideration;

(c) providing accurate sales forecasts for sites, to form the basis of a profit and loss analysis.

Our key technical response to these requirements has been the locational modelling system. This, by necessity, has been developed in an incremental way. Therefore the objectives we set and claims we make for the system have expanded in an inductive way in line with our own understanding of its capabilities and the salient issues which it can address within the company.

Data sources

Tesco acquired a *population database* of the 1981 Census, defined at an appropriate spatial scale. Variables relate to household structure, economic condition, mobility and tenure. This database allows us to assess consumer demand; measures of household expenditure on different product ranges can be obtained from various national surveys and, when combined with the Census information, allow direct measures of purchasing power to be computed. In addition, profiling of catchment areas in line with the 'analogue' approach to site appraisal provides a useful validation of the sales forecasting model, as well as having implications for other management actions.

Information about the shopping behaviour of our customers is obtained from an in-store *customer survey* undertaken each year in the Tesco superstores. The aim is to interview between 8 and 10 per cent of all customers over a full week, with interview quotas being directed by traffic through the store. The data allows the delineation of catchment areas and the calculation of expenditure by population zones. When combined with information from our computerised Tesco branch information database – store measurements, product ranges, sales history, life-cycle stage, etc. – the result is a set of comprehensive store profiles.

Considerable time and effort has been expended on collecting information on the extent and quality of *competitive activity*. Unlike durable-goods shopping, where stores selling different goods may still be in competition for disposable income, the definition of our food competitors is relatively straightforward. A more vexed question is how to assess the quality of competition, which varies with both the operator and the characteristics of the store.

The inappropriateness of commercially available data sources on food retailers dictated that each competitive store had to be visited by a member of the Research Unit and a detailed questionnaire completed. The result is unquestionably the most comprehensive database on food shopping outlets in the U.K. Furthermore, the data has been brought on-line to senior management in the company using a state-of-the-art database system, and consequently competition data in any form appropriate to management actions and competition analysis is immediately available.

New developments are monitored through a network of links developed with the local authorities, commercial planning leads, local press, and field-work undertaken by our store managers. In general, we would expect to hear of any application for planning permission within two weeks of its being placed. All the relevant journals on food shopping and property development are also monitored.

A *digitised road network* has been interfaced with the other databases, which allows the computation of travel time between any two geographic points. Again considerable in-house development was required, since our evaluation of digitised networks showed that no system had an adequate density of roads for our purposes. Output from the system can be input directly to the modelling system.

The data sets are all linked together on the IBM mainframe computer at Tesco. To enable their wider use for decision-making in the company, we have designed user-friendly data retrieval systems which allow typical questions to be answered immediately; for example, the following questions would obtain an instant and accurate response.

(a) Which of our stores over 20,000 ft^2 selling-area are within 10 minutes drive time of an Asda?

(b) What are the addresses of current superstore planning applications in Yorkshire, classified by operator?

(c) What are the characteristics of the population within 10 minutes drive time of a site in Lewisham?

The forecasting model

The initial focus of the modelling system was to provide an accurate model for sales forecasting. The starting point for the model, at least in conurbation areas, was a spatial interaction model of the form:

$$\text{EXP}_{is} = \beta_0 \left(\sum_k E_k H_{ik} \right) \cdot \frac{W_s . e^{-\beta_1 t_{is}}}{\sum_m W_m . e^{-\beta_1 t_{im}}}$$

Where: EXP_{is} is the expenditure from zone i to site s;

β_0, β_1 are parameters;

E_k is the mean food expenditure by household category k;

H_{ik} is the number of households of category k located in zone i;

W_s is a measure of attraction of the proposed store s;

t_{is} is the travel time from zone i to the site at s;

W_m is the attractiveness of competitor m;

t_{im} is the travel time from zone i to competitor m.

The aim was to calibrate this model successfully using customer survey data; the result could then be used as a sales-forecasting model as well as being applied systematically to nodes in the network in order to scan areas for optimum store locations.

To explain our use and development of the model at Tesco, it is useful to distinguish three key elements of the model form:

(a) available expenditure in each zone:

$$\sum_k E_k . H_{ik}$$

(b) the denominator term:

$$\sum_m W_m \cdot e^{-\beta_1 t_{im}}$$

which can be interpreted as a measure of the accessibility of residents of zone i to superstores, or superstore availability;

(c) the quotient term, given the relative attractiveness of the proposed store, or the market penetration.

With respect to *available expenditure* for food and grocery shopping, the research objective was to identify a typology of households which successfully explained variations in food shopping expenditure. This obviously requires a derivative measure based on Census and survey information, and we found that no 'off-the-shelf' measures were appropriate to our needs. Our analysis, therefore, focused on our own customer survey data, and we found a concise life-cycle classification to explain spending. Equivalent tables were commissioned from the Family Expenditure Survey as a comparison. Iterative proportional fitting procedures were then used to generate measures of available expenditure for our zone system.

This measure proved to be a valuable analytic device in itself. The plotting of available expenditure as a map, overlaid by the locations of trading and planned stores, provides a means of 'eyeballing' areas in order to identify locations with a high-expenditure potential but low superstore availability. Overlaying maps of the catchment areas of Tesco stores, as obtained from the customer survey, allowed us to isolate geographic problems of market penetration.

The work also had implications of a sectoral, rather than a spatial, kind. The comparison of average expenditure based on our customer survey with those from the Family Expenditure Survey showed that the discrepancy between classes varied greatly. Consequently, the 'leakage' of potential revenue from the superstore varies with the type of customer, a situation which can be addressed by marketing activity.

The *superstore availability term*, contained in the interaction model, represents a more complete measure of the accessibility of residents of our population zones to superstore facilities. Simple indices, incorporating superstore availability with available expenditure, allowed initial scanning of the country to identify optimal areas for development; although more sophisticated measures are now used, these indices still provide a useful filtering device.

The attraction of any store to residents of a population zone is a function of a *composite attractiveness term weighted by travel time*; the quotient in the interaction model allows the relative attractiveness of the proposed Tesco store to be assessed. Rather than use travel time directly in this formulation, we have borrowed from transportation studies the concept of 'generalised time'. In addition to simple travel time from the population centroid of each population zone to the store, this incorporates measures of local accessibility, size and type of car park and general customer convenience around the store, translated into travel time impedance. This formulation permits the relative importance of these various attributes of store design to be assessed.

The specification of a composite attractiveness term is possibly the most problematic modelling issue; effectively, we are asking what characteristics of a store's profile, both Tesco and competitor, most influence store choice. Questions vary from what facilities must be present to establish the image of a 'complete' superstore to customers, e.g. petrol filling station, restaurant, in-store chemist, etc., to detailed issues of store operation including merchandising, movement about the store and atmosphere. It should be emphasised that the store-choice decision is taken at a household level and should properly be addressed using disaggregate modelling methods; such an approach, with the much greater insight afforded into customer behaviour, presents an opportunity for the future.

It has not proved possible to separate out the impacts of individual facilities on food turnover in such a way that they can be entered into the model form. We have, however, used qualitative research to support our conclusions, based on data analysis, that in order to achieve maximum return on investment a superstore must offer a minimum threshold of facilities, and that this threshold varies with the type of location. Operating below this threshold leads to a marked decrease in store patronage.

In reality, therefore, the composite attractiveness term which is incorporated into the model only takes account of departmental size and the 'quality' of the store; other factors must be considered by sales forecasters alongside the model results. With respect to size effects, in addition to using total sales area as a surrogate for attractiveness, a realistic relationship has been identified between sales and the food/non-food split of floorspace in stores. This has led to the concept of optimum split, as well as optimum total selling area based on customer demand and market share around the site. Before being entered into the model, square feet selling areas are converted into linear feet in accordance with the level of technology current in each store. The conversion factor is also varied in line with our subjective assessment of competitor quality. In future work an attempt will be made to distinguish the effects confounded in this term by systematically varying the subjective quality rating. The resulting model form, comprising these various elements, is non-linear and is calibrated using numerical optimisation procedures. The model is then run using an interactive computer system.

However, this only forms one element of the sales forecasting process. Before we can feel completely confident in our data sets and model predictions, the proposed site must be visited along with local competition, the relevant planning department contacted, the road network checked, and qualitative information collected. It is imperative for the credibility of the Research Unit that the sales forecasts can be fully justified to the senior directors of the company.

Conclusion

This insight into the store location approach operated by Tesco illustrates the successful amalgamation of research techniques and a commercial retail organisation. The decision-making process whereby the relevant information is utilised conveniently combines all the issues outlined.

Tesco operate a specific store-development strategy orientated towards opening approximately twelve new stores a year. In order to optimise the location of these new stores, strategic guidelines are provided by the research team for ratification by our development director and the main board. These guidelines are areas and towns deemed suitable for new store locations. In-house property executives search for available opportunities within these guidelines and regularly communicate site availability to a senior committee of directors for evaluation. This evaluation involves the research-based screening process prior to a detailed sales forecast for a particular site. Preparatory steps are then taken to develop the opportunity further; negotiations are carried out with the appropriate vendor, planning advice and technical building considerations are collected and the sales forecast input into a capital investment appraisal. All this information is subsequently presented to a main board acquisition committee for final approval. Research is represented on this committee, which regularly meets to determine the company's future development strategy.

Presuming that the opportunity meets the required financial return and that favourable planning advice is received, then Tesco would proceed and negotiations towards acquisition commence. Site acquisition may involve a competitive tender or a position of sole negotiation. The acquisition of the physical site is a delicate process handled by professional property executives and can be time consuming.

The time involved in such decision-making can vary. From the initial site opportunity through the sales forecast evaluation to an acquisition decision can all occur within less than ten days if urgent, but usually takes a little longer. It is possible, however, for a site to be acquired and to be trading as a Tesco store within as little as a year. Other opportunities may take as long as seven or eight years. Consequently, the research approach to store location at Tesco needs to be flexible but, more importantly, accurate, robust and of sufficiently high quality to aid a highly volatile process of decision-making. Few researchers face such situations where they are accountable for multi-million pound investment decisions.

CHAPTER 5
Market share analysis techniques: a review and illustration of current US practice

A. Stewart Fotheringham

The role of market share analysis in marketing

Marketing analysis – the investigation of regularities in retailing – can be divided into two major components, one having an emphasis on brand choice, the other an emphasis on store choice. Both of these components can be subdivided into choice frequency analysis and market share analysis. The types of questions investigated in each of these four research areas are described in Table 5.1. Brand modelling involves analysing and predicting either the choice or the frequency of purchase of particular brands of goods, and tends to involve input from psychology, economics and sociology rather than from geography. Store choice frequency modelling (often referred to simply as store choice modelling[1]) is also relatively aspatial, being concerned not with the store locations visited by consumers but with *frequency* of visits to certain types of store. It is also concerned with measuring store loyalty in much the same way as brand loyalty is examined in brand choice modelling. Consequently, there has also been little in the way of geographic input into store choice frequency models, although there are signs of a break-through in this area with the recent applications of the NBD (negative binomial distribution) and Dirichlet models of store choice frequency by Kau and Ehrenberg (1984) and particularly by Broom and Wrigley (1983) and Wrigley and Dunn (1984a and b).

The fourth major topic of market analysis, which I call store market-share analysis, is concerned with the questions of why and how consumers select certain stores. Geographic methodology

Table 5.1 Research areas in marketing analysis

Research area		Types of question investigated
Brand modelling	Choice frequency	What factors determine a consumer's brand choice? What decision process leads to brand choice?
	Market share	How frequently do consumers purchase particular brands? How loyal are consumers to certain brands?
Store modelling	Choice frequency	How frequently do consumers patronise particular types of store? What determines the frequency with which consumers patronise particular types of store?
	Market share	Who shops where? What factors and processes determine a consumer's selection of a particular store? What is the demographic composition of a store's market? Where is the best location in terms of maximising revenue for a new store? What will happen to a store's market if there is a change in the retailing system?

plays a critical role in this area of marketing since store market-share analysis involves explaining and predicting consumers' spatial behaviour. The probability of a consumer selecting a particular store out of a set of stores is a function of the spatial separation of consumer and store, the spatial separation of the store from its competitors, and spatial variations in store attributes or image variables. Answering the basic store market-share question of 'Who shops where?' thus forms the emphasis of this chapter. It is a quintessential geographic problem where the application of spatial concepts is not simply a useful aid but is a necessary precursor to accurate market analysis.

Having established that this chapter is concerned solely with store market-share analysis and not with brand market-share analysis, the adjective 'store' will be omitted henceforth for convenience and the term 'market share analysis' should be read as 'store market-share analysis'.[2] The chapter will also concentrate on grocery patterns as opposed to non-grocery patterns, although the framework of the modelling procedure used can be applied equally to both forms of retailing. The many uses of market share analysis are first described. An applied modelling procedure is outlined which is then used to predict consumer spatial behaviour (the choice of grocery store). Finally, this model is applied to supermarkets in Gainesville, Florida.

The importance of market share analysis

The questions raised in Table 5.1 give some idea of the importance of market share analysis. This chapter will demonstrate the application of a modelling technique to predict consumer purchasing patterns. The basic premise of the paper is that a lack of understanding of the determinants of retailing patterns can lead to sub-optimal decisions regarding the location of stores, which in turn leads to reduced profits, the inefficient service of consumers and the greater likelihood of business failures. Conversely, having a knowledge of consumer spatial behaviour and being able to answer basic questions such as 'Who shops where?' and 'What factors determine who shops where?' is necessary in order to perform the following important marketing tasks which are demonstrated subsequently for supermarkets in Gainesville, Florida.

(a) Examining the market characteristics of a store. Determining the proportion of the store's potential customers who belong to a particular age group, a particular income bracket, socio-economic class, race, etc.

(b) Relating the market characteristics of a store or stores to the sales of particular brands or types of product. For instance, consumer purchasing patterns of brands and especially products are likely to vary by race, income, age, etc., and a knowledge of a store's market characteristics would be useful at two different levels. It would be useful for individual stores to know their market breakdown as a guide to the quantities of products to carry and to help in the decision of whether or not to carry a new item. The sales potential of the new item can be gauged from the store's market characteristics. At another level, it would be useful for companies supplying particular brands of goods to have knowledge of the market characteristics of stores so that relationships between sales of particular products and socio-economic characteristics can be accurately established. This would help answer such questions as 'What is the relationship between decaffeinated coffee purchases and the income of consumers?' and 'To what extent are frozen dinners purchased more by single-person households than by multi-person households?'

(c) Determining the optimal location of a new store. This optimal location may be defined in terms of a maximum potential share of the total number of consumers in an urban area or, in the case of highly specialised stores, the maximum potential share of a certain sub-group of the population. In either case, it is necessary to know what the determinants of consumers' shopping behaviour are in order to assess the potential attraction of a new location.

(d) Predicting the market share and market characteristics a store of a given size will generate by locating in a certain location. This would be a useful evaluative tool in deciding between several potential locations for a new store.

(e) Determining the effects on sales at existing stores of opening a new store or closing an existing store.

(f) Determining the optimal size of a new store at a given location (see also Haynes and Fotheringham, 1984) or, similarly, determining the minimum profitable store size at a given location.

(g) Examining the effects of increasing store size on market share. For a company owning several stores in an urban area, this would be useful in order to determine in which store the investment in extra size would be most profitable.

(h) Examining the sales performance of individual stores with respect to their expected performances derived from the projected market share of each store.

(i) Analysing why a particular store fails.

(j) Investigating the relationship between price levels and market characteristics. It is suspected, for example, that stores in low-income areas have higher-than-average prices because they have a 'captured' or spatially immobile market. Hall (1982), for example, examined this suspicion but used a very simple market-analysis procedure; a store was assumed to capture all the consumers from the census tract in which it was located and from all neighbouring census tracts. A more accurate method of determining a store's market area is explained below.

(k) Deriving accurate trading areas for stores can aid in the application and performance of other marketing models such as the NBD model of consumer purchase frequency at particular types of stores (Wrigley and Dunn, 1984a).

Given the above applications, it is rather surprising that, of the four areas of marketing analysis identified in Table 5.1, store market-share analysis is the least frequently encountered in both applied and theoretical marketing studies. (Shepherd and Thomas (1980) similarly bemoan the lack of use of store market-share analysis.) It is especially surprising given the spatial dynamism of retailing. For example, Winn Dixie, a major food retailer with stores in fourteen states in the south-eastern and south-western US, opened fifty-two new stores in a 28-week period during 1985 and planned to open ninety-five to ninety-eight new stores while closing fifty to fifty-five during the fiscal year 1986–7 (information obtained from a Merrill Lynch Investment News Report). The limited use of store market-share analysis probably results from a lack of awareness of geographic aspects of marketing and the value of spatial modelling by the marketing profession in general. An attempt is made here to correct this situation by demonstrating the application of a spatial choice model to predict market shares and market characteristics of supermarkets in Gainesville, Florida.

The importance of mathematical modelling in market share analysis

There are two methods of store market analysis which are diametrically opposite in their approach. One relies on the local knowledge of store personnel; the other relies on mathematical models to forecast market share and market characteristics. The modelling approach is superior for two reasons.

The first is that local knowledge of market characteristics, while accurate in some instances, is fraught with uncertainty and inaccuracy. Such knowledge obviously will vary in quality across stores due to: differences in the length of tenure of the personnel providing the information; personal biases; the amount of time devoted to thinking about market characteristics; general differences in the perception of the environment by different personnel (Hanson, 1977); and differences in the interpretation of the information being requested. The application of mathematical models, on the other hand, is a much more objective approach to market share analysis and generates more consistent results.

A second advantage of the modelling approach is that, even if local knowledge of market characteristics were reliable, it would still not be possible to use such knowledge to establish the relationships between store attributes and consumption patterns and the relationships between spatial attributes and consumer spatial behaviour. Only when the latter relationships are determined through mathematical modelling is it possible to forecast accurately the effects of changes in the retailing system on market share and market characteristics. It would be extremely difficult, for example, for a supermarket manager to assess the impact on his store's sales potential of a proposed addition of 10,000 square feet to a competing store located half a mile away and the simultaneous closing of a competitor located 1 mile away. Predicting the impact of such actions with the aid of a mathematical market-share model, on the other hand, would be a relatively simple matter.

Since local knowledge of market characteristics is usually unreliable and since forecasting is one of the major uses of store market-share analysis, the remainder of this chapter describes the application of a mathematical model to predict consumers' store preferences.

An overview of market share models

Market share models attempt to answer the question 'Who shops where?' This is done by relating the probability of an individual of type m at location i selecting store j to a set of values describing store j and the spatial separation of i and j. It is of no consequence that individuals may not make daily or weekly decisions regarding store choice and that they shop mainly by habit – if this is the case, what is being modelled is the probability that an individual will form a particular habit. The modelling approaches that have been used to answer the question 'Who shops where?' are described in Figure 5.1

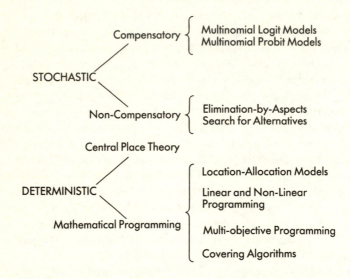

Figure 5.1 Market share models.

The market share model that will be used in this study is a multinomial logit model, which is a stochastic, compensatory model selected because it does not have the limitations of other approaches. Deterministic models of market share, such as Central Place Theory (King, 1984), and various types of mathematical programming models (Bacon, 1984), were ruled out because they rely on generally unrealistic assumptions regarding consumer spatial behaviour such as consumers patronising the nearest opportunity (with certain constraints).[3] Empirical studies of consumer purchases demonstrate that, while there is a tendency for consumers to select nearby stores, there are other factors that determine a consumer's choice of store and many consumers do not patronise the closest store to their residence. Stochastic, non-compensatory models such as Tversky's Elimination-by-Aspects model (Tversky, 1969; 1972) and Hansen's Search for Alternatives model (Hansen, 1976) allow that consumer store choice is probabilistic rather than deterministic, but they differ from compensatory models in the following manner. Compensatory models operate on the premise that a consumer's choice of a particular store is based on a variety of store attributes and that there can be a trade-off between these attributes; that is, if a store scores poorly on some attribute (such as size), this, to some extent, can be *compensated* for by scoring highly on some other attribute (such as proximity to residence) so that a consumer may trade the advantages of shopping at a large store which is across town to shop at a smaller but much closer store. Non-compensatory store choice models do not allow for such behaviour. In the Elimination-by-Aspects model, aspects or attributes of store are ranked in order of their perceived importance and each time stores are examined on an attribute, stores that do not possess an acceptable level of that attribute are eliminated from further consideration by the consumer. This process continues until only one alternative, the selected store, remains. In the Search for Alternatives model, a consumer is assumed to continue evaluating stores until one is found that is satisfactory on *all* dimensions under consideration.

Because it is usually, if not always, impossible to know exactly how consumers reach their decisions regarding store selection, it is difficult to argue for the compensatory framework over the non-compensatory framework, or vice versa.[4] However, the logit compensatory choice model has advantages over non-compensatory models (and over the probit model) in terms of ease of application, ease of calibration, ease of interpretation, and in terms of having a history of use in modelling spatial behaviour. It is also useful that the logit model has a strong theoretical basis in terms of random utility maximisation (McFadden, 1974; Williams, 1977; Williams and Ortuzar, 1982) which instills confidence in the application of the model.[5] Consequently, following similar decisions by Openshaw (1975), Gautschi (1981), and Miller and O'Kelly (1983), the multinomial logit model will be utilised in this study to examine consumer retail-choice behaviour. This model is now described.

The multinomial logit model

The probability that an individual type m (that is, belonging to a certain socio-economic group, age category, race, etc.) located at place i selects supermarket j out of a set of J supermarkets to do his/her major grocery shopping is given by the multinomial logit (MNL) formulation as:

$$P_{ijm} = \frac{\exp (V_{ijm})}{\sum\limits_{j=1}^{J} \exp (V_{ijm})} \qquad [5.1]$$

where V_{ijm} represents the observed utility an individual of type m at location i receives from selecting store j. This utility can be expressed as a linear additive function of store attributes as perceived by the individual; that is:

$$V_{ijm} = \sum\limits_{k=1}^{K} \alpha_{mk} f(X_{ijk}) \qquad [5.2]$$

where α_{mk} is a parameter relating P_{ijm} and X_{ijk}, f represents a functional form (such as logarithmic, exponential or logistic) and X_{ijk} represents the kth attribute of store j (such as size) as perceived by an individual at i. There is a total of K attributes. It is usually assumed that an individual's utility increases logarithmically as an attribute increases so that f is usually defined as a natural logarithm. This implies that the addition of a fixed quantity to one of the store-attribute variables has a greater impact on an individual's utility, and hence on the probability the individual will select that store, when that attribute is small than when it is large. For instance, an addition in size of 5,000 square feet to a supermarket is likely to have a greater impact when the store's original size is 5,000 square feet than when it is 30,000 square feet. When the store is already large, the addition of 5,000 square feet is likely to add little to its perceived attractiveness. Hence, equation [5.3] can be written as:

$$V_{ijm} = \sum_{K=1}^{K} \alpha_{mk} \ln (X_{ijk})$$ [5.3]

where ln denotes a natural logarithm. Substituting equation [5.3] into equation [5.1] yields:

$$P_{ijm} = \frac{\exp \left[\sum_{k=1}^{K} \alpha_{mk} \ln (X_{ijk}) \right]}{\sum_{j=1}^{J} \exp \left[\sum_{k=1}^{K} \alpha_{mk} \ln (X_{ijk}) \right]}$$

$$= \frac{\prod_{k=1}^{K} X_{ijk}^{\alpha^{mk}}}{\sum_{j=1}^{J} \prod_{k=1}^{K} X_{ijk}^{\alpha^{mk}}}$$ [5.4]

which is the form of the multinomial logit model that will be used to analyse the market characteristics of supermarkets in Gainesville, Florida. Several tasks remain, however, before the model in equation [5.4] can be used for this purpose. Amongst other things, it is necessary to define what the relevant X_{ijk} variables are; that is, what makes a store attractive to a consumer. It is also necessary to obtain estimates of the α_{mk} parameters and to identify the person-type characteristics that influence the values of these parameters. These and other topics that arise in operationalising equation [5.4] in a retail environment are now discussed.

Operationalising the logit model in a retailing environment

To apply the MNL model described in equation [5.4] in a retail system to forecast the market share and market characteristics of each retail outlet, the following operational considerations need to be addressed.
(a) What are the relevant store attributes (often referred to as store image variables in the marketing literature) that determine a consumer's choice of store? Which attributes or image variables should be included in a model of store choice?

(b) How can prejudice, particularly racial prejudice, be included in a model of store choice?

(c) Are aggregate or disaggregate data to be used?

(d) How is the spatial separation between the consumer and each store to be measured?

(e) Are there constraints on individuals' choice sets? Do all individuals consider the same set of stores?

(f) What are the relevant person-type categories (identified by the notation m above) to include in the modelling framework? What attributes of *individuals* rather than stores affect store choice?

(g) How are estimates of the model parameters obtained?

(h) How is information on market shares and market characteristics derived from the multinomial logit model?

Each of these issues in applying market share models is now discussed. It is stressed that the answers to the questions raised here need to be tempered with parsimony in applied studies. That is, there is often a trade-off between accuracy and applicability; in order to ensure that a model can be applied with relative ease, it is usually necessary to forgo a certain degree of accuracy that could otherwise be obtained. In retailing studies, there is a need for a fairly simple model for which data are readily available and which can predict consumer spatial behaviour with reasonable accuracy. Obtaining such a model is the goal in each of the following discussions.

The identification of relevant store attribute variables

Studies of store attribute or image variables are fairly common (see Lincoln and Samli, 1979). Generally, information on store image is obtained from administering questionnaires in which consumers are asked to rank the store attributes they perceive as important in their selection of stores.[6] Louviere and Meyer (1979), for example, surveyed 100 residents in Tallahassee, Florida, and 100 residents in Laramie, Wyoming. Three attributes overwhelmed all others in frequency of response by consumers; variety of products, convenience to residence and price levels. Similarly, Schuler (1979) surveyed consumers in Bloomington, Indiana, and found that the most important store attributes were price levels, quality of merchandise, proximity of parking, quickness of service and proximity to residence. Recker and Kostyniuk (1978), from 300 completed questionnaires in Buffalo, New York, found the important store attributes to be divided into four major categories; quality of store, accessibility, convenience and service. The quality of store variables included prices of goods, variety of goods, and quality of goods. The accessibility variables were distance from residence and distance from work (the former, presumably, for major purchases and the latter for minor purchases). The convenience variables included parking facilities, proximity to other shops, convenient hours, degree of crowding in the store and the display of goods. Finally, the service variables included the acceptance of credit cards, cheque-cashing policy and the ease of returning goods.

While questionnaire surveys regarding store attributes can be useful, the danger in relying on them is that consumers may be either unaware of what affects their choice of stores or they may be unwilling to divulge certain attributes. An example of the former is the variable measuring proximity of a store to its competitors which has been hypothesised by Fotheringham (1983a; 1983b; 1986) to play an important, although possibly subconscious, role in determining destination choice. This was also described in a retailing context by Fotheringham (1985). The proximity of a store to its competitors, X_{ij3}, can be described by a weighted inverse distance measure where the weight is store size; that is:

$$X_{ij3} = \sum_h X_{ih1} \exp (\beta \cdot X_{jh2}) \qquad [5.5]$$

where X_{ih1} represents the size of store h and X_{jh2} represents the distance between store j and its competitor h. The parameter β, which is less than zero, represents a distance decay parameter (Fotheringham, 1985). With $\beta < 0$, the value of X_{ij3} will be large for a store in close spatial proximity to other stores and small for a store spatially isolated from its competitors. Inclusion of this variable in the logit model has also been shown to remove the undesirable Independence of Irrelevant Alternatives property from the MNL model (Fotheringham, 1986).

An example of the latter danger of relying on questionnaire surveys concerns racial prejudice in store choice, which consumers are very unlikely to acknowledge. In the United States, for example, whether it be an active form of prejudice or simply a feeling of discomfort at being conspicuous, whites tend to be deterred from shopping at stores in predominantly black neighbourhoods, and blacks tend to be deterred from shopping at stores in predominantly white neighbourhoods (Lloyd and Jennings, 1978). Similar consumer behaviour is likely to occur if the population is segregated by some trait other than race.[7]

The store attribute variables identified above fall into four categories:

(a) those that are impossible to quantify, such as the ease of returning goods, the friendliness of store personnel and the display quality of goods;

(b) those that can be quantified but for which accurate data are extremely difficult to obtain, such as the degree of crowding and price levels;[8]

(c) those that are highly correlated with another, more easily measurable, variable, such as the variety of goods and the number of cashiers, which tend to be highly correlated with store size;

(d) those that suffer from none of the above problems.

This study will use only those variables that fall into the last category; these are the spatial separation of the store from the consumer's residence, store size, proximity of the store to similar stores, and the racial environment of the store. The spatial separation of the store and the consumer's residence will be measured by distance, which is a surrogate for a consumer's travel time and for the rate of information decay. Consumers are likely to be more familiar with local stores (Hanson, 1977) and are more likely to patronise stores with which they are familiar. The store size variable is a surrogate for the variety of merchandise available, and also possibly for general price levels since prices tend to decrease with increasing store size. The rationale for the inclusion of the other two variables is described above.

The selection of store attribute variables to include in the MNL model is a good example of the concept of parsimony in modelling (see Figure 5.2). While improvements in the accuracy of the model could undoubtedly be made by including more store attribute variables, the improvement would be so small relative to the extra efforts needed in terms of data collection that such

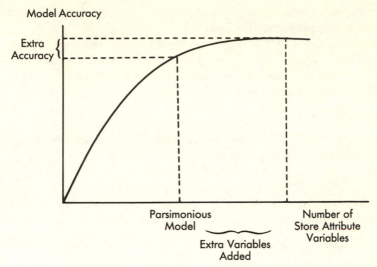

Figure 5.2 Parsimony in a retail choice model.

efforts are generally unjustified. The model is deemed to perform sufficiently accurately in predicting consumer spatial behaviour with only the four store attributes described above. There are three major advantages to this relatively simple modelling approach. The first is that it is easy and cheap to collect the data; the second is that the lack of multicollinearity between variables removes the necessity for complex calibration techniques such as ridge regression (Timmermans, 1981); and the third is that the interpretation of the parameter estimates in the model is free from the confusion created by variables being highly collinear (Fotheringham, 1982).

Modelling racial prejudice in consumer spatial behaviour

Consider two individuals, one black and one white, at the same location, selecting a destination for grocery shopping. Racial prejudice is evident in consumer spatial behaviour whenever, *all else being equal*, the probability of the white person selecting a store in a black neighbourhood is lower than the probability of the black person selecting a store in a black neighbourhood, and vice versa. To the author's knowledge, such behaviour has not been modelled explicitly in retailing studies and the following methodology is an attempt to incorporate a component of store choice modelling previously ignored.

To model the effect of racial prejudice on store choice, different specifications of the MNL model need to be used for different racial groups. Assume that there are only two racial groups, blacks and whites. For whites:

$$V_{ijm}{}^{w} = f(p_j{}^{b}) \qquad\qquad [5.6]$$

where $p_j{}^{b}$ is the proportion of black population in the neighbourhood or zone in which store j is located. Similarly, for blacks:

$$V_{ijm}{}^{b} = f(p_j{}^{w}) \qquad\qquad [5.7]$$

Since the range of units of $p_j{}^{b}$ and $p_j{}^{w}$ is a constant $(0 - 1)$, f is most appropriately defined as an exponential function so that:

$$f(p_j{}^{b}) = \exp(\phi_w p_j{}^{b}) \qquad\qquad [5.8]$$

and:

$$f(p_j{}^{w}) = \exp(\phi_b p_j{}^{w}) \qquad\qquad [5.9]$$

where $\phi_w < 0$ and $\phi_b < 0$ and are parameters denoting the degree of racial prejudice by whites and blacks, respectively.[9] If $\phi_w = 0$, then, in terms of store choice, there is no racial prejudice by whites; if $\phi_b = 0$, there is no racial prejudice by blacks. Increasingly negative values of either indicate increasing racial prejudice.

To see the effect of varying ϕ, consider a system of zones in which the proportion of white population in each zone is 1.0. For notational convenience, assume that, except for racial differences, the population is homogeneous so that the m subscript can be dropped. Consider the selection of store k in one particular zone. Under these conditions, there will be no evident racial prejudice and:

$$P_{ik}\,(\text{no}) = \frac{V_{ik}}{\sum\limits_{j} V_{ij}} \qquad\qquad [5.10]$$

where V_{ik} is a function of store attribute variables as described in equation [5.2]. Since the population of the region is 100 per cent white, the race variable, P_j^b, is 0 for each V_{ij}.

Consider what happens to P_{ik} as the proportion of blacks in the zone in which store k is located increases and racial prejudice exists. Then:

$$P_{ik}(\text{yes}) = \frac{V_{ik} \exp (\phi_w p_k{}^b)}{\underset{j \neq k}{\underset{j}{\sum}} V_{ij} + V_{ik} \exp (\phi_w p_k{}^b)} \qquad [5.11]$$

If the number of stores is large, then:

$$P_{ik}(\text{yes}) \simeq P_{ik}(\text{no}) \exp (\phi_w p_k{}^b) \qquad [5.12]$$

so that the term $\exp (\phi_w p_k{}^b)$ can be interpreted as the approximate proportional reduction in the probability that a white consumer will choose store k because it is in a black zone. Equation [5.12] can be rewritten as:

$$P_{ik} \simeq C \exp (\phi_w p_k{}^b) \qquad [5.13]$$

where C is the probability that individual i will select store k without racial prejudice. The effect of ϕ_w on P_{ik} is demonstrated in Figure 5.3. The parameter $\phi_w < 0$ can then be seen as an index of racial prejudice; the more negative is ϕ_w, the greater is the rate of decrease in the probability that a white individual at i will choose store k when store k is located in an increasingly black zone. A similar interpretation would be given to ϕ_b. As mentioned above, because p_b and p_w have constant ranges, the parameters ϕ_b and ϕ_w will be invariant to changes in spatial scale and can therefore be compared directly across different geographic areas. It is expected that in reality the values will be somewhere in the range of 0 to -1.5 as depicted in Figure 5.3.

Aggregate and disaggregate approaches to modelling consumer spatial behaviour

The retail choice model described in equation [5.4] can be applied at two levels. If the model is used to predict the behaviour of *individuals*, then the application is said to be at a disaggregate level. If the model is used to predict the behaviour of *groups* of individuals, then the application is said to be at an aggregate level. The former is more accurate because in dealing with groups of individuals, information tends to be lost in the aggregation

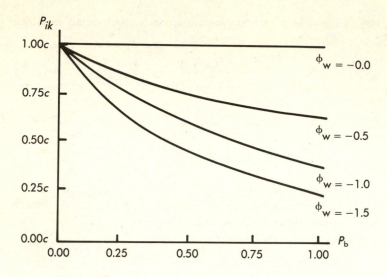

Figure 5.3 Demonstrating the effects of racial prejudice on consumer spatial behaviour.

procedure. For example, if a disaggregate model were applied, information on individual's exact residential locations would be used, whereas a common aggregation procedure is to group individuals by geographic location into zones and assume that the location of the population in each zone can be represented by some central point.

Unfortunately, while the disaggregate application is superior in terms of model performance, it is often not feasible to obtain such detailed data and for this reason the majority of applications of destination choice models have been at the aggregate level. The modelling procedure followed in this chapter is at the aggregate level where the data needed to apply the model are readily available in Census documents. Consequently, in the choice model described in equation [5.4], p_{ijm} is the proportion of the population of type m in zone i that selects store j.

The measurement of spatial separation

Three measures of spatial separation are needed to apply the spatial choice model described in equation [5.4]. These are:

(a) the interzonal separation of individuals and stores;
(b) the intrazonal separation of individuals and stores;
(c) the spatial separation between stores to calculate the store competition variable.

While travel time could be used for all three measures, it is generally not feasible to obtain accurate travel times for even a small urban system.[10] Geographic distance is thus usually used as a travel proxy (Koppelman and Hauser, 1978; McCarthy, 1980) and can easily be obtained from coordinates by the following metric:

$$d_{ij}{}^P + (|x_i - x_j|^P + |y_i - y_j|^P)^{1/P} \qquad [5.14]$$

where the coordinate of place i is (x_i, y_i). If $P = 2.0$, then the distances calculated are straight line; if $P = 1.0$, the distances are rectangular. It is more realistic in urban areas, particularly in the US where roads are commonly arranged in a grid system, to use rectangular distances as measures of spatial separation. Thus, by simply having information on locations of zone centroids and stores, equation [5.14] with $P = 1.0$ can be used to derive realistic measures of spatial separation for categories (a) and (c) above.

It is inaccurate, however, to use equation [5.14] to calculate the distance between the centre of a zone and a store located within that same zone (an intrazonal distance). The reason for this becomes clear when one considers a store located at the centre of the zone; the distance in equation [5.14] would be zero, when in reality the average distance travelled by consumers would obviously be non-zero. This is a problem caused by using aggregate data and assuming the population to be clustered in discrete points rather than being distributed continuously across space. As a result, a different formulation is needed to calculate intrazonal distances.

Measures of intrazonal distances for zones of various shapes have been provided by Eilon, Watson-Gandy and Christofides (1971) and this study uses two of these measures for calculating rectangular distances. Eilon *et al.* demonstrate that if a zone is circular and the population is distributed evenly throughout the zone, then the minimum intrazonal distance would occur when the store is located at the centre of the zone. This minimum distance is equal to $0.846r$, where r is the radius of the zone.[11] The maximum intrazonal distance, $1.423r$, would occur when the store is on the perimeter of the zone. Consequently, if zones are approximately circular, the following formula can be used for intrazonal distances:

$$d_{ij} = 0.846(1.432/0.846)^{z/r} \cdot r \qquad [5.15]$$

where z is the distance between the store and the centre of the zone.[12] The equivalent intrazonal distance formula for zones that are rectangular and of length a and width b is:

$$d_{ij} = (1/4 + z/4q)\ (a + b) \qquad [5.16]$$

where:

$$q = [(a/2)^2 + (b/2)^2]^{1/2} \qquad [5.17]$$

and where z is distance of the store from the centre of the rectangle.[13]

Thus, in the modelling example that follows, if zones are approximately circular, equation [5.15] is used to calculate intrazonal distances; if zones are approximately rectangular, equation [5.16] is used. As zones become increasingly irregular in shape, inaccuracies in calculating intrazonal distances will obviously increase.

Activity-constrained choice sets

One disadvantage of using the MNL model to predict store choices is that it often produces non-zero probabilities for choices that are, in reality, never evaluated by consumers. That is, consumers probably do not consider all of the J stores available to them in an urban area; rather, they make their selection from a constrained choice set, J^* (Openshaw, 1975; Landau et al., 1982). Generally, in destination choice models, the set J^* is defined in geographical terms. Specifically, consumers generally select stores only from those within a certain distance from their residence; stores further away are never considered and, consequently, are not part of their choice sets. Such activity-constrained choice sets can be modelled easily within the framework by setting all distances that are greater than a pre-selected critical value equal to some large number. This in effect removes stores at such distances from a consumer's choice set and ensures that the predicted probability of a consumer selecting such a store is virtually zero.

The influence of personal characteristics on consumer spatial behaviour

On page 132 four variables were selected for inclusion in the store choice model. These were the distance from a consumer's residence to a store, the size of a store, a variable depicting the racial composition of the zone in which the store is located, and a store competition variable. Each of these variables has an associated parameter which can vary by person-type. The discussion in this section centres on which of these parameters is likely to vary systematically between person-types and on what these particular person-types may be.

In fact, there is relatively little empirical evidence regarding systematic variation across person-types in parameter values associated with the above variables. An exception to this is the distance parameter, which appears to vary systematically by income group. Generally, individuals with higher incomes appear to be less constrained by distance in making spatial choices than are people with lower incomes (Davies, 1969; Potter, 1977). This is probably because individuals with higher incomes tend to be more familiar with their urban environment (Horton and Reynolds, 1971; Smith, 1976) and they have greater rates of car ownership (Thomas, 1974).

Consequently, in the following application of the store choice model, the only disaggregation by person-type that is made is in terms of income and it is only the distance-decay parameter that is made income-dependent.

Parameter estimation and the value of surveys

To utilise a store choice model in predicting market shares, it is necessary to obtain estimates of the model's parameters. This can be done in one of three ways. The first is to rely on the results of previous studies and to employ parameter values that are in accordance with values found in other systems. This should only be done, however, if each variable is written in terms of a power function or if the range of each variable is fixed so that parameter estimates are spatially transferable. However, it is still necessary to make the assumption that individual consumer behaviour does not vary across systems. While this procedure of operationalising equation [5.4] is the least reliable method, it has the advantage of being the simplest and cheapest. It is also the only method that can be used if a survey of consumers is not undertaken.

The second and third methods of operationalising equation [5.4] rely on obtaining information on either individual's preferences or behaviour in the system in which the model is to be used. The easiest to administer is a survey of individual's *preferences* for stores since this can be conducted in an experimental setting. Individuals are not asked which stores they actually patronise, but are asked to give some indication of their preference rankings for hypothetical stores having various characteristics. In this way it is possible to obtain sufficient information on revealed preferences to obtain estimates of the parameters associated with various store image variables (Cadwallader, 1975; Louviere and Meyer, 1979). Two potential problems exist with this approach, however. One is that there is not necessarily a strong relationship between people's revealed preferences and their actual choices. A second is that, as mentioned on page 131, individuals may make their choices in part subconsciously and so cannot reveal their true behaviour (as in the case of store competition), or they may be unwilling to reveal their true preferences (as in the case of racial prejudice).

The third method of obtaining parameter estimates is to conduct a survey of consumers' shopping habits through both store-based and home-based interviews. Data are then available on the actual store choices of consumers and on the characteristics of the consumers making these choices. Calibration of the model can be undertaken by either maximum likelihood estimation (Batty, 1976; Williams and Fotheringham, 1984) or, if the data are aggregated into proportions, by least squares regression (Nakanishi and Cooper, 1974). While this approach is the most accurate and preferred method of obtaining parameter estimates, it is not without its problems. It is very time-consuming and expensive to elicit the required information from a sufficient number of individuals in order to obtain reasonably accurate parameter estimates. Ideally, in order to account for any possible spatial differences in consumer behaviour, this survey process should be undertaken separately in every retailing system in which the model is to be applied. Also, care has to be taken not to introduce bias into the store-based surveys. As Shepherd and Thomas (1980, p. 35) note, for example, random surveys of consumers at stores tend to over-estimate local consumers who shop frequently but who purchase only small amounts.

Unfortunately, in the application of the model that follows, survey data were not available to calibrate the store choice model so that the results rely on the accuracy of previous studies and the transferability of parameters. However, this does not detract from the results because the object of the application is to demonstrate the types of information on market characteristics that *can* be obtained from geographical modelling if accurate survey data are available.

The derivation of market shares and market characteristics from the store choice model

Once operationalised, the store choice model in equation [5.4] can be used to predict the proportions of individuals belonging to each sub-group in each origin zone shopping at particular stores. These proportions are then multiplied by the appropriate sub-group populations and aggregated by store. This yields data from which the market share and market characteristics of each store can easily be calculated.

To see how this is done, consider the following example. Suppose that it is predicted from the store choice model that the proportion of zone 1's low-income white population who patronise store 12 is 0.4. If zone 1's low-income white population is 600, then the number of low-income white shopping at store 12 is $600 \times 0.4 = 240$. The equivalent number can be calculated for all zones and the process repeated for all person types. The total number of individuals predicted to patronise store 12 as a proportion of the total population in the region will be store 12's market share. The market characteristics of store 12 are derived by calculating the percentage of individuals in each person-type category out of store 12's total market.

The application of the store choice model to derive market

shares and market characteristics with the above operational considerations is described in the marketing program MARKET1 which has been written by the author. The flowchart for this program is given in Figure 5.4. One useful aspect of the program that will be exploited in the subsequent market analysis of supermarkets in Gainesville is that it allows the user to assess the impacts of closing and opening stores in the system.

A market analysis of supermarkets in Gainesville, Florida

The modelling framework described above was applied to supermarkets in Gainesville to predict both the pattern of major grocery purchases in the city and the market characteristics of each supermarket. There are thirteen supermarkets within the city limits and three that lie just outside.[14] The spatial distribution of supermarkets is shown in Figure 5.5, which also describes thirty-nine neighbourhoods that form the origin zones in the study. Detailed socio-economic data are available for each of the neighbourhoods from the 1980 US Census. Data on the supermarkets were obtained from a grocery store survey firm.[15]

Five market characteristics, especially useful in estimating total sales and sales of individual products, were derived for each store. These were racial composition, age composition, one-person versus multi-person household composition, income composition, and renters versus owners composition. There tend to be differences in purchase frequency; for example, in cuts of meat and varieties of vegetables between races; in snack food items between age groups; in convenience foods between one- and multi-person households; in speciality food items between income groups; and in pet foods between home-owners and renters. It would be interesting to examine the relationships between the purchase frequency of various food items and particular market characteristics. This could be achieved if market characteristics were predicted for a set of supermarkets that supplied detailed sales figures. Knowledge of such relationships would be useful to target the advertising of various products and also to determine sales potentials of foodstuffs at different locations.

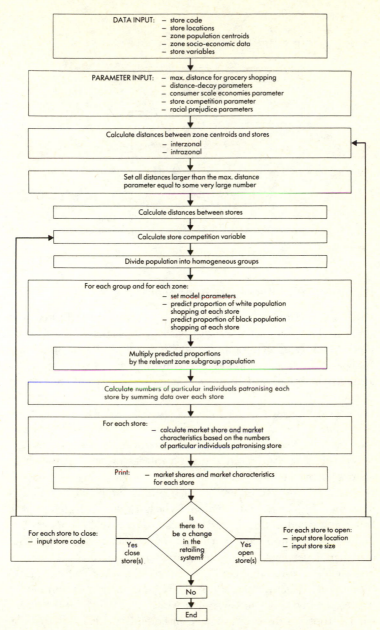

Figure 5.4 Flowchart of the marketing program MARKET1.

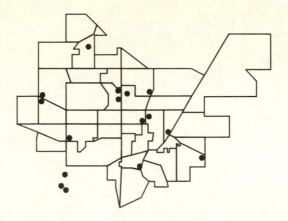

Figure 5.5 Supermarkets in Gainesville.

Population distribution in Gainesville

If the population of an urban area were evenly distributed and supermarkets were spaced at regular intervals, there would be no point in applying geographic modelling techniques in marketing analysis. However, populations within urban areas are never evenly distributed and supermarkets are never spaced at regular intervals. The distribution of supermarkets in Figure 5.5 is evidence of this latter point, while Figures 5.6 to 5.13 demonstrate that Gainesville's population of approximately 81,000 is certainly not evenly distributed. In fact, Gainesville's very uneven population distribution makes it an interesting site in which to conduct a market analysis.

Consider, for example, the distribution of black population described in Figure 5.6, which is heavily concentrated in the south-east quadrant of the city. Blacks constitute 20.6 per cent of Gainesville's population, with all other minority races totalling less than 5 per cent, so it is clear from Figure 5.6 that there are relatively few zones that could be described as racially mixed (20–75 per cent black). Neighbourhoods tend to be predominantly white, such as those in the north-west, or predominantly black, such as those in the south-east. Consequently, it is likely that the racial prejudice parameters described earlier will be non-zero.

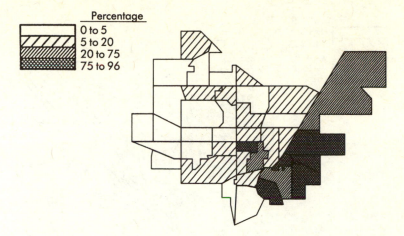

Figure 5.6 Distribution of the black population in Gainesville, shown as a percentage of neighbourhood population.

The concentrations of the low- and high-income families described in Figure 5.7 and 5.8 are, as one would expect, very dissimilar.[16] The low-income population tends to be found in two areas within the city: in the south-east, reflecting the distribution of the black population; and around the university, reflecting the

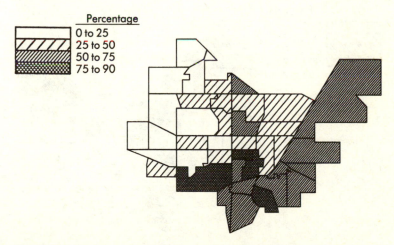

Figure 5.7 Distribution of low-income families in Gainesville, shown as a percentage of neighbourhood population.

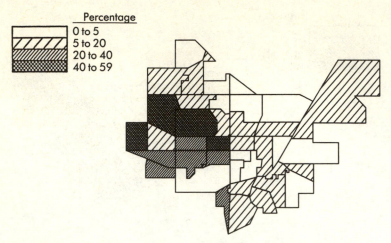

Figure 5.8 Distribution of high-income families in Gainesville, shown as a percentage of neighbourhood population.

distribution of students.[17] The University of Florida lies in the most westerly neighbourhood that has 75–90 per cent low-income families. The distribution of high-income population coincides with the distribution of white population and is strongly concentrated in the north-west.

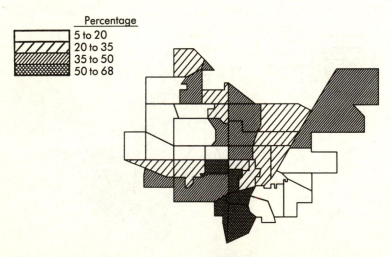

Figure 5.9 Distribution of the population aged 20–9 in Gainesville, shown as a percentage of neighbourhood population.

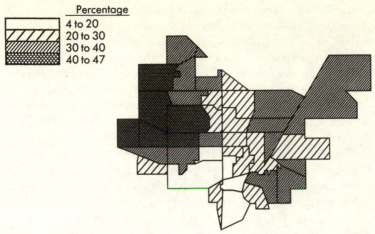

Figure 5.10 Distribution of the population aged 30–59 in Gainesville, shown as a percentage of neighbourhood population.

The distributions of age groups given in Figures 5.9 to 5.11 are also strongly localised in certain areas. Young, independent adults (aged 20–9) tend to be located close to the university and along a major north–south axis through the geographic centre of the city. The population aged 30–59, traditionally home-owners,

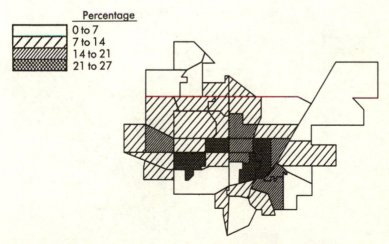

Figure 5.11 Distribution of the population aged 60 or over in Gainesville, shown as a percentage of neighbourhood population.

is heavily concentrated in the suburban areas in the north-west of the city and, to a lesser extent, in the south-east and east.[18] The elderly population tends to be located in the older residential neighbourhoods close to the centre of the city and the density of elderly population decreases fairly regularly as distance from the centre of the city increases. That these age cohorts tend to exhibit distinct and separate concentrations within the city is important in understanding consumption patterns, which are usually quite different across age groups.

The two population sub-group distributions described in Figures 5.12 and 5.13 – one-person households and renters – show some similarities with concentrations primarily along a north–south axis in the centre of the city. There is a heavy concentration of renters in the southern part of the city, particularly around the university, as one would expect, but most students share accommodation and so the proportion of one-person households around the university is quite low.

Quite clearly, these very distinctive concentrations of population sub-groups in Gainesville will produce markedly different market characteristics for each of the supermarkets described in Figure 5.5. In turn, these different market characteristics will lead to different sales potentials for each store. The prediction of the market characteristics of each supermarket is now undertaken.

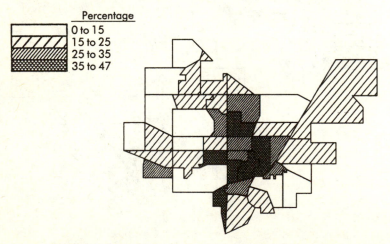

Figure 5.12 Distribution of one-person households in Gainesville, shown as a percentage of neighbourhood population.

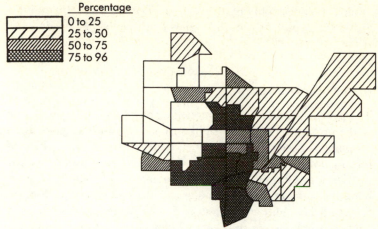

Percentage	
	0 to 25
	25 to 50
	50 to 75
	75 to 96

Figure 5.13 Distribution of rented dwellings in Gainesville, shown as a percentage of neighbourhood occupied housing units.

Parameter values for Gainesville

As noted earlier, the objective of this study is to demonstrate the types of marketing information that *can* be obtained through the geographic modelling of consumer spatial behaviour. Consequently, the absence of survey data on Gainesville's consumers is not particularly important. The parameter values chosen for the following market analysis demonstration were:

Store size parameter	=	1.5
Store competition parameter	=	-0.5
Racial prejudice parameter (whites)	=	-1.0
Racial prejudice parameter (blacks)	=	-1.0
Distance parameter (low-income group)	=	-1.8
Distance parameter (medium-income group)	=	-1.5
Distance parameter (high-income group)	=	-1.2.

These values were felt to represent reasonably accurately the behaviour of consumers in Gainesville.

The only other parameter to be input is the maximum distance threshold to define consumers' activity-constrained choice sets. A maximum driving time of 20 minutes (cf. Openshaw, 1975) was used, which translates into a distance of 6.7 miles assuming an average driving speed of 20 miles per hour. Therefore, in the model, the probability of a consumer selecting a supermarket for grocery shopping beyond 6.7 miles from his or her residence is zero.

Market analysis results

The primary outcome of the modelling procedure is the prediction of the proportion of each neighbourhood's sub-group population shopping at each supermarket. To demonstrate the nature of information that can be obtained in this type of analysis, the predicted proportions of the total population of each neighbourhood shopping at three particular stores are described in Figures 5.14 to 5.17. Quite clearly, store 8 is predicted to draw heavily from the low-income black neighbourhoods, store 5 from the university area, and store 10 from the wealthier north-west suburban neighbourhoods. The full effects of these widely different markets are evident in Table 5.2, which describes the *predicted* market characteristics of the three stores.[19] On the basis of these figures, store 10 could be classified as serving predominantly white suburban home-owners with medium to high incomes; store 8 as serving predominantly black suburban

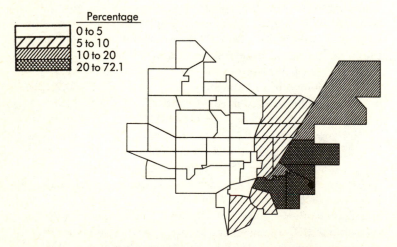

Figure 5.14 The predicted proportion of each neighbourhood in Gainesville shopping at store 8, Winn Dixie, shown as a percentage of neighbourhood population.

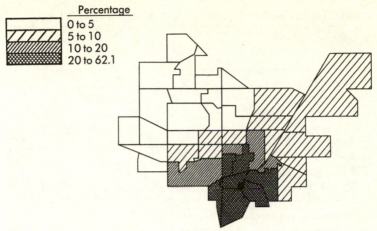

Figure 5.15 The predicted proportion of each neighbourhood in Gainesville shopping at store 5, Winn Dixie, shown as a percentage of neighbourhood population.

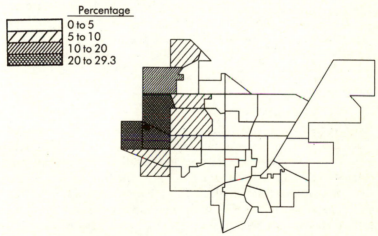

Figure 5.16 The predicted proportion of each neighbourhood in Gainesville shopping at store 10, Publix, shown as a percentage of neighbourhood population.

families with low income; and store 5 as serving predominantly young renters with low incomes.

While such information is obviously useful to supermarkets, the greatest utility of the modelling framework is when it is used

Table 5.2   A market comparison of three supermarkets

Market characteristic	Store			Gainesville Ave
	10	8	5	
Store size (000 ft^2)	20.0	19.0	24.3	21.2
Population served	3,867	7,772	9,479	5,086
Population served/1000 ft^2	193	409	390	239
Market share	4.8	9.6	11.7	6.3
% Black	7.0	60.9	23.7	20.6
% Age < 20	32.5	38.7	29.2	31.1
% Age 20–9	22.8	24.5	42.3	32.4
% Age 30–59	35.5	27.7	19.6	26.8
% Age ≥ 60	9.2	9.1	8.9	9.7
% One-person households	16.8	19.0	25.7	23.7
% Low income[1]	23.7	58.7	56.7	26.8
% Medium income[2]	50.4	34.8	33.1	58.7
% High income[3]	25.8	6.5	10.3	14.5
% Renters	31.0	50.5	70.2	49.6

Locations:
10 = Publix, NW 16th Blvd
 8 = Winn Dixie, Hawthorne Rd
 5 = Winn Dixie, SW 16th Ave

1 1980 Annual family income < $15,000.
2 1980 Annual family income $15,000–35,000.
3 1980 Annual family income ≥ $35,000.

for forecasting. To demonstrate this, four sites that seemed plausible locations for the opening of a new supermarket were examined. For each potential location, a full market analysis was carried out, the results of which are presented in Table 5.3. On the basis of potential market share, location C would be the recommended site for the new supermarket. However, other factors should also be considered. For instance, the market of a new store at location C would be dominated by low-income renters (presumably students) who may not spend as much money on grocery shopping as do other segments of the population. By examining a large number of potential sites throughout an urban area, it would be possible to generate a revenue or market-share surface which would be a valuable aid in searching for a general area within the city to locate a new store (Haynes and Fotheringham, 1984). Once a site is chosen, the market share model can also be used to determine the optimal size of a new store simply by obtaining estimates of the market share for a variety of store sizes and comparing these figures with projected operating costs (Haynes and Fotheringham, 1984).

A slightly different type of prediction is undertaken in the following scenario. Suppose a major supermarket chain in Gainesville – Publix – wanted to increase the size of one of its four stores by 10,000 square feet but has not decided at which store the addition would be most profitable. The predicted market share of each store with the proposed addition is given in Table 5.4. In terms of increasing both the market share of a particular store and Publix's overall share of the Gainesville market, the addition should be built on to store 1. This action is predicted to attract

Table 5.3 Market analysis of four possible locations for a new supermarket in Gainesville[1]

Market characteristic	Location			
	A	B	C	D
Population served	3,716	4,952	5,670	4,829
Market share	4.6	6.1	7.0	5.9
% Black	7.0	29.8	18.4	11.5
% Age < 20	33.6	28.7	30.2	32.4
% Age 20–9	23.9	32.6	42.7	32.4
% Age 30–59	35.7	26.0	18.7	25.6
% Age ≥ 60	6.8	12.7	8.5	9.6
% One-person households	15.8	28.9	30.8	23.6
% Low income[2]	25.0	51.8	52.5	36.9
% Medium income[3]	58.6	38.8	35.7	40.9
% High income[4]	16.4	9.4	11.8	22.2
% Renters	29.3	55.8	68.1	47.4

Locations:
A = NW 39th Ave and NW 34th St
B = SE 11th St and SE 7th Ave
C = SW 2nd Ave and SW 13th St
D = W Univ. Ave and SW 22nd St

1 Supermarket size in each case is 20,000 ft^2 (approximate average size of supermakets in Gainesville).
2 1980 Annual family income < $15,000.
3 1980 Annual family income $15,000–35,000.
4 1980 Annual family income > $35,000.

Table 5.4 Determining the optimal Publix supermarket to receive an additional 10,000 ft^2 of retail space

Addition made to store	Original market share (%)	New market share (%)	Change in market share (%)	Old total Publix market share (%)	New total Publix market share (%)
1*	6.8	11.6	+ 4.8	23.9	28.1
2	7.2	11.5	+ 4.3	23.9	27.8
9	5.1	9.2	+ 4.0	23.9	27.5
10	4.8	7.9	+ 3.1	23.9	26.5

*Optimal location for addition.

Locations:
 1 = N Main St
 2 = SW 34th St
 9 = NW 13th St
 10 = NW 16th Blvd

another 4.8 per cent of Gainesville's population to store 1 and another 4.2 per cent to Publix supermarkets as a group.[20]

Continuing with this scenario, suppose the Publix addition is built at store 1. It would be of interest and value to all other supermarkets to know what effects such an addition might have on their sales. The predicted market shares of each supermarket before and after the addition to store 1 is built are given in Table 5.5. It is clear that the proposed addition will have the greatest impact on store 5, which is predicted to lose 1.1 per cent of the Gainesville market. Armed with this information, the owners of store 5 may be able to minimise their loss by more aggressive advertising or by increasing the size of their own store.

One final application of market share modelling that is demonstrated here concerns a business failure. During the summer of 1985, a large supermarket owned by the Winn Dixie chain closed in Gainesville due to low profits. It is useful to analyse why this business failed by estimating its market characteristics while in operation. This can easily be done by adding this store to the existing data set and re-running the analysis. The market characteristics of the failed store (17) and three other Winn Dixie supermarkets that are successful are listed in Table 5.6. The estimated market share for store 17 is not

Table 5.5 Predicted effects on all supermarkets of adding 10,000 ft^2 to store 1

Store	Original market share (%)	New market share (%)	Change in market share (%)
1	6.8	11.6	+ 4.8
2	7.2	6.9	− 0.3
3	3.2	3.0	− 0.2
4	11.6	11.1	− 0.5
5	11.7	10.6	− 1.1
6	6.3	6.0	− 0.3
7	6.9	6.4	− 0.5
8	9.6	9.1	− 0.5
9	5.1	4.9	− 0.2
10	4.8	4.7	− 0.1
11	4.9	4.4	− 0.4
12	5.1	5.0	− 0.1
13	3.5	3.3	− 0.2
14*	5.7	5.5	− 0.2
15*	4.3	4.2	− 0.1
16*	3.5	3.4	− 0.1

*Stores outside city limits.

particularly low (7.6 per cent), but the store was large and the ratio of population served to unit area is not very high (229 per 1,000 square feet). On the basis of these figures, store 17, while not appearing to be a particularly profitable store, does not give any strong indication of being a business failure. However, the store differed from other Winn Dixie supermarkets in three critical market categories. Because it was located in the western part of the city, its market consisted of far fewer blacks, fewer low-income consumers and a greater percentage of high-income consumers than the successful Winn Dixie stores. These differences hint strongly at why store 17 failed. Winn Dixie supermarkets in Gainesville have, and tend to nurture due to their product lines, an image of serving low-income black consumers. A Winn Dixie store in a predominantly white medium- to high-income area, such as store 17, would probably not attract as many customers as might otherwise be expected. A detailed market analysis such as is presented here would have highlighted this point and might have prevented the locational decision that eventually led to a business failure.

Summary

The objectives of this chapter have been to demonstrate the application and the utility of geográphic modelling in market analysis and to show the type of information that can be obtained from the spatial analysis of consumer behaviour. The discussion has been limited to a particular type of market analysis, store market-share analysis, and the relationship between this and other types of market analysis. Above all the *practical* uses of

Table 5.6   Predicted market characteristics of the four Winn Dixie supermarkets prior to the closure of store 17

Market characteristic	Store number			
	5	7	8	17
Store size (000 ft^2)	24.3	24.0	19.0	27.0
Population served	8,828	5,343	7,408	6,195
Population served/1000 ft^2	363	223	389	229
Market share	10.9	6.6	9.1	7.6
% Black	24.3	19.6	61.9	10.1*
% Age < 20	29.0	29.5	38.8	31.6
% Age 20–9	42.4	31.4	24.3	33.6
% Age 30–59	19.7	28.6	27.8	26.0
% Age ≥ 60	9.0	10.4	9.1	8.9
% One-person households	25.7	23.9	18.9	22.4
% Low income[1]	57.0	42.4	58.9	35.1*
% Medium income[2]	33.0	46.9	34.7	44.5
% High income[3]	10.1	10.6	6.4	20.5*
% Renters	70.4	48.1	50.4	50.3

*Major differences

Locations:
  5 = SW 16th Ave
  7 = N Main St
  8 = Hawthorne Rd
 17 = W University Ave

1 1980 Annual family income < $15,000.
2 1980 Annual family income $15,000–35,000.
3 1980 Annual family income > $35,000.

modelling consumers' spatial behaviour have been stressed. The basic tenet of the chapter is that such modelling is useful in providing input to many types of business decisions by both store owners and food suppliers. For the former, the modelling techniques described here can be used to forecast sales at locations that are being considered for a new store. For the latter, information is provided through predicting the market characteristics of stores which can then be correlated with the sales of various products. Such information could be used to target advertising at particular consumer groups.

The final sections of the chapter have described the application of a store choice model to calculate market shares and market characteristics. Operationalising such a model raises many questions not usually asked in purely theoretical work, and this is illustrated by means of an application of the modelling framework to supermarkets in Gainesville, Florida. A market analysis algorithm, MARKET1, which is used for this purpose, is also described.

The only new theoretical work described in this chapter concerns the modelling of racial prejudice in store choice. It would be interesting to pursue this topic if the necessary data were available to estimate racial prejudice parameters. These data could be obtained from a survey of shopping patterns in an urban area. Such a survey, not available for the Gainesville study, is recommended for the application of the modelling framework outlined here.

Finally, the market analysis undertaken in this study has been in terms of supermarkets. The analysis, however, could equally be applied to non-grocery stores, to banking facilities, to fast-food restaurants, or to any other type of outlet serving the general public. Geographic modelling thus has much to offer the retailing sector and, given its utility, it is an area in marketing that is under-developed and under-utilised.

Notes

1   The lengthier terminology 'choice frequency modelling' is retained here because of the potential confusion the name 'choice modelling' creates with modelling the spatial choice of stores, which is the domain of store market-share analysis.

2 It is important to distinguish between store and brand market-share analysis because, while some concepts are common to both, others are not. In particular, the spatial component in brand market-share modelling is completely absent. Unfortunately, researchers in marketing, typified by Batsell and Polking (1985), tend to be unaware of store market-share analysis so that their use of the term 'market share analysis' implies only brand market-share analysis.

3 As Shepherd and Thomas (1980, p. 23) note of the application of Central Place Theory, 'the detailed limitations and constraints on its behavioural assumptions suggest that further investigation of consumer spatial behaviour is most likely to progress through an alternative framework'.

4 It is useful to note, however, that in one of the few comparisons of the behaviour of compensatory and non-compensatory spatial choice models, the former model proved slightly superior (Timmermans, 1983).

5 While it is well known that the logit model contains what is known as the Independence of Irrelevant Alternatives property (Sobel, 1980; Tye *et al.*, 1982; Wrigley, 1985) and that this property is undesirable in retailing situations (Fotheringham, 1985), it has been demonstrated recently that this property can easily be removed within the logit framework (Fotheringham, 1986).

6 Some store image questionnaires can be very detailed. Timmermans *et al.* (1982), for instance, report a store image questionnaire that took some interviewees two hours to complete.

7 Segregation may not simply be racial. In Northern Ireland, for example, retailing patterns are likely to be affected by the distribution of Catholics and Protestants, with Catholics less likely to patronise stores in predominantly Protestant areas and vice versa.

8 While it is possible to obtain a price index for each store for a general basket of goods, such indices can fluctuate due to time-limited specials and random variations in price mark-ups. Such indices also do not take into account the effects of couponing, discounts for large purchases, stamps and other similar savings incentives that stores may offer consumers.

9 While the exponential, $\exp(\alpha X)$, and power, X^α, functions tend to be very similar, the exponential function is usually preferred when the parameter is negative. Under such circumstances, as the variable tends to zero, the exponential function tends to one, whereas the power function tends to positive infinity. However, a disadvantage of the exponential function is that the value of the parameter α is a function of the scale at which the variable X is measured. If X were distance, for example, and were measured in miles and kilometres, $|\alpha \text{ miles}| > |\alpha \text{ (km)}|$. In a power function, the parameter α is independent of the units in which X is measured. Hence, in a model where the variables are in a power format, the parameters are spatially transferrable; they are not when the variables have an exponential

format unless the ranges of the variables are constant, which is the case when X is a proportion.

10 There is also no guarantee that travel time is the most accurate specification of spatial separation, particularly if what is being measured by spatial separation is information decay.

11 Since zones will rarely be exactly circular, it is best to calculate r from:

$$r = (\text{Area of zone}/\pi)^{0.5}$$

12 When $z = 0$, $d_{ij} = 0.846r$; when $z = r$, $d_{ij} = 1.423r$; when $0 \leqslant z \leqslant r$, $0.846r \leqslant d_{ij} \leqslant 1.423r$.

13 When $z = 0$, $d_{ij} = (a + b)/4$; when $z = q$, $d_{ij} = (a + b)/2$; when $0 \leqslant z \leqslant q$, $(a + b)/4 \leqslant d_{ij} \leqslant (a + b)/2$.

14 To be included in the analysis, a supermarket had to be at least 10,000 square feet in area. This definition excluded variety and convenience stores that play a minimal role as destinations for major grocery purchases.

15 In the context of work undertaken by the author for General Foods Corporation, similar data were made available for every supermarket in Florida.

16 Low-income families are defined as having an annual family income of less than \$15,000 in 1980. High-income families are defined as having an annual family income of over \$35,000 in 1980.   ·

17 Approximately 33,000 students attend the University of Florida and so have a large effect on the demographic composition of the city and, consequently, on retailing patterns.

18 Although not shown, the distribution of population aged less than 20 correlates very highly with the distribution of the population aged 30–59, strongly indicating that these are typical suburban families.

19 The predicted market share of store 10 is somewhat misleading. This is the predicted share of the population within the city limits of Gainesville that patronises store 10. However, store 10 is on the edge of the city and draws people from areas outside the city not accounted for in this study.

20 Since the addition to store 1 draws consumers from some of the other Publix stores, the overall Publix market share does not increase by as much as store 1's market share.

CHAPTER 6
Store and shopping-centre location and size: a review of British research and practice

Alan G. Wilson

Introduction

There are a number of ways in which a review can be organised, ranging from a chronological presentation of work done (with some evaluation) to a conceptual framework to which individual contributions can be attached; or on another axis, from commercial application as the prime focus to academic viewpoint. I have chosen to emphasise a particular conceptual framework as being the most effective basis for the argument in an attempt to lend coherence to this particular presentation (rather than to claim unique validity). This approach has the advantage that it is then relevant to any point on the commercial–academic spectrum and can be used to situate and appraise a variety of applications and research studies of each kind. The review is 'British' in the sense that much of the research described was carried out in Britain, but inevitably there are some antecedents and follow-up research in other countries to which it is also appropriate to refer.

It is also useful at the outset to emphasise that I have treated this chapter as a review of ideas and practice and worked on the basis that the argument will be more readable if I do not also make it a detailed literature review at the same time. There are relatively few references cited in the text, therefore, but I have tried to compensate by providing an extensive bibliography on the relevant aspects of retailing.

The objective is to focus on *either* store *or* shopping-centre location and size. On the whole, these are best treated as separate problems but, as we will see, it is possible in principle to link the two scales – though at the expense of raising difficult research problems. The discussion will be presented, therefore, in terms of retail *facilities* (or units) and most of the analyses can then be applied at either of the two scales.

It is only possible to understand location and size issues properly by relating possible sites to markets, that is to demand at residential (or workplace) locations and the flows (which should also be related to transport costs) from origins to facilities. This basic underlying conceptualisation is shown in Figure 6.1. The principal agents in the system of interest are therefore consumers and retailers, and they are connected by expenditure flows. The retailers' operations will be influenced by relationships with a variety of other kinds of agents – manufacturers of goods, wholesalers, distributors and transport firms, developers, financiers and land owners. Town planners and transport planners will also be involved. We will focus on consumers and retailers, however – interpreting the latter as developers if we are working at the scale of 'centres' – but within a framework where explicit connections to the interests of other kinds of agents can be pursued. The system of interest will be referred to as the *retail system*, defined in an appropriate way for a particular study.

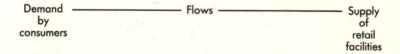

Figure 6.1 The relation of possible sites to markets.

We then make a major distinction between *analysis* and *application*. The argument is that a good analytical framework is vital if any applied study is to be successful. We attempt to provide this framework with analysis based on modelling concepts. There are thus two major sections of the chapter: the first is devoted to analysis and modelling; and the second to applications. This also helps us to keep a clear line of argument on the prior assumptions which have to be made in different types of study: 'pure' analysis, interpreting history and predicting development in terms of 'likely' behaviour of retailers; studies for one retailer against a set of assumptions about the likely behaviour of competitors; and so on. These are important distinctions which will be pursued when we review different kinds of application below.

We proceed, therefore, with two major sections on analysis and applications and then follow with some concluding comments, including a discussion about priority areas for further research and development.

Analysis and modelling

Preliminaries

In any particular piece of analysis (or indeed application) it is necessary to define the system of interest, and especially the level of resolution at which it is viewed. We have argued that there are three main elements to a model – demand, flow and facility supply. We would expect demand to be related to per capita expenditures and to residential, say by zone i, (and possibly workplace) populations; and that these quantities should be disaggregated by type of goods, say g, and person (or household) type, say m. We would expect the retail facilities to be characterised in relation to location (say j), goods available and (possibly) type of shop, say h. This would imply that the flow terms were characterised by g, m and h and perhaps should also be related to transport costs by mode (say k). Note that each of these indices could in principle be a list. Thus, we might have $m = \mathbf{m} =$ (car ownership, social class, household structure).

The key variables thus defined are shown in Figure 6.2. Already, the flow array has five dimensions and there is, in addition, transport mode k. Important judgments have to be made in any analysis or application on how much information is necessary and on how much can be feasibly handled, in the hope that both are compatible! In the following, we will simplify slightly, but still keep a good degree of realism, by dropping the store type category, h, and transport mode, k, though noting how they can be added back if necessary (cf. Wilson, 1983, for the details). We also neglect trips made from workplaces, for simplicity of exposition, on the same basis.

We thus have demand characterised by E_i^{mg}, the flows by S_{ij}^{mg} and retail supply in terms of revenue, D_j^g, and attractiveness, W_j^{mg}. We will show later how these supply variables are functions

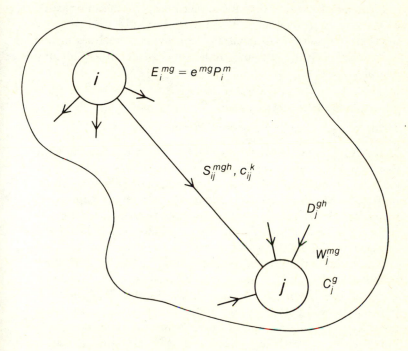

Figure 6.2 The key variables.

of an array of variables, X_{jk}^g, $k = 1, 2, 3 \ldots$, which characterise actual supply – floorspace, goods stocked, and so on.

This articulation of levels of disaggregation and a corresponding set of algebraic variables provides the beginnings of a conceptualisation for an analysis. (Note also that we have implicitly assumed the existence of appropriate residential and retail zoning systems. This is convenient for both practical (data) reasons and, as will become clear, for analytical reasons.)

It can now be argued that any analytical approach can be stated and discussed in relation to these main arrays of variables. We first examine some traditional and approximate analyses in this light and then proceed to assemble the elements of a modelling approach.

Traditional and approximate analyses

In this sub-section we briefly review the approaches (and, in some cases, contemporary variants of them) which precede the existence of modern modelling techniques, dating from before the mid-1960s say. We also include some more recent approaches which can be seen as generating useful approximations for key variables in appropriate circumstances where the full detail and power of modelling is not necessary.

It is useful in this context to distinguish the 'centre' and 'store' problems. The former has its traditional analytical roots in Central Place Theory (Christaller, 1933; Losch, 1940) as exemplified in the work of someone like Berry (1967). There are useful notions of hierarchy and use of concepts like the 'range of a good', but essentially the theory is based on non-overlapping market areas and has a very rigid underlying geometry. It can be used to give an idea of structure at a broad scale, but in general can be considered outmoded by the types of model to be presented below.

At the store location scale a variety of techniques are in common use, which range from the almost wholly intuitive to the beginnings of formal modelling. Simplest of all is a reliance on the experience of senior staff, with no formal analysis. A close relative of this is the so-called parasitic method; allow larger stores to do the job for you and simply locate near to them. But we can then progress to a range of ideas which do involve some kind of formal analysis. Applebaum's analogue method is popular: evaluate a potential site by finding a similar site elsewhere with a similar shop, and build up a sales forecast by comparison. Other methods involve calculating indices of some kind. Towsey (1972) cites Lichfield's Index of Shopping Effectiveness, which essentially involves calculating per capita expenditure in a town divided by per capita expenditure for its region and using that as an indicator of site value. There is another which estimates 'retail saturation', and Bucklin's (1971) index which is, in effect, a rule of thumb for estimating market potential. Multiple regression models provide a means of estimating potential and taking advantage of more data. There has even been an attempt to make sense of a mound of data in the retail context using factor analysis (Davies, 1973). The most detailed of all the traditional analyses, however, is the painstaking identification and measurement of trade areas: estimating demand for each of a large number of small areas, and then allocating this to possible sites. A variety of rules have been used for this. In many cases, there is still an attempt – even with Converse's use of Reilly's (1929; 1931) gravity model to establish 'break points' (cf. Huff, 1964) – to delineate sharp market-area boundaries.

The imperfections of any of these approaches can be readily seen simply by setting them against the algebraic framework established earlier for the description of a retail system. This made it clear that there should be three major elements of any analysis – demand, flow and supply (or attraction). The only acceptable contribution to contemporary methods from traditional analyses is the estimation of demand in some trade-area analyses. The other methods do not make any detailed estimate of the market or, when they do, they do not account for overlapping market areas. Again, none of the methods, except trade-area analysis, makes any explicit estimate of flows. Some of the methods – the Lichfield index, for example – can be seen as representing approximate methods for measuring site attractiveness.

It does not need a detailed investigation to reveal the weaknesses of the non-modelling methods. The history of the alternative approach now spans more than twenty years. It is based on the flow models developed by Huff (1964), Harris (1964) and Lakshmanan and Hansen (1965). In that period there has been a tremendous advance in technical capability associated with this kind of model, and with alternatives which can be reviewed within that framework. Perhaps because of the relative difficulty of implementing the models, their use is far from universal. However, the rest of this narrative uses this approach as a foundation and demonstrates the technical capability which is now available.

The organisation of the rest of the argument

The construction of flow models, with associated estimates of demand and attractiveness, are basic to further development and we consider this topic next. Additionally, it has now become possible to analyse the *structure* of whole retail systems and to provide important new insights on this basis. These ideas are presented in two sections, the first concerned with an updated comparative statics, the second a fully dynamic approach. We complete the section on analysis by showing how an integrated approach can be built up, taking advantage of the range of forecasts and insights which can be generated.

Flow models

We briefly noted the early history of these models in the 1960s and that considerable development has taken place since then. Space is not available to give a detailed account of this history and so the presentation is focused on a particular, if broad, formulation which is representative of the position which has now been reached.

We begin by presenting a model in very general terms which exhibits the main functional interrelationships involved. We use the variables defined earlier, adding the vector notation $\mathbf{X}_j^g = \{X_{j1}^g, X_{j2}^g \dots \}$ of the components of supply for convenience.

$$e_i^{mg} = e_i^{mg}(e_i^{mgo}, \{\mathbf{X}_j^g\}, \{c_{ij}\}) \qquad [6.1]$$

This functional relationship indicates that per capital expenditure at i is a function of some 'latent demand' estimate e_i^{mgo}, together with the pattern of supply, $\{\mathbf{X}_j^g\}$, as perceived from i and mediated through the travel cost vector, $\{c_{ij}\}$.

Then, of course:

$$E_i^{mg} = e_i^{mg} P_i^m \qquad [6.2]$$

Attractiveness can be written:

$$W_j^{mg} = W_j^{mg}(\mathbf{X}_j^g, \alpha_j^{mg}) \qquad [6.3]$$

where α_j^{mg} is a vector of parameters, α_{jk}^{mg} being associated with $\mathbf{X}_{jk}^g$, which measures the strength of each factor as a component of attractiveness for each income group. Travel impedance can be formally written as:

$$f_{ij} = f(c_{ij}, \beta^{mg}) \qquad [6.4]$$

where β^{mg} is a parameter which measures ease of travel for the m-group for good g and f is a function which declines with c_{ij} to an extent determined by β^{mg}.

These elements can then be combined into a flow model as follows:

$$S_{ij}^{mg} = \frac{E_i^{mg} W_j^{mg} f_{ij}}{\sum_k W_k^{mg} f_{ik}} \qquad [6.5]$$

The denominator ensures that:

$$\sum_j S_{ij}^{mg} = E_i^{mg} \qquad [6.6]$$

It also has the important effect of representing the effects of competition between retailers in the attraction of consumers – as a subtle combination of store/centre attractiveness and the travel cost function which relate these to distance from each residential zone.

The flow model can be used to predict revenue:

$$D_j^g = \sum_{im} S_{ij}^{mg} \qquad [6.7]$$

To complete the formal picture, we should also recognise that travel cost should itself be thought of as a generalised cost made up of a number of components:

$$c_{ij} = m_{ij} + at_{ij} + be_{ij} + p_i^{(1)} + p_j^{(2)} \qquad [6.8]$$

m_{ij} is the out-of-pocket money cost, t_{ij} the travel time, e_{ij} the 'excess time', e.g. spent waiting in bus queues, $p_i^{(1)}$ the origin costs, and $p_j^{(2)}$ the terminal costs such as parking charges. Alternative functional forms may, of course, sometimes be appropriate.

To fix ideas, it is useful to present the model with specific functional forms for e_i^{mg}, W_j^{mg} and f_{ij}. Assume that e_i^{mg} is, in fact, constant. This is a reasonable assumption for an urban area with well-defined m-groups. (For a specification of a fully-elastic demand model, see Wilson, 1985.) Take:

$$W_j^{mg} = (X_{j1}^g)^{\alpha_1^{mg}}(X_{j2}^g)^{\alpha_2^{mg}} \ldots \qquad [6.9]$$

for a sequence of factors of attractiveness, and:

$$f_{ij} = e^{-\beta^{mg}c_{ij}} \qquad [6.10]$$

Then the flow model can be written:

$$S_{ij}^{mg} = (e_i^{mg} P_i^m) \frac{\{(X_{j1}^g)^{\alpha_1^{mg}}(X_{j2}^g)^{\alpha_2^{mg}} \ldots \} \, e^{-\beta^{mg}c_{ij}}}{\sum_k \{(X_{k1}^g)^{\alpha_1^{mg}}(X_{j2}^g)^{\alpha_2^{mg}} \ldots \} \, e^{-\beta^{mg}c_{ik}}} \qquad [6.11]$$

We now have a fully-specified flow model. The X-factors are determined by retail management and planning – of all retailers in competition, or considered *en masse* in centres. The transport system is reflected in the c_{ij}'s; e_i^{mg} and P_i^m can be determined from surveys and forecast in subsidiary models, and the α and β parameters can be estimated. All terms on the right-hand side of equation [6.11] are therefore known. Flows can be calculated; total revenues can be calculated from equation [6.7]. There are, of course, subtleties in use, but we postpone a discussion of these until the section on applications.

Structural models and comparative statics

We now pose a further question. At any time, is there potentially a stable equilibrium retail structure? To answer this, the analytical issue has to be posed in a certain way. We have to add hypotheses about retailer behaviour and then pursue the implications of competition along with all the other properties of demand, travel and the alternative patterns of supply. For ease of presentation, consider a single person-type and a single good-type, and assume that attractiveness can be measured through a single factor – floorspace (defined as W_j and appearing as an attractiveness function raised to the power α). The flow model then becomes:

$$S_{ij} = \frac{E_i \, W_j^{\alpha} e^{-\beta c_{ij}}}{\sum_k W_k^{\alpha} e^{-\beta c_{ij}}} \qquad [6.12]$$

The complexities of the real world can be added again when the basic principles which lead to the new insights have been explained. Revenue attracted is:

$$D_j = \sum_i S_{ij} = \sum_i \frac{E_i \, W_j^{\alpha} e^{-\beta c_{ij}}}{\sum_k W_k^{\alpha} e^{-\beta c_{ij}}} \qquad [6.13]$$

We now need to define the retailer's cost of supplying facilities in j, say C_j. We can assume this is a function of W_j for simplicity and that it refers to the same period, say a year, as D_j:

$$C_j = C_j(W_j) \qquad [6.14]$$

Then a simple hypothesis has to be added on retailer/developer behaviour which will help us to tackle the question as to whether there are stable patterns which are representative of various types of situation, as follows. If $D_j > C_j$, we expect W_j to grow, and vice versa. If there is an equilibrium, it occurs when:

$$D_j = C_j \qquad [6.15]$$

That is (using equations [6.13] and [6.14]), when:

$$\sum_i \frac{E_i \, W_j^{\alpha} e^{-\beta c_{ij}}}{\sum_k W_k^{\alpha} e^{-\beta c_{ij}}} = C_j(W_j) \qquad [6.16]$$

If we make the even simpler assumption that cost is linear (and this turns out not to affect the character of the argument), with

$$C_j(W_j) = k_j W_j \qquad [6.17]$$

for constants, k_j, then the simultaneous equations [6.16] become:

$$\sum_i \frac{E_i \, W_j^{\alpha} e^{-\beta c_{ij}}}{\sum_k W_k^{\alpha} e^{-\beta c_{ij}}} = K_j W_j \qquad [6.18]$$

These equations are highly non-linear; each term in the sum on the left-hand side has a denominator which involves all the W_ks – in effect, because of the complexities of competition between retailers across space. But they can be solved numerically for the equilibrium pattern, $\{W_j\}$, and it is possible to manipulate them so as to gain considerable and important analytical insights (cf. Harris and Wilson, 1978). These can be summarised in the following points.

(a) There is, typically, a 'global' equilibrium for a given set of parameters and exogenous variables which has the greatest possible number of non-zero W_js for that situation and which can be interpreted as the pattern which maximises consumers' surplus.

(b) There are many other stable equilibria which can be constructed by setting some of the non-zero W_js of the global solution to zero, or vice versa – and any of these are likely to occur in reality because real retailers will not necessarily locate their facilities precisely in accord with the model! However, each of these could be said to represent a *typical pattern*, say in terms of overall number and size of facilities, for that parameter set.

(c) As parameters change – as they do, with shifting population distribution, new transport facilities, new αs or βs, and changing incomes – then it can be shown that even if these changes are slow and smooth, there can be *jumps* in the type of pattern of critical parameter values. The shift from corner-shop food retailing to supermarkets is thought to be an example of this kind (cf. Wilson and Oulton, 1983).

This all means that retailers and developers should be aware of these underlying structures, both in relation to new and existing stores and centres. An example for an idealised grid, with an even distribution of population and ubiquitous and even transport access, is shown in Figure 6.3. These are alternative patterns for different α and β values. Clearly, higher α and lower β imply fewer, larger stores or centres. Figure 6.4 shows the importance of transport costs through the effect of emphasising cheaper travel to the centre. Figure 6.5 shows the effect of varying land prices, and Figure 6.6 a now realistic-looking structure derived by combining both of these additional features. Through this kind of fine-tuning it is beginning to be possible to simulate a real system, as shown for examples from Leeds in Figure 6.7. Finally, in a different way, the effects of jumps in pattern at critical parameter values are shown for a region of Nottingham in Figure 6.8.

It is now possible to add back all the necessary detail for a more realistic structural model. There are three aspects to this.

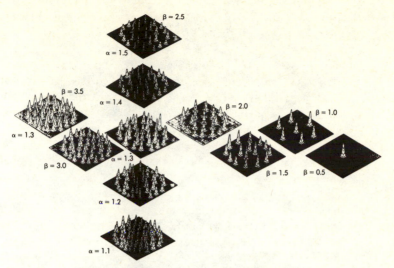

Figure 6.3 Alternative retail structures for varying α and β. (*Source*: Clarke and Wilson, 1983.)

First, to shift to an appropriate level of disaggregation, re-introducing person types, *m*, and types of goods, *g* (and possibly store types, *h*). This would involve giving an account of the attractiveness function in terms of *X*-factors, and these should include terms which represent, for a good *g*, the proximity of stores selling other types of goods. This allows the inclusion of agglomeration effects in relation to consumers' scale economies and, together with other features, lays the foundations for this style of modelling functioning as a replacement for Central Place Theory.

The second area of elaboration relates to the adjustment mechanism. In the example above, the basis of the mechanism was profitability, but only size of store or centre was adjusted. In reality, there would be some possibility of adjustment of prices of goods sold; additionally, a land rent distribution would evolve to reflect the comparative advantage of different locations. These mechanisms can be added to the comparative static structural model, but in this chapter we show how to include them in a full dynamic model – with the equilibrium solution as a byproduct – in the next sub-section below.

Thirdly, it is obviously necessary to refine the account of

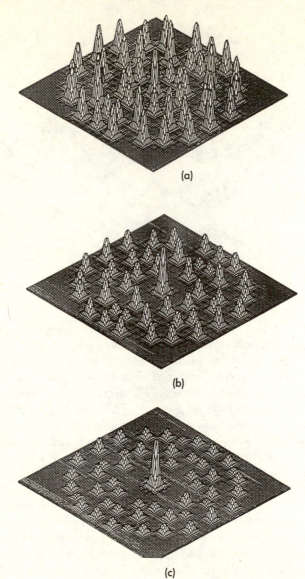

Figure 6.4 Retail structures: effects of decreasing transport cost to city centre, where $\alpha = 1.3$ and $\beta = 2.5$. (a) City-centre trips 0.95 cheaper. (b) City-centre trips 0.85 cheaper. (c) City-centre trips 0.75 cheaper. (*Source*: Clarke and Wilson, 1983.)

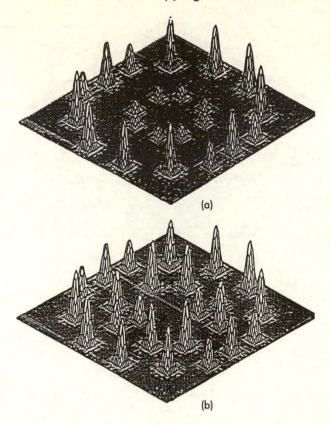

(a)

(b)

Figure 6.5 Retail structures: effects of a land-price surface.

(a) $k_j = \dfrac{1}{c_{ij}}$

(b) $k_j = c_{ij}^{-0.5}$

(*Source*: Clarke and Wilson, 1983.)

retailers' costs, rather than simply assuming them to be proportional to floorspace. The different components would all have to be brought to a common time period – say a year – and would include land, floorspace (i.e. buildings), labour, interest on capital, costs of goods for sale and costs of other inputs.

We will discuss in the next sub-section but one the effects of combining all these elements into an integrated attack on the task of building an effective retail model system.

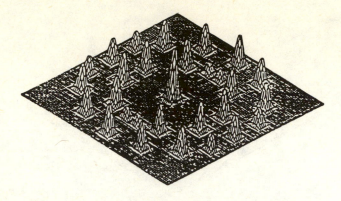

Figure 6.6 Retail structures: land prices and cheap travel to centre in combination:

$$k_j = \frac{1}{c_{ij}} \text{ , city centre travel 0.75 cheaper}$$

(*Source*: Clarke and Wilson, 1983.)

Dynamics

For simplicity of exposition, we now revert to the aggregated example of the previous sub-section. The equilibrium condition which generated the structural model arose from a hypothesis about directions of change in W_j relative to profitability $D_j - C_j$. It can be argued that retail systems will never in practice be in

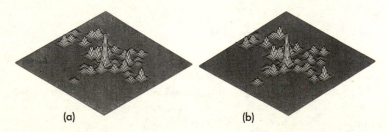

(a)   (b)

Figure 6.7 Leeds retail distribution. (a) Actual structure, 1961. (b) Structural model prediction, incuding land price variation. (*Source*: Clarke, 1986.)

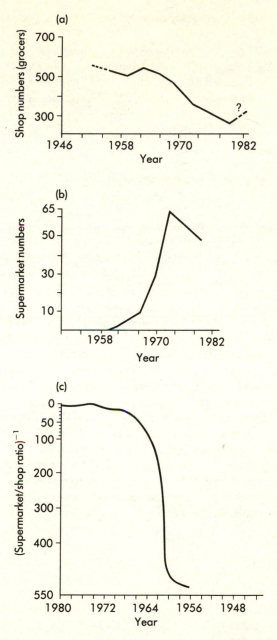

Figure 6.8 Food retailing in Nottingham. (a) Number of grocers in Nottingham. (b) Number of supermarkets in Nottingham. (c) An index of supermarket dominance. (*Source*: Wilson and Oulton, 1983.)

equilibrium because parameters and exogenous variables are continually changing – even though the trajectories will be influenced by underlying equilibria. It is therefore appropriate to write down a fully dynamic model. If $\dot{W}_j$ is the rate of change of W_j with respect to time, then a formal dynamic representation of the hypothesis we have been using is:

$$\dot{W}_j = \epsilon(D_j - C_j)\,F(W_j) \qquad\qquad [6.19]$$

This obviously has the equilibrium condition:

$$D_j = C_j \qquad\qquad [6.20]$$

The factor $F(W_j)$ determines the form of the trajectory to equilibrium, particularly for small values of W_j, when $D_j - C_j$ may differ substantially from zero. Usually, it is taken as either 1 or W_j.

Again, these equations, either as differential equations or difference equations, can be solved numerically – but there is also a new analytical result which can be derived, building on the work of May (1976). This shows that the parameter ϵ (or, more precisely, ϵD_j) can be critically large, and that when these values are exceeded, periodic or even chaotic oscillatory behaviour sets in and equilibrium is impossible to achieve. This could be interpreted as retailers or developers 'over-reacting'.

It is at this point, again in relation to the simple example, that we can show how to introduce prices and rents – say p_j and r_j. Suppose on good sites, p_js are decreased to attract more revenue but that land owners can increase r_js. Then a term like p_j would appear as one of the X-terms in the attractiveness function, W_j, and $r_j W_j$ would be a term in retailers' costs, C_j. An extended dynamic model can be written formally as:

$$\dot{W}_j = \epsilon_1(D_j - C_j)\,F_1(W_j) \qquad\qquad [6.21]$$

$$\dot{p}_j = -\epsilon_2(D_j - C_j)\,F_2(p_j) \qquad\qquad [6.22]$$

$$\dot{r}_j = \epsilon_3(D_j - C_j)\,F_3(r_j) \qquad\qquad [6.23]$$

Experiments conducted with such a model show that realistic price and rent surfaces can be generated (cf. Wilson, 1985; Birkin and Wilson, 1985).

It should be noted that in this presentation of dynamics, it is still being assumed that consumer behaviour patterns are in equilibrium – so consumers are supposed to respond rapidly to any supply-side changes. This is, on the whole, a reasonable approximation, but it is worth noting that a more complete dynamic model can be constructed which does not rely on this approximation using the master equation formulation (Haag and Wilson, 1986).

Alternative hypotheses and approaches

It is worth remarking that many different derivations of the flow model presented here are available. These range from argument by analogy with gravity models via entropy maximising to random utility theory. Perhaps seven or eight distinct cases can now be identified. They are viewed in Macgill and Wilson (1979) and, for most practical purposes, can be considered equivalent. However, there are also alternative models, such as Stouffer's (1940; 1960) intervening opportunities model. This seems to have lost popularity in recent years and, in any case, its main features can be captured with a variation of the cost function in a spatial interaction model (cf. Wilson, 1967; 1970).

This argument perhaps sounds complacent. It is not intended to be because there are many important research issues which will be taken up in the concluding section. There are also continuing new developments to the basic model; Fotheringham's (1983a; 1983b; 1985) competing opportunities model falls into this category. It can be interpreted in the terminology of this chapter as introducing a new kind of X-factor into the attractiveness function. He has also explored the effects of his innovation on the structural and dynamic models.

It can also be the case that a shift to extremes of scale can demand a new modelling approach. Wrigley and Dunn (1984a; 1984b; 1984c; 1985), for example, confront the problem of modelling brand choice within stores using longitudinal data, and they use statistical (NBD and Dirichlet) models.

The central feature of the argument, however, is that the principles for retail modelling are well established, though in any particular study a lot of detailed model design and fine-tuning need to be done.

Integrated analysis

In this sub-section we summarise the steps to be taken to establish sound foundations for a modelling exercise. First, it is necessary to establish a level of resolution which is appropriate to the problem in hand. This will establish the sets of categories m and g, and the spatial units. Detailed decisions then need to be taken on:

(a) demand;
(b) attractiveness;
(c) retailers' costs;
(d) transport generalised costs.

The flow model can then be run and the structural and dynamic models used to investigate the stability of overall retail structures at one time or at a sequence of points in time. This modelling framework will then provide the basis for a wide range of applications, and it is to these we now turn.

Applications

Introduction

There have been many applications of the range of ideas discussed above, but far more of the 'traditional' form than model-based. It is interesting to speculate at the outset on the reasons for this. These are no doubt many and varied, but the most important almost certainly relate to data availability and the effectiveness of the associated computer programs; the data were often not available without large-scale special surveys and the computer programs were not easy to use. To this, it might be added that experience was not available in relation to the fine-tuning of models. It can be argued now that the situation has changed quite fundamentally. The data are available commercially for many applications, and it is now possible to develop user-friendly computer programs of the type to be described here. It should now be possible for the community to gain the necessary experience relatively rapidly. It is appropriate, therefore to proceed in this section on the basis that model-based applications will be the main feature of retail planning in the future.

At the end of the previous section, we summarised the steps to be taken as the foundation of a model-building exercise. We now focus on the uses to which such a model can be put. The argument proceeds in three steps. First, we discuss model outputs and performance indicators; secondly, we discuss the desirability of an interactive computer package for analysis and planning; and thirdly, we review the range of possible applications.

Outputs and performance indicators

If the problem is one of store location from the retailer's point of view or centre location from the developer's point of view, then the most important output is probably the revenue attracted. The problem may also be looked at from the point of view of a town planner who may be interested not only in the efficiency of stores and centres, but also the effectiveness of delivery or access in relation to the residential population. This preliminary argument suggests there are two kinds of indicators, relating to facilities and residences; an extensive list of indicators can be developed. First, we introduce some basic concepts first used in the field of health services planning.

Consider the variables for an aggregate retail model together with some additional variables as displayed on Figure 6.9. We can take $(S_{ij}/S_{i*})P_i$ as the proportion of P_i which is served by j and, hence, in relation to the flow matrix $\{S_{ij}\}$, we can define the *catchment population* of j as:

$$\Pi_j = \sum_i \frac{S_{ij}}{S_{i*}} P_i \qquad\qquad [6.24]$$

This leads to new indicators of facility efficiency such as $(D_j - C_j)/\Pi_j$, profits per head of catchment population.

But we can also do a similar calculation in reverse:

$$\hat{W}_i = \sum_j \frac{S_{ij}}{S_{*j}} W_j \qquad\qquad [6.25]$$

can be taken as the notional square footage used by residents of i. Then W_i/P_i can be taken as a measure of effectiveness of delivery of retail services to a residential population in i.

Thus, while a retailer may be most interested in profitability and efficiency at his or her own site, the planner may be further interested in the equity of residential effectiveness indicators.

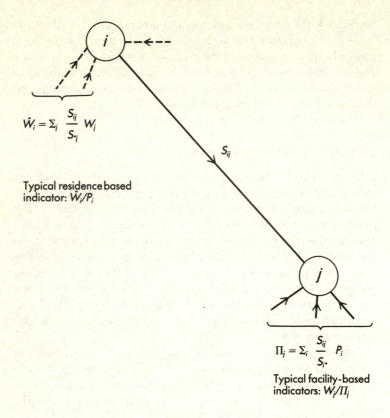

Figure 6.9 Residence- and facility-based performance indicators.

These new indicators can be combined with older ones such as the Hansen (1959) accessibility and concepts of market potential. Typical indicators to be considered can be summarised as follows.

(a) Residential zone
* Accessibility
* Transport expenditure
* Consumers' surplus

(b) Facility location
* Market potential
* Cost per head of catchment population
* Profit per head of catchment population
* Revenue per head of catchment population

* Price index
* Rent index

This brief analysis shows that, even when the focus is on retailers or developers alone, it is necessary to look at a set of indicators, and this means in turn that there is no simply-defined optimum to seek. This, therefore, suggests that the decision-maker or planner needs to be an integral part of the computer system and it is to this that we now turn.

An interactive analysis and planning system

Software is now available which will accept data files, run any part (or all) of the model system described above, and then allow the user to re-run with on-line modifications to any of the inputs. For any run, any desired performance indicators can be selected for on-line output (with hard copy available if required).

This means that in any of the tasks of store or centre siting or sizing, or of performance appraisal, it is possible first to calibrate the models for the existing situation and then to make conditional forecasts by running the flow model for any selected site and reviewing the indicators. Experience shows that the identification of sites is relatively straightforward. It is then possible to use the structural model interactively as a design tool. Given everything except the W_js, what would the equilibrium $\{W_j\}$ pattern look like? This test can also be carried out with some W_js fixed at existing values. Further, it is possible to study the stability of any proposed plans by running the dynamic model (if necessary, one iteration at a time).

This is a reasonably complete description of the running of the system when it is being used by a town planner in relation to whole centres, but even then some kind of sensitivity testing will be needed to explore the consequences of alternative behaviour patterns of retailers. The situation may involve an even wider range of sensitivity testing when the system is being used by a single retailer or developer who has to take possible alternative responses of competitors into account. Ideally, a series of 'competition' scenarios should be developed, and each possible site location tested for each scenario (and with a series of sizes for each). Such a layout of model runs is shown in Figure 6.10. The

		Competition Scenarios		
		Scenario 1	Scenario 2	Scenario 3
	Size 1			▨
Location 1	Size 2			
	Size 3			
	•			
	Size 1	▨		
Location 2	Size 2	▨	▨	▨
	Size 3			
	•			
	Size 1			
Location 3	Size 2		▨	
	Size 3			▨
	•			

Figure 6.10 Hypothetical schedule of model runs for site location and size and sensitivity testing. The shaded blocks indicate model runs with 'acceptable' performance indicators; location 2, size 2, is thus relatively robust.

interactive system could easily be used to organise a set of runs of this type. It is hoped, then, that at least one site shows itself as satisfactory against a range of indicators over a good range of scenarios. Such an example is shown on Figure 6.10 – location 2.

To conclude, it should be emphasised that the decision-maker at the computer terminal is an integral part of the system, and that human experience may be crucial both in interpreting the indicators and in devising the next plan to be tested. What the system offers is accurate predictions and associated sensitivity testing.

The future

Research issues

Introduction   Much research remains to be done, but this can mostly only be achieved by a wider range of experience – the testing of variations on the basic model. It has been argued that a good starting point has been achieved. In this section, therefore, we outline some of the issues which can be tackled, either within university research or, even, in commercial applications from which lessons can be learned. We consider in turn:

(a) variants of the basic flow model;
(b) issues associated with the structural and dynamic models;
(c) alternative models; and
(d) issues associated with applications.

The basic model   It may turn out to be important to experiment with other levels of disaggregation, and particularly to introduce store types explicitly. We have also mentioned the importance of developing elastic demand models, and this involves a new issue of defining a measure of 'perceived price' in a residential zone (see Wilson, 1983). More detail can be added to demand estimation using micro-simulation methods (Clarke, 1984). There will always be scope for explaining new terms in the attractiveness and generalised travel-cost functions. A good research topic is to find a good measure of store quality (within a well-defined category).

Structural and dynamic models   There are a number of problems associated with the representation of retailer behaviour and particularly of competition. At one level there is the difficult mathematical problem of handling the notion of a 'backcloth' in relation to a store or centre, within which the whole set of competitors' locations is being changed and appraised simultaneously (cf. Wilson and Clarke, 1979). There is another problem associated with the present equilibrium model. It does, in a sense, assume a perfect market for retailer behaviour. In practice, there will be imperfections and there is the possibility of developing a new model with an entropy-dispersion term relating to the W_js (cf.: Wilson, 1985; Birkin and Wilson, 1985). Alternative hypotheses could also be considered for retailer behaviour, or, alternatively, to use the model in relation to a particular retailer to estimate size or pricing policy which would provide some degree of protection against competitors' reponses. A further refinement along these lines involves using the dynamic model to test the effects of such policies in a time sequence, and extending the set of performance indicators to include a full related financial appraisal.

Further extensions are possible, for example by introducing more agents; we have already shown how to incorporate price indexes and land rents in this way. It would also be possible to include wage rates in appropriate circumstances.

Alternative models and extensions   In the argument so far, we have assumed the model-based analyses apply either to systems of stores or systems of centres. A more ambitious project involves combining the two scales so that it would be possible to predict centre distributions and store mixes within each centre. Research to date, however, suggests that there are difficult mathematical problems to be solved in achieving this step and, of course, there would then be very heavy data requirements.

A different kind of extension involves representing hierarchical structures. In one sense, the model system presented achieves this and thus replaces Central Place theory. This is because the range of structures across different types of goods will mimic central place systems, though without any of the rigidities. However, within a g-type, there may still be some kind of hierarchy and it is useful to explore varients of the Nystuen and Dacey (1961) matrix analysis method for this, and the outcomes can be added to the set of performance indicators. An example of such a plot is shown in Figure 6.11.

Research issues in applications   Again, what is first needed is a wider range of experience with sets of performance indicators. However, it should be noted that batteries of performance indicators contain large numbers of numbers and are not always easy to analyse. Progress has been made for health-care systems with the development of intelligent performance indicator programmes and it will be possible to apply these ideas in the retailing field.

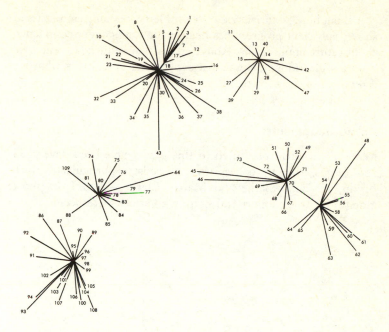

Figure 6.11 A hypothetical plot of principal flows to dominating centres. (After Nystuen and Dacey, 1961.)

Prospects for the future

It has been argued that the model approach at the very least provides a conceptual framework for the analysis and planning of store or centre location and size. This facilitates the appraisal of other methods. However, the ease of availability of both data and software should make it feasible for model-based studies to become the norm rather than the exception in the future. An appropriate version of the basic flow model should always be available for forecasting sales and market penetration and we have seen that it is also possible to use structural and dynamic models to obtain different kinds of insights – particularly in relation to stability and competition and therefore risk analysis. All these analyses are most useful in a planning context if available through a user-friendly interactive system within which the decision-maker is an integral part of the system.

Although substantial research problems remain, as discussed above, sufficient progress has been made to engender confidence about future applications. Above all, further refinement will arise from a wider range of practical experience, and this is what we can now look forward to.

Acknowledgments

Many of the ideas presented in this paper have been developed and discussed with colleagues in Leeds – particularly Mark Birkin, Graham Clarke and Martin Clarke – and I am most grateful for this support and help in a variety of respects.

CHAPTER 7
Stated preference techniques and the analysis of consumer choice

John J. Bates

Introduction

Forecasts of consumer demand are a major element in the commercial assessment of any new investment, since success in the market-place is the principal (and many would say the only) arbiter of the correctness of an investment decision. In all but the simplest form of demand forecast, there is an implied trade-off between two or more factors. The aim of this chapter is to demonstrate how our knowledge of such trade-offs can be improved.

To put the discussion in context, consider the following simple example. Suppose we had found out, from previous research, that the two most important factors affecting consumers' choice of store were its accessibility and its range of products. Then it is clear that a store with high accessibility and a wide range of products is likely to be much more popular, other things being equal, than a store with poor accessibility and a restricted product range. If there were no constraints involved, all retailers would aim for the former category.

However, in most cases there are costs attached to providing what the consumer wants, which may mean that the retailer's best strategy is not to provide everything at the highest level, but to reach a compromise; for example, high accessibility with a relatively restricted product range, or poor accessibility with a wide product range. In this way there is an implied trade-off between product range and accessibility.

The importance of this resides in the fact that the rate of trade-off between these two factors which best expresses the *consumer's* preference may be different from the trade-off implied by the relative costs that the *retailer* would incur when investing to improve the two factors. The more the retailer understands his consumers' preferences, the more he will be able to offer a better product for a given investment cost.

Mathematical models are commonly used to help in forecasting how human behaviour will alter in the face of external changes. We now go on to present a 'family' of models which have proved particularly useful. After this, we will illustrate their application using examples from the field of transport planning, where the author's main experience lies.

Random utility theory

Over the last fifteen years there has been considerable development in a branch of econometrics known as discrete choice analysis, within the general context of an approach called random utility theory. Put in straightforward terms, the theory assumes that people are able to compute some metric of preference, which we refer to as utility, for each possible alternative under consideration, and that they choose the alternative with the highest utility. The random utility approach attempts to find a formula for this utility in terms of well-defined attributes of the alternatives, but allows for the fact that there will be random effects as well.

The general practice is to assume that utility is linear in the relevant factors, though this is by no means essential. In the first place, we will make this assumption in order to keep the examples simple.

A simple example of this is the question of choice of travel mode (e.g. car or rail) for a particular journey. It is reasonable to suppose that the choice will be made on the basis of, at least, the cost of the journey by the different available modes, and the time it takes. It is then hypothesized that a trade-off exists between these two factors (and, indeed, any other factors that might appear important) so that in certain circumstances people would be prepared to countenance a slower journey because it was less expensive.

This suggests a utility formulation of the following kind:

$$U_{\text{car}} = a_{\text{car}} + b_1 \, \text{cost}_{\text{car}} + b_2 \, \text{time}_{\text{car}} + \text{error} \qquad [7.1]$$

$$U_{\text{rail}} = a_{\text{rail}} + b_1 \, \text{cost}_{\text{rail}} + b_2 \text{time}_{\text{rail}} + \text{error} \qquad [7.2]$$

In this formulation, b_1 and b_2 represent the contributions of travel cost and time to utility; note that we would expect both coefficients to be negative, since people will normally be less happy with higher costs and travel times. As well as time and cost, we recognize that there will be other, possibly unknown, factors which enter into people's assessment of the attractiveness of a mode. In so far as these are constant for the population, they can be represented by the a coefficients. (There is of course no reason why further variables should not be included in the utility functions given above.) Those effects which we expect to vary across the population, but about which we have no information (either because we are unaware of them, or because we cannot measure them) are treated as random. Thus we do not claim to be able to measure 'utility' with absolute confidence, and we allow for an element of uncertainty. Obviously, the larger this element is relative to the 'deterministic' factors, the less useful the model will be!

In passing, we should point out that we are not treating the notion 'utility' as if it had absolute value. Within the econometric framework, it simply acts as an index of preference, so that if the utility of one option is higher than that of another, then the first option will be preferred. Both the origin (i.e. the point at which utility is zero) and the scale are entirely arbitrary; however, relative magnitudes are not. In fact, in the example just given, it is not possible to estimate separate a constants (known as 'alternative-specific constants') for both car and rail – only the difference can be estimated.

Random utility models of this kind have been frequently estimated within the transport research field, and are able to suggest, for instance, how much of the market might be lost if the price of one alternative increased by 10 per cent, say. In order to use a model of this kind, we need, of course, to have actual values for the coefficients b_1, etc., and this is normally achieved by the statistical process of estimation, which we now consider.

In order to obtain estimates of the coefficients, two things are required: data which will yield measurements of the variables in the equation; and a theory about the distribution of the error term. It is the error distribution which allows us to make the transition between preferences and the probability of choosing any particular alternative. A common assumption, though the reasons for making it are largely practical, is to assume that the error terms are independently and identically distributed, with the Weibull distribution (see, for example, Maddala (1983)), since this yields the well-known multinomial logit model.

The form of the model is:

$$p_i = \exp(V_i)/\sum_{j \in \mathcal{J}} \exp(V_j) \qquad [7.3]$$

where V_j is the deterministic part of the utility formulation for alternative j (i.e. excluding the random term), and p_i is the probability that i will be chosen out of the set of available options $\mathcal{J}$.

As far as the data is concerned, the traditional approach has been to conduct a sample survey, from which individual's measurements of variables such as travel cost and travel time can be obtained. However, we cannot measure *utility* directly, of course. The only observable data which relates to utility is a record of what choice was actually made. Models based on such data are known as 'revealed preference' (RP) models. Thus for a given individual we would know the costs and times of the alternatives available to him, and we would know whether he had chosen (in this case) car or train. If he had chosen car, say, we may deduce that for him the utility of car is greater than that of train. On the basis of such evidence about preferences, it is generally possible to estimate the coefficients of the utility function.

The problem with estimating such revealed preference models is that it is necessary to find a sufficiently large sample of people who do have a genuine choice, or, to put it another way, who can genuinely contemplate a trade-off between some or all of the attributes which affect choice. In the absence of identifying a suitable sample, it is not possible to estimate the model with any reliability, as we now illustrate.

The problem of estimating revealed preference models

Continuing with the simple example of mode choice in the

previous section, we can illustrate the basics of the estimation problem as follows. The discussion is taken from Bates (1983). With only two alternatives, the problem can be recast in difference formulation, and we arbitrarily define differences as 'car − train'. Then the utility model can be rewritten as:

$$DU = a' + b_1 Dc + b_2 Dt + De \qquad [7.4]$$

where c is cost, t is time, and e is the random element.

The equation $DU = 0$ represents a line in the (Dc, Dt) plane, as shown in Figure 7.1(a), the actual location and slope of the line being determined by the (unknown) values of b_1, b_2 and a'. If the size of De is small, relative to the contributions of the 'deterministic' part of the utility function, then it will be approximately the case that any observation on one side of the line will choose one alternative, and any observation on the other will choose the other. Thus, the modelling process can be seen as one of *choosing* a line which will segment the population as accurately as possible into those choosing car and those choosing train.

Consider now the data illustrated in Figure 7.1(b). Here the observations have been plotted according to their values of (Dt, Dc) and have also been coded − T for those who actually chose train, and C for those who chose car. It is clear that this data provides virtually no help in estimating the line which segments the car-choosers from the train-choosers. Each respondent has chosen the 'dominant' alternative − the one which is favoured on the basis of all the attributes, so that there is no evidence of a trade-off between cost and time, which is essential if we are to deduce the slope of the line.

The situation is not much better in Figure 7.1(c), though here there is some evidence of a possible trade-off. It is, however, only those observations near the line which make any significant contribution to the estimation. Thus it may be appreciated that what is required to calibrate a satisfactory model is not to have clearly separated population groups with distinct choices, but to have as many 'marginal' choosers as possible, i.e. respondents who might change their choice given a small change in their actual Dc and Dt, as is illustrated in Figure 7.1(d).

A way of circumventing this problem which is currently finding increasing favour within transport research (though in essence it derives from a market research technique) is the method of stated

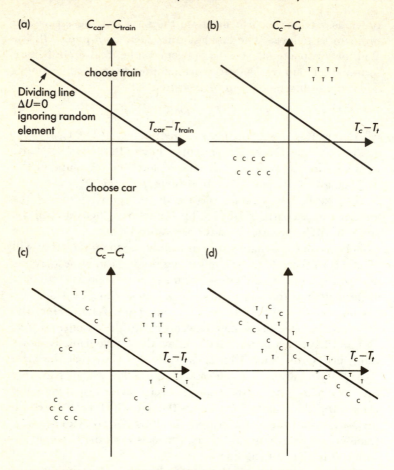

Figure 7.1 Hypothetical illustration of mode choice data.

preference (SP), in which respondents are presented with *hypothetical* alternatives and asked to choose between them, or rank them, or otherwise assess them. After deciding what variables are likely to be most important in affecting choice, an experiment is set up in which the values of these variables are systematically varied, and the respondent is offered different 'packages'. From the responses to the questions asked, it is possible to deduce the implied trade-offs between the variables in the experiment.

The method (or at least similar versions of it) has been referred to in many ways, and is also known as direct utility assessment, functional measurement analysis, conjoint analysis, trade-off analysis, so that the terminology is somewhat confusing. We do not claim any special status for the term stated preference, but we would maintain that our use of the method is compatible with the econometric framework briefly discussed in the previous section; this is certainly not true of many other applications of the technique. The advantage of our approach is that it has a statistical basis, which allows us to assess the accuracy of our estimates.

In collaboration with The MVA Consultancy, the author has now been involved in some fifteen applications of the technique, mainly, though not entirely, within the field of transport. Although each study has its own particular requirements, certain principles have emerged. In the following section the essentials of the technique are briefly described, and the subsequent section then describes a typical application.

The stated preference approach

In this section we will assume that we have already identified the variables of interest, and concentrate merely on the kind of data which is to be obtained, and how it is analysed. The crucial issues of how to identify these variables, and how the questions are to be presented to the respondent, are deferred until the next section.

Given a number of factors of interest, we wish to obtain data about relative preferences for each factor; for this we need to offer different levels of the factors so that preferences can be expressed. As was explained in the previous section, when using RP data we are completely at the mercy of the current circumstances in which the respondents find themselves; this can lead to excessive correlation among the factors, or to too little variation. In either case, the result is an inaccurate estimate of the importance of each factor. With SP we are able to control the variation and the correlation between factors. In addition, using the statistical theory of experimental design, we are able to reduce the number of responses that are required from each individual in the sample, so as to avoid placing too much burden on respondents.

Although there are many variants on the method, the approach that we have taken most often is as follows. Typically the number of factors will be between three and five. Each factor is defined at a number of different 'levels', usually between two and four; thus a particular factor might be included at 'low', 'medium' and 'high' values, etc. Then, based on an experimental design, we construct a number of alternatives ('treatments') in which the levels of the factors are systematically varied, in a way which minimizes the correlation between the factors.

An example is given in Table 7.1, which is taken from a study carried out for the British Railways Board in order to evaluate their Pullman services. Four factors have been selected:

(a) journey time
(b) journey cost
(c) type of rolling stock
(d) quality of service

and in this example each factor has been assigned three levels, denoted as H, M and L (high, medium and low) in Table 7.1.

Each alternative is set up as a separate card (see Figure 7.2), and the respondent is given a pack of cards (in this case, nine) and asked to rank them in order of preference. In this way he displays implicit trade-offs between the levels of the various factors in the experiment. To avoid any bias, the cards are randomized for each respondent, and alphabetic codes are used to identify them so that the respondent is not led towards any pre-conceived ordering.

It is possible to analyse this ranked data by an extension of the

Table 7.1 Design of the stated preference experiment

Card	Time	Cost	Rolling stock	Service quality
1	L	L	H	H
2	M	L	H	M
3	H	L	H	L
4	M	M	M	H
5	H	H	L	H
6	L	H	L	M
7	M	H	L	L
8	H	M	M	M
9	L	M	M	L

NE

Journey time	2 hr 10 mins
Journey cost	£63 (return)
Rolling stock	Type C
Service quality	Pullman

Journey time — is the total one-way time which the train should take between your boarding and alighting stations.

Journey cost — is the return journey fare (including any supplements for seat reservation or Pullman service).

Type of carriage — is the design of carriage in which you would be travelling (the photographs help to show the difference between types A, B and C).

Type of service — this may be one of three levels of service:

standard —
    restaurant and buffet available, but no at-seat service;

executive —
    restaurant and buffet available, plus a trolley service selling drinks and snacks;

pullman —
    a high quality of service providing friendly and personal service at your seat.

Figure 7.2 Sample of a stated preference card.

conventional multinomial logit model, which is known as the 'ordered' or 'exploded' logit model (see Beggs, Cardell and Hausman (1981) and Chapman and Staelin (1982)), based on a formulation such as:

$$U_i = \sum_k b_k X_{ki} + e_i \qquad\qquad [7.5]$$

where X_{ki} represent the values on the cards (or transformations thereof), and b_k are the coefficients to be estimated. In spite of the assumption of linearity, this formula is reasonably general, and by appropriate use of dummy variables and transformations can allow a variety of relationships to be estimated, including interactions between variables.

It is theoretically possible to calibrate separate sets of coefficients for every respondent in the sample, and in many of the market research applications of this kind of technique this has in fact been done. However, we do not recommend such an approach, principally because it relies too heavily on the particular characteristics of individuals in the sample, and because the accuracy with which such individual-specific coefficients can be estimated is low. We feel that it is far more in keeping with statistical sampling theory to estimate population means and variances by conventional methods, but at the same time to take advantage of segmentation possibilities.

To expand on this point, rather than carry out separate estimations for each individual, it is preferable to begin with some hypotheses about the kinds of variations that are likely, and to test these statistically. Thus, in the example given, we might hypothesize that businessmen are less concerned about the cost of travel than private travellers, or that females are more concerned about service quality than males. We would then segment the coefficient(s) on the variables concerned according to the number of distinctions we wished to make, and see whether they were significantly different.

To take the first case, the variable associated with cost would be expanded into two separate variables, with the following form:
(a) cost, if traveller is a businessman; otherwise zero;
(b) cost, if traveller is not a businessman; otherwise zero.
As well as all the other coefficients in the utility function, which in this case we have assumed are not segmented, the estimation process would give us *two* coefficients on cost. If our hypothesis is correct, the coefficient on cost for businessmen should be smaller (in absolute terms) than the coefficient for private travellers. Standard statistical tests are available to test such a hypothesis. If the hypothesis that there is no difference between the two coefficients cannot be rejected, then we should not distinguish the two segments. Note that while in the examples given each segment consists of two categories, there is in fact no such restriction; thus we could have, for instance, a segmentation of employed persons, housewives, retired people, children, or one of social class indicators (A, B, C1, C2, etc.).

Such an approach is extremely flexible, and allows all kinds of market segmentation to be carried out; it is possible to have more than one segmentation on a given variable, or for a given segmentation to apply to more than one variable. In each case we have a testable hypothesis. The result is that we can distinguish different rates of trade-off between factors according to market segments, which can have major implications for marketing and product design.

The ability to distinguish significant differences of this kind has implications for sample size. As a general indication, we would not normally consider investigating segments unless there were at least fifteen to twenty respondents in that segment in our sample. In order to have a reasonable chance of distinguishing a number of segments of interest, we would normally aim for a final sample of about 200.

Clearly, the crucial issue in SP is its reliability. We have shown that it is possible to obtain some extremely interesting results about the kind of weights put on various factors by different people, but how seriously can we take such results? The author has been involved in a number of such studies, and in particular has carried out comparison between the results from models estimated on observed data and on SP data, when the same sample has responded to both types of question (see, for example, Bates (1984)). The results are generally encouraging, but there are some practical limitations, which we shall briefly list.

Most importantly, the 'packages' offered to respondents must seem realistic, and should not depart very far from their actual experience. In addition, the number of variables which can be included in the package should probably not exceed five, and not too many packages should be offered to a single respondent, as commitment and ability to perform the tasks tends to fall off. It is also advisable to have some way of weeding out respondents who have not taken the task seriously, though in practice the proportion of such people is normally only about 5 per cent.

Further useful information is provided in a review by Cattin and Wittink (1982), which generally supports these findings. They also find that methods of presentation are very important, particularly for the 'softer' variables (like 'quality of service' in our example above); particular care needs to be taken in such cases. If such variables are poorly explained, they will tend to be ignored, whereas if they are 'over-presented' the respondent may assign to them an importance which does not truly reflect his day-to-day assessment. We shall return to this in the next section.

Practical conduct of an SP investigation

Having given some indication of the kind of data that is collected, and the results which can be obtained from it, we now outline the general process according to which a typical study would be carried out. It will emerge from this that, while the analysis represents the final product, it occupies a relatively small part of the total effort.

Qualitative research

When embarking on a given project, there will normally be a specific aim in mind; sometimes it may be very clearly defined, as in, say, 'What value do passengers place on this improved type of rolling stock?', and sometimes less so, as in 'What aspects of the Pullman service contribute most to customer satisfaction?' Even when the aim involves assessing a single factor in, say, monetary units, it is unwise to leap straight into an SP experiment. It is well known that direct questions such as 'How much would you be prepared to pay to have a cleaner train?' are almost bound to elicit biased response, and in general the more the respondent can see through the point of the question, the more he will be tempted to give answers which he hopes will influence the outcome in particular ways.

Thus, regardless of the apparent simplicity of the question to be addressed by an SP approach, we consider it essential to begin with some qualitative research, which will normally take the form of in-depth interviews or group discussions, and might include some attitudinal questions. This will normally be in addition to any desk research studying other people's investigations in the field. The aim hereby is to identify the factors which people consider important in the context which we are investigating, and to understand the vocabulary which will be suitable for describing the kind of situation which we might present in the SP experiment, particularly when we are dealing with 'soft' variables.

Experimental design

Having thoroughly acquainted ourselves with the situation, the next task is to choose a list of factors for including in the SP experiment. As noted above, the experiment is normally limited to three to five factors; in cases where it is clear that more factors are necessary, it is possible to set up more than one experiment, and with a certain amount of ingenuity the experiments can be nested or otherwise combined in such a way that the analysis of the separate experiments can be carried out simultaneously. However, in most of the cases which we have dealt with, a single experiment is sufficient.

Given a decision on the factors to be included, the next decision is how many levels of each factor to include. The simplest approach is to have two levels for each factor (say, high and low) but our research strongly suggests that more reliable results are obtained by having at least three levels, unless the factor is implicitly binary-valued, since among other things, this permits the testing of non-linear relationships.

The number of levels selected for each factor is crucial for the experimental design. However, once a decision has been made, the experimental design is the simplest part of the whole process, because textbooks are available listing suitable designs for given numbers of factors and levels. The only decision to be made at this stage is how many treatments should be included and how many interaction effects should be allowed for. When the minimum number of treatments that will allow all desired coefficients to be estimated is considered too great to put to individual respondents, there are devices for 'blocking the experiment' across the sample so that although certain coefficients can no longer be estimated within any block, they can be estimated when the whole sample is taken together.

The most important and difficult part of this stage is choosing the values for the levels of the factors. We have to find a balance between values which are so close that respondents tend to be insensitive between one level and another, and values which are so far apart that they seem unrealistic. It is no point offering someone a rail journey from London to Manchester in ten minutes, when in their wildest dreams they could not imagine it taking less than, say, one and a half hours. Offering such extreme values merely makes the experiment implausible.

On the other hand, if the ranking of the cards is so obvious to everybody that they all give the same response, we will learn very little about trade-offs. In such a case, the implication is that even when individual's rates of trade-off between factors vary quite widely, the alternatives offered on the cards are too coarsely 'spaced' to reflect such variation.

In order to deal with all these issues, we normally begin by setting the central levels of the factors at something corresponding with the respondent's current experience. The other levels are then set at plausible values, and we put the experimental design through a computer simulation to see how sensitive the ranking is to the likely variation in trade-off rates which we may expect to find in the population. If it appears too insensitive, we alter the values until we are satisfied with the result. In some cases, it may be necessary to alter the experimental design as well as the values. The process requires considerable judgment, and is crucial to obtaining reliable results from the analysis.

In presenting the experiment to respondents it is of course essential that all the variables are clearly defined. In many cases this will require photographs or other visual aids, especially when trying to convey concepts like quality of service, cleanliness, etc.

The survey

Having designed a suitable questionnaire which incorporates the SP experiment, we then have to draw our sample. The nature of the SP question imposes its own constraints on surveying. In the first place, it takes the respondent a little time and concentration to complete the assessment of the hypothetical alternatives presented to him, and it is not generally practical to contact people in public places and get them to do the experiment there and then (an exception to this is when people are making long journeys). It is usually better if people can fill in the questionnaire in their homes or offices.

Secondly, if people are interviewed in their homes and asked to fill in the questionnaire while the interviewer waits, this would both impose time pressure on the respondent (which might make the responses less reliable) and waste a considerable amount of the interviewer's time.

For these reasons, we tend to use the following process. Potential respondents are contacted in a location which gives us a greater chance of their being useful to us (for instance, if we are carrying out a shopping survey, we would contact people at stores). They are then either given a short 'screening' interview at the time, or, if this is difficult, given a short pre-paid mailback questionnaire. As well as allowing us to decide whether we wished a given respondent to complete the SP question, we would also elicit basic details (age, sex, etc.) which are useful in checking for representativity. We normally ask whether respondents are willing to complete a further questionnaire; the response to this varies, but usually at least 70 per cent are willing to take part in a subsequent survey.

Those whom we screen in are then given the main questionnaire, together with the cards (either by post, or, in certain circumstances, handed it at the time of the initial contact). If we have not received the completed questionnaire within a reasonable time, we send a reminder, as we have discovered that this has quite an important effect on response. Of those who are given the main questionnaire, the proportion who respond and give useful information turns out to be extremely constant, at about 50 per cent. Because of the possibilities of response bias, we carry out a number of tests for representativeness.

Analysis

After certain checks on the quality of the data, which allow us to weed out 'frivolous' responses, the analysis begins along the lines set out in the previous section. We start with simple models, which indicate the relative importance of each factor in the experiment, and then gradually build up through investigation of market segments.

As a result of the analysis we are able to find out the way in which different market segments react to the various factors. When one of the factors included relates to price, it is possible to convert the value placed on each factor into monetary units. If price elasticities of demand are available from other research, these can be used to suggest likely elasticities to the factors under investigation.

Conclusions

In this chapter the nature of models based on stated preference data and their particular advantages have been outlined. The approach which we have adopted permits the statistical testing of hypotheses, can obtain valuations of different factors in terms of relative importance, and facilitates the process of market segmentation.

All in all, SP allows useful models of behaviour to be built on the basis of much smaller samples. None the less, it is not an 'off the shelf' technique, and the design and piloting of the experiment needs to be carried out with considerable care. Its particular advantage is that it allows areas of trade-off behaviour to be investigated where it is difficult to identify large enough samples of people who are facing such trade-offs in real life.

CHAPTER 8
Stated preference analysis and new store location

Laurence Moore

Introduction

The recent history of British retailing has seen a marked increase in the scale of operation, resulting from an escalation in the concentration of retail capital, and the increased mobility of the consumer. Allied to the stimulus provided by the decentralisation of the population, these changed circumstances have led to the proliferation of large out-of-town superstores. The retail multiples have pursued aggressive expansion policies with, for example, Sainsbury's investing £188.6 million in site acquisition and development in 1985–6, a year in which they opened fifteen new stores.

In the early stages of this change in the retail environment there were a number of 'easy' sites available, where market potential for superstores, retail warehouses and speciality stores was high, and there was little competition. Little attention was paid to the use and development of techniques to optimise store locations, as sub-optimal locations still promised good returns. However, in the 1980s circumstances changed and, as Bowlby, Breheny and Foot (1984a) suggest, the changed retail environment, with its high stakes, fierce competition, and increasing marginality of available sites, is in need of accurate, sophisticated, predictive methods of store performance analysis.

In this chapter a methodology will be described that has been developed to address the problem of assessing the optimal location of a new store. This methodology uses the disaggregate models of shopping behaviour discussed elsewhere in this volume by Fotheringham and Bates. A predictive dimension is added to these models by the use of 'stated preference' data, whilst the forecasts produced from the models take advantage of the highly disaggregate demographic and socio-economic databases that are now available.

Improving predictive capability

Disaggregate discrete-choice models have been shown in numerous applications to be effective in the modelling and explanation of observed patterns of shopping behaviour (see for example Richards and Ben-Akiva, 1975; McCarthy, 1980). However, in order to improve the predictive capability of these models, their scope must be expanded beyond the description of behaviour in existing choice contexts to include the forecasting of behaviour in choice sets which contain alternatives which may lie beyond the domain of current experience. The most obvious application is forecasting the patronage of a possible new store, but equally such hypothetical alternatives may refer to existing stores with varied characteristics.

An example of a possible application is illustrated in Figure 8.1, which is a map of a hypothetical medium-sized city that we shall call Storesville. This city has sixteen existing medium-large supermarkets, but Nicebuys, a large multiple-store grocery chain, has identified Storesville as an under-provided city, and believes that it offers great potential for retail development. Three sites have been identified as being suitable for development and likely to receive planning permission from the council. Nicebuys wish to identify the best site of the three and the optimal size and design of any new store. They would also like to know how investment expenditure may best be allocated at their three existing supermarkets in Storesville, as they wish to enhance their trading image in the city. This example will be used throughout the chapter to aid explanation of the methodology.

Preference data obtained from consumers on choice sets containing such hypothetical choice alternatives are known as stated preference data. Respondents in such a choice experiment are asked to indicate (or state) their preference between hypothetical alternatives, without references to their real-life choices. This is in contrast to revealed preference data, which

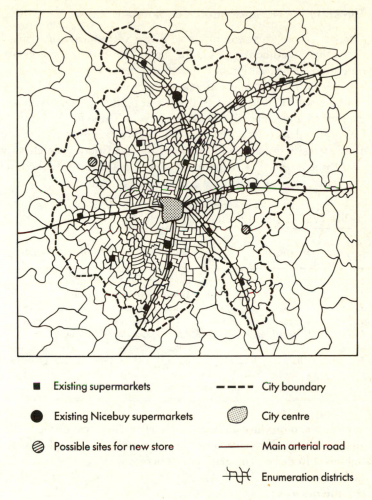

Figure 8.1 Plan of Storesville.

- ■ Existing supermarkets
- ● Existing Nicebuy supermarkets
- ⊘ Possible sites for new store
- – – – City boundary
- ⬭ City centre
- —— Main arterial road
- ⊥⊔⊢ Enumeration districts

relates to observed choices actually made by consumers and which, until recently, has been considered by many to be the only legitimate source of choice data. However, there is a wide literature concerning the theoretical development and empirical usage of stated preference data, and the validity of hypothetical choice data is now well established (see Moore (1985) and Timmermans (1984) for reviews of the literature).

The stated preference choice experiment

Chapter 7 in this volume by Bates introduces the stated preference methodology so, in order to avoid unnecessary repetition, the execution of a stated preference choice experiment will be illustrated using the example shown in Table 8.1. This example will then be used to discuss several important issues of experimental design. The choice design in Table 8.1 is termed a full-profile design. It is structured in such a way that each of the alternatives is described in terms of four attributes, which vary over three levels. The respondent is then asked to study the nine alternatives and to indicate a preference between them.

Table 8.1 A stated preference choice design

Alternatives (stores)	Parking	Attributes Distance	Prices	Range of goods
1	Free, easy	< 2 miles	Cheap	Wide
2	Free, easy	2–5 miles	Moderate	Limited groceries
3	Free, easy	> 5 miles	Expensive	Groceries only
4	Charged, easy	< 2 miles	Moderate	Groceries only
5	Charged, easy	2–5 miles	Expensive	Wide
6	Charged, easy	> 5 miles	Cheap	Limited groceries
7	Charged, difficult	< 2 miles	Expensive	Limited groceries
8	Charged, difficult	2–5 miles	Cheap	Groceries only
9	Charged, difficult	> 5 miles	Moderate	Wide

In order to produce and execute such a choice experiment, the analyst will need to have considered a number of complex issues that arise in design construction. These are:
(a) the selection of attributes;
(b) the description of attributes;
(c) the experimental design;
(d) the presentation of the choice experiment;
(e) the measurement of preference.

The selection of attributes

It is essential that the hypothetical choice experiment presented to the respondent is a realistic representation of the real-world choice situation that it hopes to simulate. It is therefore vital that, if the experiment is to have external validity, the attributes used to describe the hypothetical alternatives should be the attributes that the consumer in fact uses to discriminate between alternatives in the real world. Attribute identification is thus a key process, and should be carried out with reference to three sources:

(a) previous literature;
(b) managerial interests;
(c) preparatory fieldwork.

Previous literature   Previous studies of shopping behaviour have aimed to discover the key attributes in store or shopping-centre choice. Here is a sample of studies, and the attributes that they identified.

(a) Timmermans *et al.* (1982): distance, price of goods, choice range, service, quality of goods, parking facilities.
(b) Timmermans *et al.* (1984): number of shops, location relative to home, parking facilities.
(c) Schuler (1979): price, quality, service, parking facilities, distance.
(d) Blommestein *et al.* (1980): price, range of goods, service, accessibility, parking facilities, atmosphere, safety, complementary services.
(e) Louviere and Meyer (1981): price, variety of goods, convenience of location.

From this list it can be seen that distance, price, range of goods, and parking facilities are key attributes.

Managerial interests   The attributes chosen should normally be those that are of most significance to the consumer, such as the quality and price of goods. However, stated preference techniques may also be used in more managerially-oriented applications, where a retailer may wish to estimate the effect of relatively minor alterations, such as the addition of extra checkouts. In the example used in this chapter the attributes included are those that are of most importance to the consumer, whilst more managerially-oriented studies will be discussed in the final section.

Preparatory fieldwork   There are a number of methods which are used to elicit from consumers the attributes they consider important in their choice of a store. One technique involves the use of repertory grid methodology in which triads of known store-types are presented to a respondent, who is then asked to pick out a dimension over which two are similar and one is different. This technique has been successful in many applications, but in general is very time-consuming (Hudson, 1974; Timmermans *et al.*, 1982). A second technique involves in-depth interviews which include an element of factor-listing. Factor-listing is a simple procedure whereby respondents are asked to list why they prefer one alternative to another. It is usually not necessary to interview too many individuals, because, as the previous literature suggests, there is not a vast diversity in response. However, in-depth interviews should always be completed so as to discover attributes that may attain unusual importance in the particular study area, and also to obtain useful information on the most appropriate descriptions of attribute levels.

The description of attributes

Having selected the attributes which discriminate between choice alternatives, the respondent is then asked to indicate preferences between the alternatives. As the alternatives vary in terms of the levels of each of the attributes, it is of key importance that the levels used are meaningful to the respondent, and that the trade-offs between attributes that the respondent makes cover the range of choices the respondent makes in the real world. In this way the most apt specification of attribute levels must first be discovered. Then the range of variation in any attribute must be chosen in such a way that it does not overshadow the variation in any other and thus cause attribute dominance.

The experimental design

Once the relevant attributes and attribute levels have been selected, they must then be incorporated into an experimental design. The example used in Table 8.1 has four attributes at three levels which means that $3 \times 3 \times 3 \times 3 = 81$ possible different hypothetical alternatives may be described. A design with eighty-one alternatives is described as a full factorial design, as all possible alternatives are included, and such a design is capable of measuring all 'main' and 'interaction' effects. The main effect of each attribute is the effect of variations in the attribute, given that the other attribute levels remain constant. However, as Carmone and Green (1981) note, there are many instances where the attributes are not simply additive. In these cases, the attributes are said to 'interact', where the respondents' part-utility derived from one attribute depends on the level of some other attribute.

However, it is clearly beyond even the most astute respondent to indicate preferences amongst eighty-one alternatives, and so it is necessary to exploit the statistical properties of what are termed fractional factorial designs (Cochran and Cox, 1957). In this case, for example, the nine-alternative design in Table 8.1 will allow us to estimate all main effects. If we wish to include interaction effects, then twenty-seven alternatives should be included in the design. However, the complexity of the respondents' task can be reduced by splitting the twenty-seven alternatives into three blocks of nine alternatives, as shown in Table 8.2.

The value of this design is that it enables the analyst to obtain twenty-seven observations on each individual, which is sufficient data to permit analysis at the individual level. A further advantage of the twenty-seven-alternative block design is that a number of interaction effects may be estimated from the data. This allows us not only to look at the significance of interactions between car parking and distance, or car parking and range of goods, or any other interactions we may expect; it also allows tests of the 'independence from irrelevant alternatives' assumption of the multinomial choice model that will be used in the subsequent analysis of the preference data (see Wrigley, 1985, pp. 313–18).

The major problem is that the block design may represent a choice task too repetitive for the respondents. However, the effect of boredom with the repeated design will be counteracted by learning effects, where the respondents become more familiar with the choice task and the terminology of the experiment, and can clearly decide their preferences. However, the importance of these effects may be minimised by randomising the order of presentation of the blocks, and the data may be analysed to test for their significance.

Table 8.2 A twenty-seven alternative three-block design

Block	Parking facilities	Distance	Prices	Range of goods
Block 1	F E	<2	C	W
	F E	2–5	E	L
	F E	>5	M	O
	C E	<2	E	L
	C E	2–5	M	O
	C E	>5	C	W
	C D	<2	M	O
	C D	2–5	C	W
	C D	>5	E	L
Block 2	F E	<2	E	O
	F E	2–5	M	W
	F E	>5	C	L
	C E	<2	M	W
	C E	2–5	C	L
	C E	>5	E	O
	C D	<2	C	L
	C D	2–5	E	O
	C D	>5	M	W
Block 3	F E	<2	M	L
	F E	2–5	C	O
	F E	>5	E	W
	C E	<2	C	O
	C E	2–5	E	W
	C E	>5	M	L
	C D	<2	E	W
	C D	2–5	M	L
	C D	>5	C	O

This design was obtained from Cochran and Cox (1957). Attribute descriptions are abbreviated here, but are the same as those in Table 8.1.

The presentation of the choice experiment

Generally, the best method of presenting the experiment is to describe each alternative on a card, in terms of both a pictorial representation of the alternative and a short verbal description of each attribute (see the example in Chapter 7, this volume).

However, it is difficult to imagine how a picture representing range and price of goods, distance and parking facilities may be drawn, and so in this context it may be necessary to rely solely on verbal descriptions.

The measurement of preference

Respondents may be asked either to rank alternatives in each design in order of preference, or to attach an abstract measure of preference, for example marks out of twenty, to each alternative. The latter approach produces richer data, but it is unreliable and taxing for the respondent. Thus, ordinal data are preferred.

Level of analysis

Current models of discrete choice calibrated using revealed preference data are often termed disaggregate, in recognition of the fact that data are available at the individual level. However, in standard cross-sectional studies it is not possible to calibrate such models for each individual separately, because of the lack of repeated observations of individual choice patterns. In calibrating cross-sectional revealed preference models, some assumption must therefore be made about the consistency of the postulated utility function over the population; this is the problem of taste variation.

However, when stated preference data are available this is not the case. Stated preferences provide a *number* of observations on each individual and allow the calibration of truly individual models. These repeated observations may be obtained either by presenting respondents with a series of hypothetical choice sets, and asking them to indicate their most preferred alternative in each choice set; or alternatively by asking the respondent to go beyond simply choosing the most preferred alternative, and to rank all the alternatives in a single-choice set in order of preference.

The former strategy was used by Hensher (1984) in a study to forecast attendance at a proposed Expo exhibition in Australia. However, the strategy is liable to suffer problems associated with dominant attributes. Only a limited amount of information can be obtained from the first choice in a stated preference experiment, as the best alternative is likely to be the same for a large proportion of the sample, and any departure from that will probably concern another alternative where the dominant attribute is at its best level. Thus, very little information is obtained as to how the respondent evaluates the other attributes.

Consequently, it is preferable to use data from an experiment where respondents are asked to rank all alternatives in a choice design in order of preference. This is even more the case where a block design is used, as this will provide more observations for each individual, without presenting them with too unwieldy a choice task.

Given these repeated observations on each individual, it is therefore possible to calibrate truly individual models which will account for all heterogeneity. The problem here is that these individual models are of limited use for inference to the population. What is needed therefore is a compromise between the two extremes, of the individual model on the one hand and the general model on the other. Such a compromise can be achieved by calibrating the model separately for market segments, which are groups of people with similar preference structures. The majority of heterogeneity is accounted for by the differences between the preference structures of each market segment, whilst external application is achieved by identifying these homogeneous groups in the population.

Having identified the market segments as the preferred level of analysis, it is now necessary to investigate how these groups of like-minded individuals should be identified. It would be possible simply to specify market segments *a priori*, and disaggregate the analysis into groups pre-defined in terms of socio-economic characteristics such as income, life-cycle stage or car-ownership. On the other hand, the ability to calibrate individual models may be exploited by defining market segments in terms of groups of individuals with similar preference structures.

Analysis of the stated preference data at the individual level

The aim of any stated preference experiment is to understand how individuals choose between different alternatives. It is assumed that the individual evaluates the utility to be derived from each alternative, and chooses the alternative with the highest utility. In order to discover the respective influence of each attribute on the respondent's utility, we need to know how the individual combines the part-utilities of each attribute into some overall measure of satisfaction with each alternative. Algebraically, we need to have information on the form of the function (f) that maps the vector of attribute values $\mathbf{x}$ on to a utility value for alternative a:

$$U_a = f(\mathbf{x}) \qquad\qquad [8.1]$$

where:

$\mathbf{x} = (x_1, x_2, x_3 \ldots x_k)$
$U_a = $ Utility associated with alternative a

There are many different rules by which the individual may derive an overall utility (reviewed by Green and Srinivasan, 1978, so it is best to adopt the following general and unrestrictive form, which will accommodate many combination rules:

$$U_a = \beta_{0a} + \sum_{k=1}^{K} \beta_{ka} x_k \qquad\qquad [8.2]$$

This is a linear-in-the-parameters form where the parameters represent the weight of attribute k in the valuation of alternative a.

We may then incorporate these utility values as the deterministic element of the multinomial logit (MNL) choice model, noting that the random error in a stated preference context relates to faulty perception of the alternatives, as well as unexpected idiosyncratic preferences:

$$P_{ai} = \frac{\exp(U_{ai})}{\sum\limits_{s=1}^{A} \exp(U_{si})} \quad a = 1, 2 \ldots A \qquad\qquad [8.3]$$

where $P_{ai} = $ probability of individual i choosing alternative a out of choice set size A.

It should be noted at this stage that the remainder of the chapter assumes that the attributes have linear effects. This is essentially for the sake of simplicity, as it is well within the capability of the methodology to handle non-linearities, by virtue of the unrestrictive form of the model and the ability of the block design to detect interaction effects. For example, the distance attribute in Table 8.1 may well have non-linear effects, and will quite possibly have an S-shaped distance decay. This may be accommodated in the model using higher-order or transformed values of distance (squared, cubed, logged, etc.), and these may be tested for significance.

A direct translation of the conventional use of the observed-choice – (revealed preference) – data MNL model to stated preference data would involve the modelling of the respondent's first choice. However, the stated preference approach provides us with much richer data than merely the one alternative preferred above all others. As a result a modelling approach has been developed that exploits the extra information that stated preference data contains, and which also allows estimation of an individual model. This method is known as the exploded logit model.

The exploded logit model

The exploded logit approach is used to analyse data from stated preference experiments where an individual is asked to rank N alternative attribute combinations in order of preference. If we assume that ranking behaviour is related to choice behaviour, then the ranking of N alternatives may be viewed as N-1 choice decisions. The first choice is made out of all N alternatives, the second out of N-1, etc., until the $N-1$th choice is made out of the final two alternatives. Thus, a ranking of nine alternatives is seen as eight choices. We may then derive the following model form, originally derived by Beggs, Cardell and Hausman (1981) from an earlier proof by Luce and Suppes (1965), that the conditional probability for a given subset of the choice set being ordered as:

$$P_r(u_1 > u_2 \ldots > U_R) = \prod_{r=1}^{R} \frac{\exp(U_{ri})}{\sum_{s=r}^{A} \exp(U_{si})} \quad [8.4]$$

where:

r = Level of ranking
R = Depth of ranking analysed ($R \leqslant A - 1$)

This derivation depends on the key assumptions that the choices are independent, with independent and identically distributed error terms, and can be treated as separate observations. However, this assumption is somewhat dubious, as the less-preferred alternatives will be subject to greater error variance than the high-ranked alternatives. This is because respondents in a hypothetical choice experiment will give greater attention to the more preferred alternatives and will give less thought to those which are lower ranked, as the choices at this level seem increasingly irrelevant to them. It is therefore important that one investigates the effect of depth of ranking on the model results.

The original stimulus for the development of the exploded logit approach was to utilise the larger number of independent choice observations that the stated preference experiment contains. However, as noted above, it would appear that some of these extra observations are subject to higher error variance. What is needed is a compromise, where choices are modelled only up to the point where the data become less reliable. As a result there is a need to find the optimum depth of ranking, beyond which the analysis should not be extended. There are a number of methods of investigating the optimal depth of ranking, and these are reviewed by Chapman and Staelin (1982). For the purposes of this chapter we will simply note that Chapman and Staelin's empirical example, Bates and Roberts (1983) and the author have all found the optimal depth of ranking to be approximately half the possible observations. Thus, in a nine-alternative design, we would expect the first five rankings to be of adequate reliability.

Given that this is so, a three-block design with a total of twenty-seven choice alternatives will provide fifteen reliable observations for each individual, with which it is possible to calibrate a simple model for each individual. Thus, if a stated preference experiment covered 200 respondents, one would estimate 200 models and obtain for each individual a set of coefficients relating each attribute to an overall utility value. This set of coefficients is known as the individual's preference structure.

It should be noted at this point that there is a little uncertainty as to whether fifteen observations are sufficient to calibrate accurately a multinomial logit model which contains four parameters. There appears to be no explicit statement of the minimum number of observations that will allow reliable maximum likelihood estimation, but it should be noted that Hensher (1984) was able to calibrate successfully models with four parameters based upon sixteen observations, i.e. with eleven degrees of freedom. However, these individual models are not our final models, and so inaccuracies caused by scarcity of observations will not be of major importance. Additionally, we should note that the number of parameters included in the model will have been limited by earlier considerations in the experimental design stage.

Methods of market segmentation

Market segmentation is an increasingly important theme in retail analysis. Diversification of both the supply and demand sides of the market-place has led both to increased effort in product specialisation and catchment-area targeting by the retailer, and to increased discrimination by consumers (Frank, Massy and Wind, 1972). In order to understand and model the retail market, it is necessary to identify groups of consumers that behave similarly. Once these market segments are identified, they form the optimal level of analysis, as the heterogeneity of the consumer behaviour is defined by the segmentation, and the segments themselves constitute relatively homogeneous groups of consumers ideal for predictive and explanatory modelling of store choice.

In this section, a number of methods by which multivariate statistical analyses may be used to relate the variations in individual preferences to socio-economic characteristics will be outlined. Each method is briefly described and evaluated, and it is recognised that there is no need to restrict the actual analysis to any one technique, as a variety of methods may be used and compared.

Regression of differences between individual and aggregate models against personal characteristics   Hensher (1984) estimated individual models and a conventional aggregate model. He then attempted to explain taste variation by regressing the differences between the individual model predictions and the aggregate model predictions against socio-economic characteristics. However, there is a weakness in this approach as it does not relate characteristics to different *preference structures*. Instead, it merely considers the total choice probability value, and disregards the fact that it is very possible for completely different individuals to be equally likely to shop at a particular store.

Regression of individual parameters against personal characteristics It would be posible to regress the set of estimates obtained for each parameter over all individuals against their socio-economic characteristics. This may provide useful information about the type of people who place a high value on, for example, variety of goods. However, it is not easy to see how this information can be processed into meaningful market segments, as it relates only to particular attributes and not to overall preference structures.

Relate preference structures to personal characteristics using canonical correlation The most appealing approach is to use a method of analysis that relates the *set* of socio-economic variables to the *set* of parameter estimates. Such a method is that of canonical correlation (see Clark (1975) for a discussion of this technique).

Canonical correlation is used on data that consists of two sets of variables, the predictor variables and the criteria variables. In the case of Table 8.2 there will be four predictor variables, and the values of these variables will consist respectively of the estimates for each of the four parameters derived from the exploded logit model. The criteria variables will be socio-economic characteristics. Canonical correlation operates by extracting orthogonal principal components for each set of variables, which are then located so that they account for the maximum amount of variance within each set, and at the same time, the maximum amount of covariance between each set. In other words, the correlation between the scores obtained for each set on the components is maximised. The results are then interpreted by seeing which criteria variables are most highly correlated with one or more of the predictor variables. Possible results could be that car ownership is positively correlated with parking and negatively correlated with distance, or income may be positively related to parking and range of goods, but weakly correlated with the price. Sex may not be highly correlated with any of the predictor variables and will thus not be used in market segmentation.

Given that this analysis highlights the socio-economic variables that are most highly correlated with taste variation, it is possible to use these to produce market segments. The sample of consumers can then be divided according to these groupings, and aggregate models for each group can then be calibrated using the exploded logit model. The results obtained from these models may then be tested for their fit and comparisons made between different levels of market segmentation to assess the optimal number of segments to be used, i.e. the minimum number of segments that accounts for the maximum taste variation. When this optimal level has been discovered, a choice model for each market segment will have been calibrated. These models can then be applied to external, or real-world, situations.

Derivation of store patronage forecasts

In order to illustrate the potential of this methodology in application to real-world retail problems, we will return to the Storesville example introduced earlier. Assuming that Storesville is a city in the UK, the 1981 Census small area statistics may then be used to ascertain how many people of each market segment are resident in each enumeration district. The total expected patronage of any new store $a*$ may then be calculated as the sum of the number of people from each market segment that will shop there.

For each market segment, the expected patronage is the number of people in that market segment, multiplied by the probability that they will shop there:

$$\text{Expected patronage of new store } a* \text{ from enumeration district } u = \sum_{m=1}^{M} N_{mu} P_{a*m} \qquad [8.5]$$

where:

M = The total number of market segments, m

N = Number of people in enumeration district u in market segment m

P_{a*m} = Probability of person in market segment m shopping at store $a*$

The number of people in each segment is obtained from the small-area census data, whilst the probability of patronage is obtained for each market segment by plugging utility values into the multinomial logit choice model:

$$P_{a*} = \frac{\exp (U_{a*m})}{\left[\sum_{a=1}^{A} \exp (U_{am}) \right] + \exp (U_{a*m})} \qquad [8.6]$$

where:

a = 1, 2 . . . 16 = existing stores
$a*$ = Projected new store

Each of the utility values is obtained using the parameter estimates derived from the stated preference models calibrated at market-segment level:

$$U_{am} = \beta_{1m} PARK_a + \beta_{2m} DIST_a + \beta_{3m} PRICE_a + \beta_{4m} RANGE_a \qquad [8.7]$$

where $PARK_a$, $DIST_a$, $PRICE_a$ and $RANGE_a$ are the physical values of each attribute for any existing or projected store.

The variable values relate to the physical attributes of individual stores, both the sixteen existing stores in Storesville and any possible new store. At this stage it is worth noting that it is easy to calculate predicted patronage values for existing stores from equation [8.7] and to compare these predicted values to data on actual store patronage or turnover. This allows the validity of the results to be tested and allows the testing of any scaling necessary to generalise from models calibrated on a few hundred respondents to the whole population of a particular city.

Thus, from equation [8.7] a utility value (U_{am}) may be obtained for each existing and hypothetical new store. This value is calculated separately for each market segment in each enumeration district as the value of the distance variable will be different in each case. It is worth noting that, assuming we have a negative coefficient of distance β_{2m} in equation [8.7], the utility values obtained may take zero or negative values. The distribution of these values may be directly related to store catchment areas.

The utility values derived from equation [8.7] are then plugged into the multinomial logit model, equation [8.6], to calculate probabilities for each market segment for any of the existing or possible new stores. This is repeated for each market segment in each enumeration district (equation [8.5]), and for each enumeration district in turn, to produce a total patronage prediction for each of the stores.

The simplest interpretation of the results is that the possible new store site with the highest expected patronage should be the one chosen. However, we will also be able to detect the effects of new stores on existing stores. In this way Nicebuys will be able to assess the effects of a new store on its existing operations. Thus, in our example, the possible new store in the north-east of Storesville (see Figure 8.1) may not be the best option, even if it has the highest expected patronage, as it is close to two of Nicebuys' existing stores. Furthermore, the preference structures will have indicated which attributes of a store contribute most to the utility that a consumer associates with a store, and may be used in a cost/benefit analysis for investing in existing stores or deciding the size and design of a new store.

Conclusions

The stated preference methodology outlined above has been shown to produce patronage forecasts for new and existing stores, and these may be tested for validity given data on existing patronage. The technique also enables delimitation of catchment areas, and indicates the key attributes in a store's design. Furthermore, we should note here that the stated preference methodology can be used very effectively in non-spatial applications. For example, it may be of managerial interest to ascertain how the various features of a store are perceived by the consumers. The attributes included in such an experiment may be quality, price, checkout-queuing time and staff courtesy. Such applications may be of more immediate interest to retailers, as the results may be applied generally to all stores in a retail chain, the interviews may be carried out in-store, and the problematic distance attribute is omitted. However, to limit the use of the methodology to such applications would be to ignore its potential to answer the key question of new store location.

PART 3   Models of store choice

In this section of the book one particular approach to modelling patterns of store choice by consumers is explored. This approach uses the NBD and Dirichlet models of consumer purchasing behaviour to represent and forecast patterns of store choice for frequently-purchased grocery items. It should be stressed that there is no intention here to provide a comprehensive review or treatment of the many approaches to the modelling of store choice which are available across the wide literature of marketing, statistics, economics, geography, and planning, or to model store choice for infrequently-purchased durable or fashion items. Instead, the intention is to provide just a comprehensive set of chapters on one promising method of modelling store choice; a method which has recently been felt to have considerable potential for assessing the market performance of individual stores and/or complete retail chains, and which has the potential to be linked to other retail forecasting techniques described in Part 2 of this book.

To this end, Chapters 10 and 11 by Wrigley and Dunn, and Uncles and Ehrenberg, which were specially prepared for this book, are complemented by a chapter by Kau A. Keng and Ehrenberg previously published in the *Journal of Marketing Research*, 1984. This chapter, reproduced here as Chapter 9, provides a common reference point for the other chapters in this section, and it is included to complete a self-contained group of contributions on the NBD/Dirichlet approach to store-choice modelling.

CHAPTER 9
Patterns of store choice

Kau Ah Keng and Andrew S. C. Ehrenberg

Introduction

Though retail stores have been gaining in influence over manufacturers of branded grocery products, the way consumers choose between different stores has not been studied as much as brand choice. Knowing more about store choice should help in addressing practical distribution and marketing problems and improving our understanding of the consumer.

We offer some findings about the way consumers choose between leading chains and other store groups in the United Kingdom, based on analyses of AGB consumer panel data. In the second section of the chapter we discuss three regularities related to store choice for a given grocery product class (such as instant coffee or detergent).

(a) The number of customers a chain has for the product varies markedly with the chain's market share and also with the length of time analysed.

(b) In contrast, the average purchase frequency of the product (i.e. repeat-buying loyalty) differs very little between chains and varies less with the length of the analysis period.

(c) Most customers of a given chain also buy the product elsewhere (few are 100 per cent loyal). They do so simply in line with the other chains' market shares. There is little or no noticeable segmentation.

The observed patterns are the same for different products and store groups. They are closely predictable by the same theoretical model (the Dirichlet) as applies for brand choice, with only market shares as store-specific inputs. Though retail stores differ from each other and compete for customer loyalty in many different ways, the close fit of the model shows that these various strategies and tactics have no net effect on the structure of the stores' customers' loyalty, but only on their market shares.

In the third section of the chapter we extend the analysis to the buying of the specific *brands* of the product class at each of the different chains or store groups. Here, too, there are three main findings.

(a) Brand loyalty at a store is positive but low. People also spread their purchases among other brands and stores, again simply in line with market shares.

(b) Loyalty to retailers' own-label brands is much the same as loyalty to manufacturers' brands.

(c) Penetration growth and repeat buying of a brand within a chain or store group follow the same patterns as in the population as a whole.

Background

Cunningham (1961) noted long ago that consumers' store loyalty was often not exclusive or undivided, but little quantification or extension of his results has been done. Published studies have used differing kinds of data, analytic procedures, or loyalty criteria (see Charlton (1973) and Kau (1981, Chapter 5) for reviews). Few have used individual customer's buying records over time. Major exceptions are pioneering analyses by Jephcott (1972) and more recent ones by Wrigley and his associates working in a geographic rather than marketing mode (e.g. Dunn, Reader and Wrigley, 1983; Wrigley, 1980; Wrigley and Dunn, 1984a; 1984b). However, even for *brand* choice the already-known empirical regularities are seldom described in the marketing literature. A specialist text on consumer behaviour reports that American and British repeat-buying habits are the same (e.g. Engel, Blackwell and Kollat, 1978, p. 86), yet does not actually describe these habits.

On the theoretical side, many models have been discussed for brand choice but few for store choice, and almost none for both store and brand choice together (see, e.g., Charlton, 1973; Engel, Blackwell and Kollat, 1978; Kau, 1981; and Massy, Montgomery and Morrison, 1970 for reviews). However, because the patterns of store choice observed under stationary market conditions turn out to be the same as the patterns of brand choice, the same models in fact apply. These are basically the Dirichlet model of heterogeneous buyer behaviour (e.g. Goodhardt, Ehrenberg and Chatfield, 1984) and earlier, more limited, but numerically almost equivalent, formulations such as the NBD model of repeat buying and the Duplication of Purchase Law. A brief description of these models is given in the Appendix.

Data analysed

Our illustrations mainly cover instant coffee in the UK. We have found the same results for ready-to-eat (RTE) breakfast cereals, canned soups, canned dog food and detergents (Kau, 1981). These products were chosen for their variety: food versus non-food; a single versus numerous end users; brands with similar or different product formulations; etc. Jephcott (1972) also covered toothpaste and dishwashing liquids, and Wrigley and his colleagues studied tea, butter, margarine, toilet tissue, baked beans, fabric conditioners and instant coffee (Dunn, Reader and Wrigley, 1983; Wrigley, 1980; Wrigley and Dunn, 1984a). Thus a good basis for generalization is building up, including earlier results for gasoline (petrol), where retail outlet and brand are generally the same anyway (e.g. Aske Research, 1972).

Our data come from 24-week buying records from the well-established consumer panel operation run by AGB Research in the UK (see Buck, 1982), using two regional sub-samples in Lancashire and London (each with $n = 800$ to 900 households). The markets show the usual short-term fluctuations due to promotions, but no sizeable trends over the period other than the standard seasonal one in the case of canned soup. Our unit of analysis is the purchase occasion, not the amount bought or the money spent (see Ehrenberg, 1972, Chapter 1).

The AGB buying records distinguish between groups of stores rather than individual outlets, e.g. major UK supermarket chains such as Tesco, the Co-op, Sainsbury and Kwiksave, a large 'miscellaneous' group of smaller chains, and a grouping of independent grocers. Such data on store groups cover the main marketing needs of both retailers and manufacturers, but general knowledge of UK shopping habits suggests that consumers mostly buy at just one or two branches of a particular chain. Indeed, the recent work by Wrigley and his colleagues extends the results to an *ad hoc* panel covering individual stores in a specific town (Dunn, Reader and Wrigley, 1983).

Store choice for products

In this section we describe how consumers distribute their purchases of a product within and across different chains or store groups. We address three main topics.
(a) The number of customers a particular chain has (its 'penetration') in different lengths of time, and their frequency of buying the product there.
(b) The relationship between the penetrations, average purchase frequencies, and market shares of different chains.
(c) The extent to which the customers of one chain also buy the product at other chains.
We illustrate the results with instant coffee. Fuller details, including results for other products, are given elsewhere (Kau, 1981).

Penetration growth

The cumulative number of buyers of a product at a given store group increases rapidly with the length of time analysed. Thus 2 per cent of the Lancashire population bought instant coffee at the Tesco chain in a typical week, but 21 per cent bought it there at least once in six months (the longest period analysed here).

Week-by-week repeat-buying of such a product is relatively low, about 20 per cent (as closely predicted by the NBD model – see also Jephcott, 1972; Kau, 1981; Wrigley, 1980). Thus it is mostly not the same 2 per cent buying coffee each week. Over two weeks the penetration is 3.6 per cent. It grows markedly, but less than *pro rata*, to almost 30 per cent buying at least once a year. This dramatic penetration growth may seem surprising. Tesco managers might think from their weekly sales data or counts of store traffic that they have about 400,000 instant coffee customers out of 20 million nationally in the UK, but in fact they have more than 5 million over a year.

Table 9.1 shows that such penetration growth generalizes to

Table 9.1 Penetration growth of instant coffee in eight different store groups

	1 week	6 weeks	12 weeks*	24 weeks
Anywhere				
O%	17.0	54	(65)	76
T%	16.0	50	(65)	77
Miscellaneous				
O%	4.0	15	(24)	33
T%	3.9	16	(24)	33
Cooperative				
O%	3.8	16	(20)	28
T%	3.7	14	(20)	27
Kwiksave				
O%	3.4	12	(16)	22
T%	3.0	11	(16)	21
Tesco				
O%	2.2	9	(14)	21
T%	2.0	9	(14)	20
Asda				
O%	1.4	8	(11)	14
T%	1.9	8	(11)	15
Symbol				
O%	0.9	4	(6)	10
T%	1.1	4	(6)	8
Independents				
O%	0.9	5	(7)	11
T%	1.0	4	(7)	10
Fine Fare				
O%	0.4	3	(3)	5
T%	0.5	2	(3)	5
Average store group				
O%	2.1	9	(13)	18
T%	2.1	8	(13)	17

* Used in fitting the NBD model.
O = observed; T = theoretical NBD.

other chains and store groups and that it is highly predictable from the NBD or Dirichlet model using the observed 12-week penetrations as input (see Appendix). The fit is generally to within about ±1 per cent. It is even better for the *average* store group in Table 9.1 because the discrepancies for individual chains are partly due to sampling errors.

Table 9.2 illustrates how the predictable growth pattern also holds for the other product classes covered. (Canned soup is excluded here because of its marked seasonality.)

Table 9.2 Penetration growth for four products at a store group (averages of the itemized chains or store groups)

	1 week	6 weeks	12 weeks*	24 weeks
Instant coffee				
O%	2.1	9	(13)	18
T%	2.1	8	(13)	17
RTE cereals				
O%	5.5	20	(28)	36
T%	5.4	20	(28)	36
Detergents				
O%	4.4	16	(24)	31
T%	4.4	16	(24)	32
Dog food				
O%	nt	3.6	(4.8)	6.0
T%	1.3	3.7	(4.8)	5.9
Average				
O%	4.0	12	(18)	23
T%	4.0	12	(18)	23

* Used in fitting the NBD model.
nt = not tabulated.

Frequency of purchase

The growth of penetration is paralleled by an equally predictable growth in the average number of purchases per buyer. For instant coffee at Tesco this number is from 1.0 purchase per weekly buyer to an average of 3.1 per half-yearly buyer. When we multiply this three-fold increase in purchase frequency by the nine-fold increase in Tesco's penetration (see Table 9.1), we get a twenty-seven-fold increase in cumulative sales. This increase is greater than the twenty-four-fold increase to be expected under strictly stationary conditions because of a small trend in Tesco's coffee sales. (Tesco was chosen as an illustration here because its coffee sales were less stationary than those at most of the other chains – see Kau, 1981.)

Individual consumer's frequency of buying the product varies widely about these averages. Most buyers buy the product only once or twice at a given chain, even in a period as long as 24 weeks, as illustrated in Table 9.3. The pattern is the same for different chains and products, and is well modelled by the negative binomial distribution (NBD) or Dirichlet.

Table 9.3 Frequency distribution of purchases of instant coffee at Tesco in 24 weeks

| | *Number of purchases at store* | | | | | | | | | |
	1	*2*	*3*	*4*	*5*	*6*	*7*	*8*	*9*	*10+*
Tesco										
O%	38	19	14	9	7	3	4	0	1	5
T%	42	20	11	8	5	4	3	2	1	4
Average chain										
O%	44	19	12	6	3	3	3	3	2	5
T%	43	20	11	8	4	3	2	2	2	5

O = observed percentage of buyers making 1, 2, 3, etc., purchases; T = theoretical NBD.

Average purchase frequencies for different store groups

The shares of the instant-coffee market held by the eight store groups analysed differ by a factor of about ten, as shown in the first column of Table 9.4. In contrast, the average purchase frequencies per buyer in the 24 weeks are very similar – all roughly lie within maximum limits of ±0.9 (and much less for the theoretical estimates).

The main correlate of the stores' differing market shares is therefore the different store penetrations – Fine Fare has far fewer buyers in the 24 weeks than the miscellaneous group (5 per cent vs 33 per cent). Fine Fare's customers also buy a little less

Table 9.4 Market share, penetration and purchase frequency of instant coffee

	Market share (%)	Penetration (%) O	T	Av. purchase freq. per buyer O	T
Miscellaneous	21	33	28	2.8	3.3
Cooperative	21	28	29	3.4	3.3
Kwiksave	19	22	26	3.9	3.3
Tesco	14	21	20	3.1	3.2
Asda	11	14	16	3.6	3.1
Symbol	6	10	10	2.9	3.0
Independents	6	11	9	2.4	2.9
Fine Fare	2	5	4	2.1	2.8
Average	12	18	18	3.0	3.1

O = observed; T = theoretical Dirichlet.

frequently (an average of 2.1 vs 2.8), a kind of 'double jeopardy' pattern which is already well known from brand purchasing (e.g. Ehrenberg, 1972; Ehrenberg and Goodhardt, 1979). Thus a small store group suffers in two ways – it has fewer buyers and they buy (somewhat) less frequently (an average of 3.3 for the four largest groups and 2.7 for the four smallest). The Dirichlet model also picks up this trend.

The overall picture is that a chain's instant-coffee sales over 24 weeks essentially result from a certain number of customers buying coffee there about three times on average. This finding implies a relatively low level of repeat buying, on average about one purchase of the product at the chain every two months. However, the figures in Table 9.4 show that store groups differ little in this respect, i.e. the levels of repeat-buying loyalty they attract are much the same.

Buying at other stores

Grocery stores have fairly low loyalty in the sense of generally not satisfying their customers' total needs for a product. Most buyers of a product at a given chain also buy the product at other chains very extensively. For example, over 24 weeks the average Tesco buyer of instant coffee bought instant coffee a total of 7.3 times, as shown in Table 9.5. However, only about three of these purchases were made at Tesco (Table 9.4) and about four purchases elsewhere. This result generalizes to other chains and other products and is highly predictable. Thus chains differ little in the extent to which they attract heavy users of a product class or in the proportion of their customers' total purchases that are made at their stores.

In contrast with the small double-jeopardy trend in Table 9.4, the observed purchase frequencies at *any* store in Table 9.5 tend to increase slightly with decreasing market share, from an average of about 7.3 for the four largest store groups to 7.9 for the four smallest ones (with the Symbol group being exceptional but based on a sub-sample of only $n = 84$ households). This small trend has long been established in the case of brand purchase (e.g. Ehrenberg, 1972; Ehrenberg and Goodhardt, 1979). It also occurs for store groups in the other product classes examined (detergents, cereals, soup, etc.) and is shown by the Dirichlet model.

Table 9.5 Average number of purchases of instant coffee anywhere in 24 weeks

| By buyers at | Av. no. of purchases at any store | |
	O	T
Miscellaneous	7.3	7.3
Cooperative	7.4	7.3
Kwiksave	7.1	7.3
Tesco	7.3	7.4
Asda	7.6	7.5
Symbol	8.6	7.6
Independents	7.9	7.6
Fine Fare	7.5	7.7
Average	7.6	7.5

O = observed; T = theoretical Dirichlet.

In combination the two trends in Tables 9.4 and 9.5 mean that buyers at a smaller chain have a more marked tendency to buy the product elsewhere. This is a statistical selection effect, as is implied by the specification of the Dirichlet model (Goodhardt, Ehrenberg and Chatfield, 1984). It is independent of the numbers of competing retail outlets in each chain and of their locations.

The extent of multi-store buying is greater the longer the time period and the higher the purchase frequency of the product class. For ready-to-eat breakfast cereals the typical 24-week purchase rate (both observed and predicted) averages at about four per buyer at chain X, with an average total of fourteen purchases anywhere. Buyers at X therefore make almost two-and-a-half times as many purchases of the product elsewhere in 24 weeks. Though store loyalty in general is relatively low, it exists because the number of product-purchases buyers at chain X make at X is greater than the number they tend to make at any other *single* chain.

Sole buyers

The proportion of 100 per cent loyal or 'sole' buyers at a store tends to be low, except in very short periods of time. In half a year, only 20 per cent of Tesco buyers of instant coffee were 100 per cent loyal to Tesco. Much the same was found for the other store groups, as Table 9.6 shows. (The proportion would be lower still in longer periods, as implied by the Dirichlet model.)

The low incidence of sole buyers is no great drawback because they are not especially heavy buyers anyway. Their purchase frequency of about 3.0 is close to the average for *all* buyers at the chain (Table 9.4). Moreover, sole buyers are light buyers of the product class in total as they do not buy it elsewhere.

Both sets of observed figures in Table 9.6 show downward trends with market shares, indicating a three-fold jeopardy pattern for sole buying:

(a) smaller store groups have fewer customers (Table 9.4);
(b) fewer of the customers are 100 per cent loyal; and
(c) these 'sole buyers' tend to buy the product slightly less often (excluding the 'outlier' for Symbol, based here on a sub-sample of $n = 10$ sole buyers).

The same patterns recur for the other products covered and are again already well established for brand choice (e.g. Ehrenberg,

Table 9.6   Incidence of 100-per-cent loyal buyers of instant coffee in 24 weeks

	% buyers who are sole buyers		Av. no. of purchases per sole buyer	
	O	T	O	T
Miscellaneous	20	24	3.1	3.3
Cooperative	29	24	3.6	3.3
Kwiksave	31	24	3.9	3.3
Tesco	20	22	3.0	3.1
Asda	27	19	3.8	3.1
Symbol	12	19	4.3	2.9
Independents	19	18	2.8	2.9
Fine Fare	16	18	2.7	2.8
Average	22	21	3.4	3.1

O = observed; T = theoretical Dirichlet.

1972; Ehrenberg and Goodhardt, 1979). These results are predictable from the Dirichlet model without the assumption of a 'hard core' of highly loyal buyers.

Duplication of purchase between chains

The degree to which buyers of a product at one chain patronise another chain also follows a regular pattern. It tends to be proportional to the second chain's overall penetration, i.e. to how many buyers of the product the second chain attracts from the population as a whole. Table 9.7 illustrates this finding – the higher the penetration of instant coffee in a chain, the higher its duplication with Tesco buyers. The average proportionality factor is 1.2 (i.e. average duplication 21 per cent/average penetration 18 per cent). Being greater than one, it shows that buying at Tesco does not inhibit buying instant coffee elsewhere.

Table 9.8 shows that the pattern generalizes to each of the other store groups, with numerically much the same duplication coefficient. It is the well-established Duplication of Purchase Law in action (e.g. Ehrenberg, 1972; Ehrenberg and Goodhardt, 1969a; 1979). The fit is closer for the averages than for the

Table 9.7   Percentage of Tesco buyers also buying instant coffee elsewhere in 24 weeks

	% buying at							
	Misc.	Co-op	Kwiksave	Asda	Symbol	Ind.	Fine Fare	Average
Tesco buyers (%)	45	29	23	13	14	13	7	21
Total population (%)	33	28	22	14	10	11	5	18

Table 9.8   Duplication of purchase between chains; percentage of buyers of instant coffee at chain C who also bought it at chain D in 24 weeks

Buyers at (%)	% who also bought at								
	Misc.	Co-op	Kwiksave	Tesco	Asda	Symbol	Ind.	Fine Fare	Average
Miscellaneous	(100)	32	25	29	13	16	15	8	20
Cooperative	38	(100)	21	22	19	12	13	4	18
Kwiksave	37	26	(100)	22	9	9	11	7	17
Tesco	45	29	23	(100)	13	14	13	7	21
Asda	31	38	14	24	(100)	14	9	3	19
Symbol	52	32	20	30	20	(100)	19	8	26
Independents	52	34	23	24	12	18	(100)	5	24
Fine Fare	50	23	29	27	9	16	11	(100)	24
Average	43	31	22	25	14	14	13	6	
1.2 × penetration	46	34	26	25	17	12	13	6	
Penetration	33	28	22	21	14	10	11	5	

individual figures in the body of the table, reflecting the fact that some of the variations are sampling errors (with ns about 150).

The Duplication Law pattern also holds for the other products analysed (generally with duplication coefficients of about 1.1 in 24 weeks). This finding means that there is no substantial segmentation or special clustering of particular chains in these markets (except possibly within the deviations shown). Two chains generally share the number of customers that their sheer market shares or penetration levels warrant.

Brand choice at different chains

We have noted in Tables 9.4 and 9.5 that in a reasonably long time period, such as half a year, buyers of a product at a given chain, say C, buy that product more often at other chains that at chain C itself. We now explore this finding in terms of the specific brands bought and assess the role of retailers' private-label brands.

The detailed patterns of brand choice are again those of the Duplication of Purchase Law. The coefficients confirm the existence of some store loyalty and some brand loyalty, but not in any dominant fashion. Another new finding is that penetration growth and repeat buying of a specific brand within a chain or store group also follow the NBD-type patterns that are traditional for the population as a whole.

Buying other brands and buying at other stores

In a time period long enough for several purchases of the product, most buyers of a given brand B at chain C do not restrict themselves to the one brand and store. For example, in 24 weeks:

(a) 58 per cent of buyers of Nescafé at Tesco also bought other instant coffee brands at Tesco;

(b) 72 per cent also bought other instant coffee brands elsewhere (an abnormally high figure); and

(c) 58 per cent (a different 58 per cent) also bought Nescafé elsewhere.

Therefore much multi-brand and multi-store buying occurred. Indeed, none of the Nescafé buyers at Tesco in the half year was 100 per cent loyal to both the brand and store group. (In most

Table 9.9   Nescafé buyers at a given chain C who also buy other brands or elsewhere in 24 weeks

Buyers of (%)	% buying Nescafé at stated chain C	Other brands at C	Others elsewhere	Nescafé elsewhere
Nescafé at misc.	100	65	47	43
Nescafé at Kwiksave	100	30	56	44
Nescafé at Co-op	100	42	58	58
Nescafé at Tesco	100	58	72	58
Nescafé at Asda	100	44	58	46
Nescafé at average store	100	48	55	50

other cases a few per cent were 100 per cent loyal.) Table 9.9 shows that the pattern is similar for Nescafé buyers at other store groups. The pattern is much the same for other brands of instant coffee and for the other products analysed, including own label brands, as illustrated in Table 9.10.

Amounts bought

The incidence of multi-brand and multi-store buying is not just occasional – due to some isolated promotion, say. 'Other' purchases tend to account for the greater part of consumers' total purchases of a product in a period such as half a year. For example, the average Nescafé buyer at Tesco made eight instant coffee purchases anywhere. Only about 2.5 of these purchases were devoted to Nescafé at Tesco; the rest were almost equally divided among the other three types of purchases, as shown in Table 9.11. The distributions of private-label buyers' total purchases are mostly very similar (with buying of other brands at the same store being somewhat lower). The degree of disloyalty is also much the same for the other brands of instant coffee and the

Table 9.10 Buyers of leading brand or of private label brand at chain C who also buy other brands at C or elsewhere in 24 weeks (results averaged across the different chains)

Buyers of (%)	% buying Stated brand at S	Other brands at S	Others elsewhere	Stated brand elsewhere
Nescafé at chain C	100	48	58	50
Private label instant coffee at C	100	41	53	40*
Heinz soups at chain C	100	54	45	34
Private label soups at C	100	36	48	39*
Kellogg's Corn Flakes at chain C	100	77	87	62
Private label corn flakes at C	100	85	90	53*
Average	100	57	66	50

* The other chains' private labels.

Table 9.11 Average number of purchases by Nescafé buyers and private label buyers at a given chain C in 24 weeks

Buyers of	Their average number of purchases of Stated brand at C	Other brands at C	Others elsewhere	Stated brand elsewhere	Any coffee anywhere
Nescafé at chain C	2.6	1.8	1.9	1.8	8.1
Private label at C	2.8	1.1	2.2	1.8*	7.9

* The other chains' private labels, if any.

other product class analysed, after allowances for differences in market share.

The right-hand column of Table 9.11 shows that both Nescafé and private-label buyers at a specific chain C average about eight instant coffee purchases anywhere in the 24 weeks. This finding reflects another regularity – different brands (including private label) differ little in the extent to which they attract light or heavy users of the product class.

The extent of disloyalty, however, is even higher than Table 9.11 indicates. The rates shown are averages across all buyers of brand B at chain C, yet only about 50 per cent of these buyers also bought other brands at C, or other brands elsewhere, etc. (as shown in Table 9.10). Thus the rates at which *these* consumers bought these other items were roughly twice as high as those shown in Table 9.11. For example, *all* Nescafé buyers at C bought it 2.6 times on average, but the 48 per cent who also bought *other* brands at C bought them at the rate of 1.8/0.48 or 3.8 purchases each.

Duplication of purchase within a chain

We now look in more detail at:

(a) the competition between brands within the same store group; and

(b) the competition between store groups for the same brand.

In both cases the Duplication of Purchase Law applies again. it relates the number of duplicated buyers of a brand to the brand's penetration. Within the limits of fit, no allowance need be made for more specific store or brand characteristics such as the number or size of retail outlets in a chain, its pricing or merchandising policies, any product differentiation, or other characteristics of the specific brands.

Table 9.12 illustrates how multi-brand buying within a particular chain follows the Duplication Law. The example is for ready-to-eat (RTE) breakfast cereals in the Sainsbury's chain in the London region, a product class in which every brand tends to look and taste different. The predicted duplications are 1.4 times penetration. They hold to within a percentage point or so for the average duplication (showing virtually no consistent bias) and to

Table 9.12   Brand duplication within Sainsbury's for ready-to-eat cereals in 24 weeks

Sainsbury buyers of (%)	% who also bought at Sainsbury's					
	PLCF	KCF	WB	KRK	SW	KAB
Private label corn flakes (PLCF)	—	36	24	25	17	12
Kellogg's Corn Flakes (KCF)	37	—	21	19	18	12
Weetabix (WB)	41	35	—	24	15	12
Kellogg's Rice Krispies (KRK)	56	42	26	—	13	19
Shredded Wheat (SW)	51	54	31	18	—	13
Kellogg's All Bran (KAB)	38	38	22	27	14	—
Average Sainsbury duplication	45	41	25	23	15	14
1.4 × Sainsbury penetration	43	43	25	20	14	14
Penetration in Sainsbury*	31	31	18	14	10	10

* % of all Sainsbury cereals buyers who buy the stated brand there.
Average duplication/average penetration in Sainsbury = 27/19 = 1.4.

within an average of four points for the individual figures. This scatter is small compared with the systematic differences between the columns. (The duplication coefficient of 1.4 is estimated from the average Sainsbury's duplication of 27 per cent divided by the average penetration of 19 per cent.)

A special feature of the results is that the duplication coefficients are virtually the same for the different chains, as shown in Table 9.13. For example, the coefficient is about 0.7 for instant coffee brands within each chain and about 1.3 for RTE cereals. Consumers therefore spread their purchases among the different brands in the same way within each chain.

This stability of the duplication coefficients applies only when the observed brand duplications in a chain or store group are related to the brands' penetrations among all buyers of the product class at that chain. If the brand penetrations are expressed as percentages of the population as a whole, the

Table 9.13   Coefficients of brand duplication within a chain in 24 weeks

Instant coffee (Lancashire)		RTE cereals (London)		Detergents (London)	
Tesco	0.7	Tesco	1.4	Tesco	0.8
Co-op	0.7	Co-op	1.4	Co-op	0.7
Kwik.	0.6	Sains.	1.4	Sains.	0.8
Asda	0.7	Symbol	1.2	Symbol	0.7
Misc.	0.6	Misc.	1.3	Misc.	0.7
Average	0.7	Average	1.3	Average	0.7

duplication coefficients vary with the chains' market shares and are also much higher. Thus on one hand, in Table 9.12 37 per cent of the buyers of Kellogg's Corn Flakes at Sainsbury also bought the private-label corn flakes (PLCF) there, a percentage which is fractionally higher than the PLCF's 31 per cent penetration among all Sainsbury RTE cereals buyers (the ratio is close to the overall duplication coefficient of 1.4 within Sainsbury).

On the other hand, the penetration of Sainsbury PLCF in the population as a whole is only 13 per cent. (Thus 42 per cent of the population bought RTE cereals at Sainsbury, and 31 per cent of these bought the PLCF, making 13 per cent.) The 37 per cent of Kellogg's Corn Flakes buyers at Sainsbury who also bought its PLCF is much higher than this – a duplication ratio of almost three. (This figure also applies broadly to other pairs of brands at Sainsbury, i.e. the Duplication Law continues to hold.) This finding suggests that despite the high degree of multi-store buying described before, *some* store loyalty exists; buyers of one brand at Sainsbury are about three times as likely to buy another given brand there than is the population as a whole. However, these duplication coefficients differ from chain to chain, in line with the population penetration.

Store duplication for a brand

We note in Tables 9.9 through 9.11 that buyers of a brand at a given chain tend to buy that brand also at other stores. The detailed pattern is again that of the Duplication of Purchase Law, as illustrated in Table 9.14 for Nescafé. The first column shows that roughly 30 per cent of the Nescafé buyers at each chain also bought Nescafé at the miscellaneous stores. On the right we see that roughly 10 per cent also bought Nescafé at Asda. (The predictions fit to within an average of 3 percentage points. This small scatter limits the degree to which there could be any segmentation or particular affinity between two or more chains.)

Table 9.14 Nescafé's duplication across chains in 24 weeks

| Nescafé buyers at (%) | % who also bought Nescafé at | | | | |
	Misc.	Kwiksave	Co-op	Tesco	Asda
Misc.	—	16	15	15	10
Kwiksave	24	—	15	12	6
Co-op	32	22	—	8	10
Tesco	36	19	9	—	13
Asda	26	10	12	14	—
Average Nescafé duplication	30	17	13	12	10
0.6 × Nescafé penetration	28	19	13	11	11
Penetration among all Nescafé buyers*	46	31	21	19	18

* % of all Nescafé buyers in the period who bought it at the stated chain.

The duplications in Table 9.14 tend to be a third lower than the penetration of each chain among Nescafé buyers. Thus the averages of 30 per cent and 10 per cent compare with 46 per cent and 18 per cent of *all* Nescafé buyers who bought it at miscellaneous stores and Asda in the half year.

The results generalize to the other brands of instant coffee and to RTE cereals and detergents. (Results for soup and dog food were not tabulated in such detail (Kau, 1981).) A special regularity is again the marked similarity of the between-chain duplication coefficients for the different brands in each of the three product classes, as shown in Table 9.15. They are all less than 1, so that buying of brand B at chain C somewhat inhibits

Table 9.15 Coefficients of store duplication for different brands in 24 weeks

Instant coffee		RTE breakfast cereals		Detergents	
Nescafé	0.6	Kellogg's Corn Flakes	0.7	Persil Auto.	0.8
Private labels	0.6	Private label corn flakes	0.6	Persil	0.7
Other brands	0.6	Weetabix	0.7	Ariel	0.7
		Shredded Wheat	0.7	Bold	0.9
		All Bran	0.8	Fairy Snow	0.7
		Other brands	0.9	Other brands	0.8
Average	0.6	Average	0.7	Average	0.8

buying brand B elsewhere. None the less, buyers of B at chain C are much more likely to buy B at the other chains than is the population as a whole. For example, the 30 per cent that tended to buy Nescafé at the miscellaneous group in Table 9.14 is high in comparison with the 15 per cent of the whole population who bought Nescafé at this group in the half year (Table 9.6). In that sense there *is* some brand loyalty; buyers of brand B at one chain show a special tendency also to buy B at another chain.

Brand penetration growth and purchase frequency

The growth in the cumulative number of buyers of a particular brand at a single chain and their purchase frequencies follow the same NBD patterns as those long established for brands as a whole (e.g. Ehrenberg, 1972; Ehrenberg and Goodhardt, 1979). Local merchandising practices and variable stock levels within a chain or store group therefore have no net effects on these patterns.

Table 9.16 gives an example of the penetration growth from an average week to 24 weeks of both Nescafé and private-label brands in four different chains or store groups. The fuller results for repeat buying, etc., within a chain are outlined elsewhere (Kau, 1981).

Table 9.16   Penetration growth of brands within stores

	% buying in 1 week	6 weeks	12 weeks*	24 weeks
Nescafé in				
Misc.				
O %	nt	7	(10)	15
T%	2	6	(10)	15
Co-op				
O%	nt	3	(4)	7
T%	2	3	(4)	7
Tesco				
O%	nt	3	(4)	6
T%	1	2	(4)	6
Asda				
O%	nt	3	(4)	6
T%	1	2	(4)	6
Average				
O%	nt	4	(6)	9
T%	1	3	(6)	9
Own label in				
Misc.				
O%	nt	7	(10)	15
T%	1	7	(10)	14
Co-op				
O%	nt	9	(13)	18
T%	1	9	(13)	17
Tesco				
O%	nt	2	(4)	7
T%	1	2	(4)	6
Asda				
O%	nt	2	(3)	4
T%	1	2	(3)	5
Average				
O%	nt	5	(8)	11
T%	1	5	(8)	11

* used in fitting the NBD model.
nt = not tabulated.
O = observed; T = theoretical NBD.

Discussion

The analyses of store choice in the UK summarized here show that most buyers of a product at a particular chain or store group buy it there relatively infrequently. They often also buy the product elsewhere. The results show that store loyalty exists, but is not strong or undivided, let alone exclusive. If over time a consumer fairly regularly buys different brands at different chains, it is unlikely that there is a simple answer to the traditional question about consumers' store and brand choice, namely to what extent consumers first decide on a store to visit and then on a brand to buy, or vice versa.

The way consumers spread their product-class purchases among different chains shows no sign of marked segmentation. Individuals differ in their store-choice preferences and habits, but there is no evidence that any subset of chains appeals exclusively or even very heavily to a particular segment of the UK population, at least not for the range of grocery products analysed here. Instead, the tendency for one chain's buyers of a product to 'also buy' at another chain varies primarily with the latter's market share for that product. Market shares in turn reflect differences in the numbers of customers different chains attract (i.e. their penetrations) rather than differences in repeat-buying loyalty or frequency.

The observed patterns of store choice are very simple. Moreover, they are like those for brand choice and are predictable by the same models. This finding need not be altogether surprising. Brand-choice behaviour already has been found to be of the same general form under very different conditions (e.g. for more than forty varied product fields and for different countries such as the US and UK). Yet the underlying model of brand choice and purchase incidence (the Dirichlet) requires no specific property of a brand as input other than its market share. Hence no new parameters, variables, or concepts are needed for the model to apply to store choice.

The chains and store groups analysed differ in many ways – the number, size and location of their outlets, their ownership and styles (e.g. whether uniformly-managed chains or heterogeneous groupings of independent grocers or minor chains), their layout, the number and range of products carried, the number and choice of competitive brands carried (including private label), pricing policies, purchasing strength, and merchandising and promotional practices (which often have striking short-run effects). Products also differ greatly – whether food or non-food, by type of end user and consumption habits, by degree of brand differentiation, by advertising, by promotional strategies and tactics, etc. Finally, individual consumers also differ – e.g. demographically and by lifestyle, by usership experience and habits, by exposure to advertising, by price sensitivity, by their proximity to different shops, and by their working habits and mobility.

Differences in all these factors in the market-place will generally lead to the various sales levels or market shares which the different chains and store groups achieve. The close fit of the Dirichlet or related models, however, implies that after we allow for each chain's market share there are no intrinsic differences in any aggregate aspects of customer loyalty. Such a strong causal interpretation about the role of marketing-mix and market factors seems possible because it is negative. It is based on the *non*-correlation of all the other variables with consumers' observed patterns of buying after market share is partialled out. Lack of correlation implies lack of causation.

The simplicity of the results we report depends on studying chains (or brands) covering broadly the same geographic markets, or on making suitable allowances. Somewhat spotty geographic coverage may simply show up as a low market share. Wrigley and Dunn (1984b), however, show that within a single city the normal Dirichlet or Duplication Law patterns still arise for buying at *city-centre* stores with city-wide catchment areas, and also for *suburban* stores if suitable sub-populations 'at risk' are defined in terms of access.

More generally, consumers' relatively low loyalty to any particular chain need not be seen as a failure by that retailer to satisfy the customers or to provide enough reassurance by advertising, because all store groups show much the same patterns. Nor is it a failure of retailers in general because the same loyalty patterns apply when consumers choose between manufacturers' advertised brands.

Appendix: the theoretical models

The basic model used in this research is the Dirichlet (e.g. Goodhardt, Ehrenberg and Chatfield, 1984; see also Chatfield and Goodhardt, 1975; Jeuland, Bass and Wright, 1980). It is a theoretical formulation of all aspects of buyer behaviour – i.e. purchase incidence and store choice – in an unsegmented stationary (i.e. no-trend) market.

The model is a mixture of distributions at four levels: a Poisson-gamma (NBD) mixture of distributions for the purchase incidence for the product class, compounded by multinomial distributions of brand choice mixed across consumers by a multi-variate beta ('Dirichlet') distribution. We have used it because it fits for brands, and now also for store groups, and can theoretically be shown to be the only possible model in a strictly unsegmented stationary market (Goodhardt, Ehrenberg and Chatfield, 1984).

The model is very parsimonious. There is only one input variable, which represents the size of each chain (or alternatively the sales volume of the product class, plus the chains' market shares), and only two parameters. One of them measures how much consumers differ in their consumption of the product class; the other measures how much they differ in their store or brand preferences. No other inputs are needed. In particular, the only characterization of each chain or store group is its market share.

However, the model cannot be expressed in a simple closed form and is relatively cumbersome to estimate. We have therefore often used simpler sub-models, such as the earlier NBD for penetration growth and repeat buying and the Duplication of Purchase Law. These sub-models are easier to estimate and numerically give virtually the same results as the Dirichlet (see Goodhardt, Ehrenberg and Chatfield, 1984).

The NBD model

The NBD model is long established in marketing (e.g. Ehrenberg, 1959; 1972; Ehrenberg and Goodhardt, 1979). We use it to model penetration and purchase frequency (including repeat buying) at a particular chain under stationary no-trend conditions

(Tables 9.1–9.3) and for brands within a chain (Table 9.16). The penetration b_T in a period of length T relative to some 'unit' base period (T greater or less than 1) is given by:

$$b_T = 1 - (1 + Tbw/k)^{-k} \qquad [9.1]$$

The parameter k is calculated from the corresponding expression with $T = 1$, using the observed penetration b and average purchase frequency w for that time period. (A simplifying approximation is:

$$b_T/b = Tw/\{1 + (w - 1)\}T^{0.82} \qquad [9.2]$$

e.g. Ehrenberg, 1972.)

For the distribution of purchase frequencies (e.g. Table 9.3) the probability p_r of making r purchases in a time T can be calculated by the iterative formula:

$$p_r = \left(\frac{bwT}{k + bwT} \right)\left(1 - \frac{1 - k}{r} \right)p_{r-1} \qquad [9.3]$$

in terms of the probability p_{r-1} of making $(r - 1)$ purchases.

The Duplication of Purchase Law

The Duplication of Purchase Law pertains to $b_{E/C}$, the percentage of the persons who buy an item at least once at chain C who also buy it at least once at chain E. The law expresses $b_{E/C}$ as a fixed proportion of the penetration of chain E, i.e. $b_{E/C} = Db_E$. The duplication coefficient D is the same for all pairs of chains in an unsegmented market (Tables 9.7, 9.8, 9.12–9.15).

D usually is estimated from the observed duplications, e.g. as $D = (\text{av}.b_{E/C}/\text{av}.b_E)$ across all relevant chains or store groups. The Dirichlet model leads to variable duplication coefficients for different pairs of chains, but the differences usually are only in the second place of decimals (Goodhardt, Ehrenberg and Chatfield, 1984). The Duplication Law has been widely established for brand choice (e.g. Ehrenberg, 1972; Ehrenberg and Goodhardt, 1979) as well as for the overlap of the audiences of television programmes (e.g. Ehrenberg and Goodhardt, 1969b; Goodhardt, Ehrenberg and Collins, 1975; see also Leckenby and Kishi (1984) for an application of a multinomial Dirichlet mixture). Systematic exceptions to the Duplication Law – such as markedly high (or low) duplication values for particular pairs of chains – are remarkable for their scarcity (see Ehrenberg and Goodhardt (1979) for examples).

Acknowledgment

Reprinted from the *Journal of Marketing Research*, vol. 21 (1984), pp. 399–409; published by the American Marketing Association.

CHAPTER 10
Models of store choice and market analysis

Neil Wrigley and Richard Dunn

Introduction

Over the past twenty years, there has been a profound restructuring of the British retailing industry. This is particularly clear in the case of grocery retailing, where major retailing corporations (Sainsbury, Tesco, Asda, the Dee Corporation, the Argyll Group, etc.) have emerged and have expanded spectacularly so that they now dominate the market. For example, by 1984 the five corporations listed above had built up a combined market share of 43 per cent of UK grocery sales, compared to just 21 per cent for *all* UK independent grocers taken together. The large profits (e.g. £208 million in 1985–6 by Sainsbury – the sixth year on the run in which Sainsbury's profits had increased by more than 20 per cent) and huge positive net cash flows generated by these corporations, even in periods of economic recession, have financed major investment programmes, and there is scarcely a city or major town in Britain whose retail structure has not been transformed by the building of new superstores. This in turn, has had significant consequences for a number of traditional elements within the retail structure (independent retailers, cooperative stores, city-centre retailing areas, etc.) and for typical patterns of shopping behaviour for a large proportion of the population of Britain.

The expansion programmes of the major corporations have, in their turn, generated new demands on the academic research community. In the first place, there is the need to supply skilled manpower to staff the fast-expanding in-house 'store location and research units' which many of the larger corporations have now set up, and the specialist market analysis research consultancies (e.g. CACI, Pinpoint, etc.) which have flourished outside the corporations. Secondly, there is the need to supply new techniques which can be used by these in-house units and market analysis consultancies to assess the potential of store locations and to forecast the market performance of individual retail outlets.

In this chapter, an Economic and Social Research Council-funded research programme concerned primarily with providing such methods for retail analysis and forecasting purposes will be described. The programme builds upon the most comprehensive panel survey of urban shopping behaviour ever carried out in the UK; a survey which provides a major resource for understanding the nature of urban shopping behaviour in Britain in the 1980s, and for the development and testing of a new generation of models of store choice and market analysis.

A family of models for the analysis of store choice

Many of the models of consumer purchasing behaviour which are used most widely in commercial research in Britain today have their origins in a period (the 1950s and early 1960s) in which power in the retailing industry lay in the hands of the manufacturers rather than the retailers. As such, the models were developed in response to the needs of the manufacturers and, consequently, focused on methods of *brand-choice* analysis rather than *store-choice* analysis. Perhaps the most famous of these models is the NBD model of consumer purchasing behaviour developed by Chatfield *et al.* (1966). Many properties of this model were known by the late 1950s (Ehrenberg, 1959) and it has been applied extensively in commercial studies of brand purchasing for over twenty years (see Ehrenberg, 1972). During that period the NBD model has progressively been generalised (e.g. Chatfield and Goodhardt, 1975) to the point where it is now effectively subsumed as a special case of a more comprehensive model of consumer purchasing behaviour known as the Dirichlet model (Goodhardt *et al.*, 1984).

Although, in practice, the NBD model and its generalisations have been applied almost exclusively to the study of brand-purchasing behaviour, it has long been felt that such models may have equal validity and utility as models of consumer purchasing at stores or shopping centres. Indeed, an unpublished regional-level pilot study of the fit of the NBD model to purchasing behaviour at particular store-groups in the UK by Jephcott (1972) prompted one researcher to speculate that 'if these kinds of results can be extended it looks as though most of the present theory of brand-choice can be directly transferred to store-choice also' (Ehrenberg, 1972, p. 249).

In the intervening years the potential significance of this possible extension and transfer has increased. Beginning in the 1960s with the decline of resale price maintenance, and increasing in pace in the 1970s, a major shift in power has occurred in the British grocery retailing industry away from the manufacturers of grocery items and towards the rapidly expanding retail corporations. In its turn, this has led to a growing perception of the need to shift the focus of models of consumer purchasing behaviour from their traditional manufacturer/brand-choice orientation to a retailer/store-choice orientation. To this end, further exploratory studies of the possibility of transferring the NBD model from the context of brand-choice to store-choice were conducted in the UK by Wrigley (1980), Kau (1981) and Kau and Ehrenberg (1984). The results of these studies were both very similar and very encouraging. They suggested that consumer purchases of frequently bought non-durable goods (e.g. food and toiletries) at particular store-groups or store-types are highly predictable using the same models that had previously been successfully applied to the study of brand-choice. Unfortunately, a common limitation of these exploratory studies was that they all involved (by default) some element of aggregation: individual stores into store groups in Kau and Ehrenberg's regional-level studies; and individual stores into store types in Wrigley's urban-level investigation. If the NBD model and its generalisations were to provide models of the choice of *individual* stores, and the basis of a new generation of methods for forecasting the market performance of individual stores, then it was essential to establish how well the models performed at such a micro-level. In other words could the models be used to analyse and forecast the market performance of individual stores located across the wide spectrum of urban and suburban settings typical of British cities?

The Cardiff Consumer Panel

Assessment of the performance of the NBD and Dirichlet models at the level of individual stores required a geographical database of considerable size and detail. Ideally, continuous records of all aspects of the daily food and grocery shopping behaviour of a sizeable number of households located in a single city over, at least, a six-month period were required. Moreover, it was essential that such records contained information on the *locational* characteristics of such behaviour; in particular, the name and location of each store and shopping centre visited on each and every shopping trip. Unfortunately, no publicly accessible database of the required size, length and locational detail existed in the UK and so, with ESRC-funding, it was necessary to design and conduct a new and extensive consumer panel survey oriented to the needs of geographers, planners and retailers. This survey (see Wrigley *et al.*, 1985; Guy *et al.*, 1983) was conducted in the city of Cardiff over the six-month period January to July 1982, and is believed to have been the most comprehensive panel survey of urban shopping behaviour ever carried out in the UK.

The households included in the Cardiff Consumer Panel were located in eight sub-areas of the northern and eastern sectors of the city (see Figure 10.1) and were selected via a multi-stage stratified random design. The eight sub-areas included a large variety of housing types within both the private and public sectors of the market, and they were representative of a wide range of locational, accessibility and socio-economic conditions.

The time span of the survey was twenty-six weeks and consisted of a twenty-four-week main monitoring period plus a two-week 'running in' period. Six-hundred-and-five households were initially recruited to the panel, and these were reduced by a 'panel attrition' rate of 20 per cent to 481 households by the end of the main monitoring period (see Wrigley *et al.*, 1985). Finally, a further twenty-seven households whose purchasing records were non-continuous were removed from the data files, leaving a total of 454 'continuous reporting' households whose purchasing records constitute the final database used for analysis purposes. Detailed demographic, socio-economic and attitudinal information was obtained on each of these households, and this information shows that the 454 households used for analysis

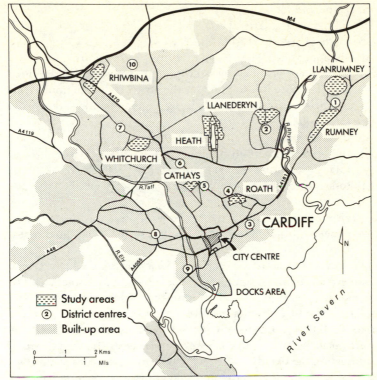

1 Countisbury Avenue 2 Maelfa 3 Leo's, Splott 4 Albany Road
5 Crwys Road 6 Whitchurch Road 7 Merthyr Road
8 Cowbridge Road East 9 Clare Road 10 Hoel-y-deri

Figure 10.1 The location of the study areas and district centres in Cardiff.

purposes include substantial numbers of virtually every type of population sub-group used in the description and analysis of urban shopping behaviour (including the old, the immobile and the unemployed).

In each of the households belonging to the Cardiff Consumer Panel the principal ('discretionary') food and grocery shopper was designated as the 'panellist' and that member of the household was trained by an experienced market research fieldworker to record all aspects of his/her shopping behaviour in a specially-designed weekly diary. From the diary, the following information could be obtained for each visit to each store:

(a) name and location of the store;
(b) time, day and date of the visit;
(c) mode of transport to the store;
(d) shopping trip origin and 'store tour' information, i.e. subsequent destinations on the same trip could be identified and therefore information on the structure of shopping trips could be recovered by chaining together information from different diary pages;
(e) a list of products purchased at the store;
(f) the brands of certain products purchased;
(g) total expenditure on food and grocery products at the store;
(h) total expenditure on non-food/non-grocery products at the store;
(i) an identification of whether the store visit was made by the panellist, other household member, or non-household member.

The basic information on each store visit was then reduced to one (sometimes two) computer records of eighty characters and, across the twenty-four-week monitoring period, this produced a total of 83,548 computer records covering expenditure of more than £250,000 and visits to over 1,000 different stores. Panellists were paid a minimum of £25, in stages, for successfully completing the twenty-four-week monitoring period. In addition, a considerable amount of money and effort was spent on panellist and fieldworker control, and on error-detection systems, in order to produce what is believed to be an unusually 'clean' data set of very high quality – a data set which is now available to all researchers via the ESRC Data Archive at the University of Essex.

Evaluation of the models of store choice

As soon as the Cardiff database became available for analysis in September 1982, an ESRC-funded programme of research on models of store-choice was started. The first and primary aim of this research was to assess the performance of the NBD and Dirichlet models as models of purchasing behaviour at individual stores and shopping centres. Full details of this research programme are provided elsewhere (e.g. Wrigley and Dunn,

1984a; 1984b; 1984c; 1985; Dunn *et al.*, 1983; 1986; Dunn and Wrigley, 1985) but its main features can be summarised as follows.

Testing the assumptions of the NBD model

Although the NBD model has a remarkably successful record as a model of brand-purchasing behaviour, its assumptions have been subject to considerable debate in the statistics and marketing literature. In the extension of the model to the context of purchasing at individual stores it was necessary, therefore, first to establish that these assumptions remained valid in the new context.

The two main assumptions of the NBD model of store purchasing behaviour are as follows.

(a) For any particular product, different consumers are assumed to have different average purchasing rates at any individual store and these purchasing rates are assumed to have a gamma distribution across consumers.

(b) For each consumer, the number of purchases made at a particular store in successive equal time-periods are assumed to be independent and to follow a Poisson distribution. This, in turn, implies that inter-purchase times at the store are exponentially distributed.

From these two assumptions it follows that the frequency distribution of purchases at a particular store in any single time-period should have a negative binomial distribution across the sample as a whole. (Note that this is an empirically testable deduction, *not* an assumption.)

Results of testing these assumptions and deductions using the Cardiff Consumer Panel data are reported in Dunn *et al.* (1983). The following findings are of most importance.

(a) The Poisson assumption appears to hold for the great majority of buyers, and it is only very heavy buyers who have significantly more regular inter-purchase times than expected under the Poisson assumption.

(b) The fit of the negative binomial distribution is particularly good for individual stores, especially stores which occupy an accessible central location in the city (see Table 10.1). For

Table 10.1 The fit of the NBD at individual stores: purchases of toilet tissue at particular stores in 24 weeks

| | Central stores | | | | Suburban stores | | | | | |
| | Tesco City Centre | | Leo's Superstore | | Co-op, Countisbury Avenue | | | International, Maelfa | | | |
Number of purchases	O	T	O	T	O	T City-wide sample	T Local sample	O	T City-wide sample	T Local sample
0	326	326	366	366	371 (43)*	371	43	409 (10*)	409	10
1	43	43	29	27	12	22	16	7	12	6
2	20	22	13	14	10	11	10	6	6	5
3–4	23	24	14	15	12	13	14	8	7	7
5–6	18	13	5	8	8	8	9	2	4	5
7–9	9	11	7	8	11	8	9	2	4	5
10–14	5	8	8	7	15	7	10	5	4	6
15–19	6	4	8	4	4	4	5	8	2	4
20+	4	3	4	5	11	10	10	7	6	7

* The observed number of non-buyers for the local sample is shown in parentheses. The local sample size is 126 for Co-op, Countisbury Avenue, and 55 for International, Maelfa. The city-wide sample size is 454.
O = Observed, T = theoretical.

suburban stores, certain small but consistent discrepancies occur which are largely attributable to the differential accessibility of consumers and which can be removed by refitting the model to the 'relevant population', i.e. a sub-sample of the panel members who reside in the local trade area of the store.

Taken together, these conclusions indicate that the assumptions of the NBD model hold up very well in the new context of purchasing at individual stores, though the model must be fitted with due sensitivity to the geography of the retail environment in the study area.

NBD model predictions of the market performance of individual stores

From the NBD model, predictions of seven important indices of the market performance of individual stores can be obtained (Wrigley and Dunn, 1984a). Table 10.2, for example, shows, for one particular product, the observed and predicted levels of market penetration for eight of the most frequently-visited stores by the Cardiff panellists, and the growth in market penetration from periods of one week in length to twenty-four weeks. Table 10.3 shows the observed and predicted average purchase frequencies of the same product across the same time periods; similar tables can also be obtained for the proportions and sales importance of light and heavy buyers at particular stores, the incidence and purchasing frequency of repeat buyers and new buyers at particular stores, and the structure of repeat buying at individual stores conditional upon previous purchasing levels.

Often, as in Tables 10.2 and 10.3, the NBD predictions are found to be extremely close to the observed figures (though sometimes the fit can be marginally improved for suburban stores by calibrating the model on a sub-sample of panellists who reside in the local trade area of the store). As such, it is clear that the model provides a wide range of market-relevant predictions which can be exploited for forecasting purposes. However, the NBD predictions also have a second role to play; that of providing a series of benchmarks or reference points (often termed 'stationary norms') which can be used to isolate observed values which are

Table 10.2 Growth of market penetration: the percentage of households in the Cardiff Consumer Panel who buy instant coffee at particular stores in time periods of various lengths

Period of length (in weeks)

Store	1		4		8		12		24	
	O	T	O	T	O	T*	O	T	O	T
Tesco, City Centre	3	3	9	9	12	(12)	15	15	22	20
Kwiksave, Merthyr Road	4	4	9	9	12	(12)	13	14	17	18
Tesco, Albany Road	3	2	7	7	10	(10)	12	12	16	16
Kwiksave, Albany Road	3	2	7	7	10	(10)	12	12	16	16
Leo's	2	2	5	5	8	(8)	9	9	12	12
Co-op, Countisbury Ave.	2	2	5	5	7	(7)	8	8	11	11
Lipton's, Countisbury Ave.	2	2	4	4	7	(7)	8	8	10	10
International, Maelfa	2	2	4	4	6	(6)	6	7	8	9

O = observed values, T = theoretical NBD predictions.
* Eight-week values used in calibration.

Table 10.3   Growth of frequency of buying: the average number of purchases per buyer of instant coffee at particular stores in time periods of various lengths

Period of length (in weeks)

	1		4		8		12		24	
	O	T	O	T	O	T*	O	T	O	T
Tesco, City Centre	1.0	1.2	1.5	1.6	2.1	(2.1)	2.5	2.6	3.5	3.8
Kwiksave, Merthyr Road	1.0	1.3	2.0	2.1	3.0	(3.0)	4.1	3.8	6.6	6.0
Tesco, Albany Road	1.0	1.2	1.6	1.7	2.4	(2.4)	3.0	2.9	4.2	4.4
Kwiksave, Albany Road	1.0	1.2	1.6	1.7	2.3	(2.3)	2.9	2.8	4.4	4.3
Leo's Superstore	1.0	1.2	1.7	1.8	2.5	(2.5)	3.1	3.1	4.5	4.7
Co-op, Countisbury Ave.	1.1	1.3	1.9	2.0	2.8	(2.8)	3.6	3.6	5.4	5.5
Lipton's, Countisbury Ave.	1.0	1.2	1.7	1.7	2.3	(2.3)	2.8	2.8	4.4	4.2
International, Maelfa	1.1	1.3	1.9	1.9	2.7	(2.7)	3.6	3.4	5.7	5.2

O = observed values, T = theoretical NBD predictions.
* Eight-week values used in calibration.

significantly 'greater than expected' or 'less than expected'. In other words, the NBD predictions can be used to identify atypical (and/or non-stationary) patterns of store-purchasing behaviour, and these anomalies (which may result from product promotion strategies or weakness in the market performance of the store) can then be the object of more detailed analysis.

An example of this second role of the NBD predictions is illustrated in Table 10.4. Here the patterns of repeat buying across five product fields at one particular store (Leo's Superstore) conditional upon levels of purchasing in the previous eight-week period are shown. A significant shortfall of repeat buyers can be observed, and this appears to be due entirely to light buyers (those who bought just once in the previous eight-week period) failing to repeat buy as often as expected. Subjecting this anomaly to more detailed analysis reveals that it was caused by a series of promotion campaigns undertaken by the store. These campaigns succeeded in attracting households to the store for a single, perhaps exploratory, visit but, in general, failed to retain them; in that sense they failed to convert the households into regular customers.

Table 10.4   Repeat buying patterns at Leo's Superstore: the percentage of households who buy particular products at the store in one eight-week period (t) by purchasing level in the previous eight-week period $(t - 1)$

| | *Households who in the first eight-week period (t–1) were* | | | | | |
| | *Non-buyers* | | *Once-only buyers* | | *More-than once buyers* | |
Product field	*O*	*T*	*O*	*T*	*O*	*T*
Fabric conditioners	2	2	38	45	88	82
Instant coffee	3	3	34	46	88	82
Margarine	5	4	20	48	80	86
Toilet tissue	4	4	39	48	83	86
Baked beans	5	4	28	48	83	85

O = observed, T = theoretical.

Multi-store purchasing patterns and the Dirichlet model

The NBD model, which treats individual stores (or brands) separately, is a special case of the more comprehensive Dirichlet model. This more general model (see Goodhardt *et al.*, 1984; Wrigley and Dunn, 1984b) combines sub-models of purchase incidence and the probability of selecting a particular store (or brand). As a result, it takes account of multi-store (multi-brand) purchasing patterns and, in addition to being able to provide all the predictions associated with the NBD model, provides other predictions. These allow the assessment of such issues as:

(a) the linkages which exist between individual stores (or brands);
(b) the degree of store (or brand) loyalty in the market;
(c) the amount of store (or brand) switching which is occurring;
(d) the number of 100-per-cent-loyal or 'sole buyers' which individual stores (or brands) are likely to have in periods of different length.

The model is derived from five distributional assumptions: two concerning store (or brand) choice; two concerning purchase incidence; and one concerning their interrelationship. The two purchase-incidence assumptions are the usual Poisson and gamma assumptions of the NBD model, and to these are added two assumptions concerning the probability of selecting particular stores (or brands). For store choice these are that:

(a) each consumer i has a fixed set of probabilities $(P_1, P_2 \ldots P_{\mathcal{J}})_i$ of shopping at store $1 \ldots \mathcal{J}$; and that
(b) these probabilities vary from consumer to consumer and are distributed across consumers as a multivariate beta or Dirichlet distribution.

The final assumption states that the store-choice and purchase-incidence components of the model are independent; this implies that the distribution of store-choice probabilities is the same for light, medium and heavy buyers.

Although some initial extensions of the Dirichlet model from its original context of brand purchasing to purchasing within store-groups at a regional level in the UK were made by Kau and Ehrenberg (1984), research on the Cardiff Consumer Panel data has provided the first application of the model at the level of individual stores. Results of the work confirm the often remarkable predictive accuracy of the Dirichlet model, and its ability to provide a series of benchmarks ('stationary norms') which allow the atypical patterns of purchasing behaviour to be identified and investigated. As in the case of the NBD, it is important to calibrate the Dirichlet model on a relevant geographical sample. For stores in suburban centres this generally means a sub-area of the city, whilst for city-centre stores a city-wide context is usually appropriate.

Fitting the Dirichlet model to the Cardiff data has highlighted the marked degree of switching between stores to buy the *same* product or brand of a product which occurs amongst urban consumers. For example, in a six-month period, Cardiff panellists tend to buy a given product two or three times more often at *other* stores than at a given store, and typically, as Table 10.5 shows, more than 70 per cent of consumers in a twenty-four-week period are *not* store-loyal even for purchases of just a single product-field. However, within this overall high level of store switching, a feature which is termed duplication of purchasing, is, in general, highly predictable. As Table 10.6 shows, 'duplication' is defined as the percentage of buyers at a particular store who buy at other specified stores in the same time period.

Table 10.5 The percentage of buyers of the product-field instant coffee amongst the Cardiff panellists who buy at 1, 2, 3 . . . stores in 24 weeks

Number of stores	% of buyers	Number of stores	% of buyers	Number of stores	% of buyers
1	27.6	5	5.8	8	0.5
2	30.1	6	4.3	9	0.0
3	18.0	7	1.3	10+	0.0
4	12.4				

The main feature of Table 10.6 is the relative stability within columns; a stability which is observable at particular geographical scales and which can be predicted by the Dirichlet model when calibrated on a corresponding geographical sample. In the majority of cases, this stability indicates that there is no marked linkage in patronage terms between pairs of stores. However,

Table 10.6   Store duplication of purchase in 24 weeks by panellists located in the Rumney/Llanrumney sub-area of Cardiff for the product-field instant coffee

Buyers at	Who also bought at				
	Co-op, Countisbury Avenue	Liptons, Countisbury Avenue	International, Countisbury Avenue	Tesco, City Centre	Leo's
Co-op, Countisbury Avenue	—	42	34	28	24
Liptons, Countisbury Avenue	47	—	38	22	20
International, Countisbury Avenue	55	55	—	29	16
Tesco, City Centre	52	37	33	—	26
Leo's	60	45	25	35	—
Average duplication	53	45	33	29	22
Predicted duplication	52	47	32	28	21
Penetration	40	36	25	21	16

Duplication = the percentage of panellists who, having bought at a particular store, also buy at another store.

stores which exhibit unusual levels of linkage can be clearly picked out in such tables by high or low duplication values, and these stores can then form the basis of further investigation.

A high degree of store or brand switching by urban consumers implies complex patterns of store and brand choice interaction, and there seems to be no clear evidence of store choice preceding brand choice or the reverse. In this context, the Dirichlet model has a second potential use; to model either brand choice within a given store, or store choice for a given brand. Using the Cardiff data, Wrigley and Dunn (1984c) have adopted the former approach and have used a within-stores Dirichlet model to help unravel some of the complex interactions between store and brand choice. They suggest that the 'within-stores Dirichlet' may have great potential value in a two-stage approach to the analysis of store and brand choice and that it has immediate practical utility in the assessment of specific market promotions, either of the store as a whole or of specific brands within the store.

As an example of the latter possibility, consider Table 10.7 which shows the duplication of purchase patterns of individual brands of baked beans purchased by a sub-sample of just seventy-

Table 10.7 Brand duplication in 24 weeks within a small suburban store (Co-op, Countisbury Avenue) for the product-field baked beans

Buyers at Co-op, Countisbury Ave., of brand	Who also at Co-op, Countisbury Ave., bought			
	Heinz	*HP*	*Private label*	*Crosse & Blackwell*
Heinz (43)	—	37	35	21
HP (34)	47	—	35	27
Private label (33)	46	36	—	27
Crosse & Blackwell (23)	39	39	39	—
Average duplication	44	38	36	25
Predicted duplication	46	37	35	25
Penetration	55	44	42	30

Figures in table are percentages.
Overall sample size from which table generated = 78. Numbers buying each particular brand shown in parentheses.

eight Cardiff panellists, within one small suburban store (Co-op, Countisbury Avenue). Despite the very small number of panellists buying each particular brand, both regularities associated with duplication of purchase tables are present:

(a) the figures within each column of the table are roughly constant; and

(b) the average duplication of the brands is predictable.

Most importantly, specific marketing promotions within the store for particular brands can then be assessed against these benchmark regularities. For example, a promotion of the store-group's own private label of the product (or the store-group's own-brand products in general) might draw differentially from other brands, and this ability of the store's own-brands to erode the competition of national brands differentially (within the particular context of an individual store) would show up clearly in a pattern of unusually high or low duplication figures.

Introducing exogenous variables into the NBD and Dirichlet models

The NBD and Dirichlet models in their conventional form do not incorporate individual-level exogenous variables relating to the socio-economic, demographic, attitudinal and locational characteristics of the panel members or to the attributes of the stores visited. However, such information will normally be recorded in consumer panel surveys, and there is considerable potential in attempting to introduce this information into the models. A second objective of the ESRC research programme was to extend the NBD and Dirichlet models in this fashion. It was believed that these extensions would considerably increase the potential of the models, since they would:

(a) permit identification of those characteristics of consumers which significantly influence their purchasing behaviour;

(b) allow a behavioural input into the stochastic models; and

(c) allow the predictions of the models to be disaggregated and made conditional upon the values of the exogenous variables.

Essentially, the technique for incorporating exogenous variables into the NBD and Dirichlet models relies upon making certain parameters of the models functions of a set of explanatory variables (see Wrigley and Dunn, 1985, for further details). A maximum likelihood estimation procedure is then used to determine the appropriate specification of the set of variables for the particular sample of consumers in question. Following this, disaggregated versions of all the usual predictions of the models are obtained, i.e. predictions which are conditional upon the set of exogenous explanatory variables – the individual-level characteristics of the panel members, and/or the stores visited.

Tables 10.8 and 10.9 show typical examples of the type of disaggregated predictions obtained from the extended NBD and Dirichlet models. In these cases only categorical exogenous variables have been used (household type, car ownership, employment status of the housewife) and this is equivalent to dividing the total Cardiff sample into sub-groups. Such tables can be used with great effectiveness to assess any weaknesses (or strengths) in the market performance of individual stores *vis-à-vis* particular market segments; for example, does the Tesco city-centre store have any unexpected weaknesses in its ability to draw patronage from two-wage-earner car-owning households, or is patronage from this market segment in line with what might be expected? In this way one can 'target' such market segments for selective store promotions, and can operationalise the promotion by linking to the ACORN-type census clusters marketed by firms such as CACI, Pinpoint, etc.

A second major use of the extended NBD and Dirichlet models is to forecast the effect of changes in urban planning and retail policy. For example, the extended models can be used to forecast the store-choice or shopping-centre-choice effects which might follow from:

(a) changes in the urban transport system which alter the accessibility of particular stores or shopping centres;
(b) the development of new areas of housing.

In addition, it is possible (though this work is still in the development stage) that the extended NBD and Dirichlet models can be linked to 'stated preference' (experimental choice) methods (see Chapters 7 and 8) to provide improved techniques for forecasting the effects on store or shopping-centre choice which follow from the opening of new retail outlets or shopping centres, or from the closure of existing elements within the retail system.

Table 10.8 Disaggregated NBD predictions: penetration growth of the Tesco store in Cardiff city centre, product-field baked beans

Household type	Time period (weeks)											
	1		4		8		12		24		
	O	T	O	T	O	T	O	T	O	T	O	T*
Whole sample	4	4	10	11	16	(16)	19	19	25	25
Households with children	5	4	12	12	17	(17)	21	21	27	27
Adult families	4	3	10	10	15	(15)	19	19	25	25
One- or two-person households	2	2	6	6	10	(10)	13	12	18	17

O represents observed values; T represents theoretical predictions.
* The eight-week values were used in calibration.

Table 10.9 Disaggregated Dirichlet predictions of market penetration for particular market segments of the panellists in one sub-area of Cardiff (Rumney/Llanrumney); product-field, baked beans; time period 24 weeks

Store	Household type[1] whole sample		A		B		C		D	
	O	T	O	T	O	T	O	T	O	T
1 Co-op CA	62	63	59	49	48	56	56	69	73	74
2 Liptons CA	46	46	35	36	52	49	39	40	53	54
3 International, CA	39	38	41	39	32	31	44	48	39	38
4 Leo's Superstore	25	25	35	38	32	26	28	24	14	16
5 Tesco CC	23	23	26	31	24	18	33	32	16	18
6 Other stores	64	63	74	63	64	70	50	56	63	62

[1] The household types are (with sample size in parentheses): A, car-owning with wife in employment (34); B, car-owning with wife not in employment (25); C, no car and wife in employment (18); D, no car and wife not in employment (49). The whole sample size is 126.

Conclusion

The results of recent research in the UK confirm that the NBD and Dirichlet models of buying behaviour can usefully and successfully be transferred from the study of brand choice to the study of store choice. Furthermore, the NBD and Dirichlet models can be extended to incorporate a wide range of exogenous variables relating to the demographic, socio-economic, attitudinal and locational characteristics of consumers or to the attributes of stores or shopping centres visited. Both conventional and 'extended' NBD and Dirichlet models provide a wealth of market-relevant predictions and/or benchmarks for the assessment of the market performance of stores, and the models have great potential for academic researchers, retailers and urban planners. The task is now to build on these initial results and to develop a package of methods which can be adopted as standard tools of market analysis by the store location and research units of the major retail corporations.

CHAPTER 11
Patterns of store choice: new evidence from the USA

Mark D. Uncles and Andrew S. C. Ehrenberg

Introduction

Large amounts of data are collected by market research companies describing store choice; these show where consumers shop, how often, whether a product is bought at several stores, and whether they return to the same outlets as before. We are beginning to acquire an understanding of these and many related topics about buyer behaviour. Moreover, with the spread of scanner panels at chains and individual stores the research effort is set to expand. Commercial interest is increasing too, especially now that national retailers have such a high profile in the grocery trade.

Our aim is to describe some patterns of consumer behaviour which are relevant to retailers and marketers. Illustration is in terms of the US coffee market using data from the MRCA consumer panel. To this end, a short account of the retail distribution system is first provided. We then investigate how consumers behave; this is done by looking at store patronage, how often customers buy at a store and elsewhere, the effect of increasing the analysis period and similarities between stores.

A special feature of our approach is the use of theoretical predictions which are consistent with observed behaviour. The Dirichlet model provides a working framework enabling us to derive theoretical norms. From the fit between actual and theoretical patterns we conclude that consumer choices are essentially regular, generalisable and predictable. Indeed, store choice is regular in a way that has been established over many years for brand choice, and this is true of the UK and US.

Our findings are presented in the third section. They show that:

(a) at a single chain the number of buyers increases quite fast with lengthening analysis periods, whereas the growth in purchase frequency is relatively slow;

(b) sales across leading chains and other store groups differ mainly because they have different numbers of buyers, rather than because their average purchase frequencies differ much;

(c) most buyers at one chain buy more of the product from other chains;

(d) generally two chains only share the number of customers that their sheer market shares warrant.

These results depend on the unique role of market share, rather than on a detailed knowledge of the marketing mix. The only other major consideration is where the trading areas of two chains do not coincide.

Finally, we discuss the utility of the results and remark upon some topics where active research is being pursued.

Background

New evidence from the United States is used to study some aspects of store choice. Data for 1981 come from the on-going diary panel operated by MRCA. Our attention here is focused on sales of instant coffee, although we have found the same regular patterns among many other products, including ground coffee. Within the coffee market the instant sector has been expanding, largely because of consumer preference for convenient decaffeinated brands. Of all coffee purchases on the MRCA panel, about 40 per cent are for instants, a third of which are decaffeinated varieties.

Brands which dominate the retail market include Maxim (General Foods), Taster's Choice (Nestlé) and High Point (Procter & Gamble). Most supermarkets and convenience stores stock a variety of brands – national, regional and own-label. Retail margins on instant coffee average only 12 per cent (gross). However many retailers see coffee as a 'traffic builder' and some have increased the shelf space devoted to this product (Harvard Business School, 1982; Katz and Shapiro, 1984).

Here we treat separately those chains which sell the largest amounts of instant coffee. Most important among major operators is the Kroger Co. Nationwide, its market share is 4.3 per cent. Other major store chains include A & P, Safeway, Winn Dixie and Lucky Stores, with market shares ranging from 3.7 per cent to 2.2 per cent. Apart from these chains several other categories of store are distinguished. Other named chains (NCs) have market shares just below the retail leaders; they tend to be large and have marked regional strengths (such as Jewel Food Stores, half of its sales coming from Illinois alone). Next are unnamed chains (UCs); usually these are of local importance. Co-ops, discount stores and cash-and-carry warehouses, such as Super Valu and K-Mart, are grouped together. A miscellaneous category covers health-food stores, drug stores and non-grocery outlets.

It is against this background that we examine consumer behaviour within the retail coffee market. Specifically, the principal regularities underlying consumers' choice of where to shop are identified. We do this by responding to six marketing questions. Two refer to buying at individual chains.

(a) How many customers does a chain have?

(b) How often do they buy instant coffee there?

A further three questions apply to buying among different chains.

(c) How often do they buy it elsewhere?

(d) How do chains differ in these respects?

(e) What groupings of chains (partitioning) shows up?

Findings are summarised by asking.

(f) What explanatory variables do we need?

Results

How many customers does a chain have?

The number of households who buy instant coffee at a store, at least once, in a single time period is what we mean by patronage. There are about 100 million households in the United States and the data show that 68 million of these buy instant coffee, at least once, in forty-eight weeks (a year). Alternatively, the number of households buying a product is expressed as the percentage of all buyers, so 68 per cent of households buy in one year. With increasing time periods the number who buy at least once rises;

10 per cent buy instant coffee in one week, 46 per cent in twelve weeks and, as we have seen, 68 per cent buy in a year.

A & P, an individual chain, captures 3.7 per cent of the retail instant-coffee market, and sells both national and its own-label items. Roughly 300,000 households shop at A & P in one week, and a similar number shop there during the next week under stationary conditions. But many of these are not the same buyers; we are seeing new buyers at the chain, week by week. Therefore, patronage rises twenty-fold from just over 300,000 households in an average week to almost 6 million annually (5.5 million, more precisely). Patronage growth flattens off because the pool of potential new buyers at A & P tends to dwindle; this is purely a facet of the increasing length of time span.

A smooth relationship exists between patronage and lengthening time periods. This raises the question: Are we observing a pattern that is general and predictable? Repeated observation over many years has shown that patterns of brand penetration are both general and predictable, and sufficient evidence exists now to confirm that patterns of store patronage are like those for brand penetration. The NBD model has long provided the necessary theory (Ehrenberg, 1972). Recently a major extension has been made, giving what we know as the Dirichlet model (Goodhardt *et al.*, 1984). In practice, these models give almost identical predictions of patronage.

Reconsidering A & P, in a week 0.3 million households are observed to patronise this chain (0.3 million predicted), 2.4 million in an average quarter (2.5 predicted), while annually 5.5 million shop there (5.5 million predicted) – there is no discrepancy between observed and predicted patronage in the latter case. The form of this theoretical relationship and the array of observed deviations is plotted in Figure 11.1. The fit is close and the data are very adequately described by theory.

Thus, patronage is the number of customers that a chain has. With increasing time periods patronage maps out a slowly declining growth curve, the form of which is predictable. These predictions offer good descriptions of observed behaviour.

How often do they buy instant coffee there?

Buying frequency depends on the number of visits to a store when

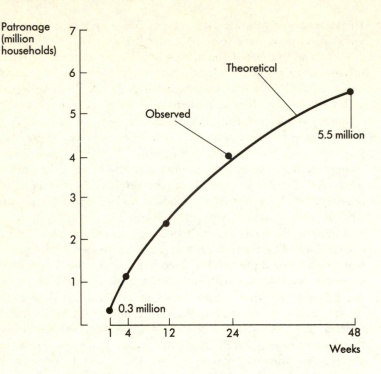

Figure 11.1 Patronage growth at the A & P chain. Millions of households buying instant coffee, at least once, in increasing time periods, at A & P.

instant coffee is bought. Buyers at A & P purchase instant coffee there 3.0 times annually. Yet among those who buy in an average week only 1.2 purchases are made (and even this frequency is unusually high). As was true for patronage, with time periods of increasing duration the frequency of buying rises. Growth in the average number of purchases, however, is much shallower than for patronage. In rounded terms:

Each week   about 0.3 million buy it 1.2 times.
Over a year   almost 6.0 million buy it 3.0 times.

Patronage increases twenty times whereas frequency rises no more than two-and-a-half times. As more households buy at A & P, at least once, their rate of buying does not increase *pro rata*. This confirms that some additional buyers have a minimal effect on sales. Indeed, there is a spread of purchase incidence rates. Many buyers visit the store just once and others seldom repeat their purchases there. Sales strategies will be affected by these variations. Retailers, therefore, need to determine how often buyers patronise their stores, and then distinguish between 'heavy' and 'light' buyers.

The basic relationships are summarised by the sales equation:

Sales = Patronage × Average Purchase Frequency

Weekly sales at A & P are roughly 0.36 million purchases (0.3 million × 1.2 times = 0.36 million). Annual sales amount to 18 million purchases (almost 6.0 million × 3.0 times = 18 million). This represents about a fifty-fold increase in cumulative sales from the average week to a year.

These patterns of consumer behaviour are predictable from the Dirichlet model. Purchase frequencies at A & P are 1.2 times weekly (1.1 predicted) and 3.0 times annually (3.0 predicted). In the annual record there is a perfect fit; indeed across all time-lengths the fit is close. Because the model fits so well, sales can be predicted too; at A & P 0.36 million items are sold each week and 17 million sold during the year, both predictions being almost equivalent to observed figures.

We see, therefore, that average purchase frequency refers to how often households buy instant coffee at a store or chain. The growth of these frequencies with increasing time is shallow, but predictable. Sales are calculated from the product of patronage and rates of buying.

Light and heavy buyers It is worth pausing to think why frequencies exhibit only a shallow rise and what are the implications for retail sales. Here we refer to the total usage of instant coffee, then we show that many customers buy at several chains. The first point to note is that many customers are infrequent buyers of the product, regardless of which store they choose. Confining ourselves to an average quarter for the moment, we find that 41 per cent of instant coffee buyers make just one purchase and only 20 per cent are heavy buyers making at least four purchases (in total).

At a single chain the proportion who are light once-only buyers is even greater; 64 per cent of customers at A & P buy instant there just once during a quarter, and a mere 7 per cent buy at least four times. This is predictable too:

> 64% buy there only once   (64% predicted)
> 21% buy there twice   (20% predicted)
> 9% buy there three times   (8% predicted)
> 7% buy there more often   (8% predicted)

Generally, purchase frequencies are heavily skewed towards once-only buying, and predictably so. This scatter reflects the range of light and heavy buyers. Deviations from the purely statistical pattern of light and heavy buying might be put down to the difficulty of reaching some stores in the choice set on a regular basis (distance, access to transport, etc.), but this effect will be slight.

The large proportion of light buyers and relatively low rates of repeat-buying at individual chains raise a number of questions. For instance, is the total usage of instant coffee light? And do customers choose to shop at several store groups? That many customers buy elsewhere is something we study next.

How often do they buy it elsewhere?

Generally buyers at one chain also buy instant coffee from other chains. Customers patronising A & P in a year buy the product there 3.0 times; however these customers buy the product much more often (9.8 times) in total. The difference of 6.8 purchases indicates how often they buy it elsewhere. More than twice as many purchases are made elsewhere as at A & P.

Extensive switching between chains indicates that customers are not particularly loyal. Indeed, after forty-eight weeks just 11 per cent of customers at A & P are sole buyers there, and most of these are infrequent or once-only buyers. In fact customers purchase more often from other chains than from a specific chain – 6.8 times as against 3.0 times in the case of A & P. And Dirichlet predictions replicate this – 6.3 times elsewhere compared with almost 3.0 times at A & P itself.

Switching between chains is largely predicted without making special assumptions – the Dirichlet model describes the data very well. Only where discrepancies exist might we wish to distinguish principal trips destined for distant supermarkets from 'topping up' visits at local grocers, or refer to store trading hours, what else is bought on a trip, retail stocks, and so forth. Patterns of switching are usually far simpler than is suggested by all these possible influences.

What we are revealing is the extent of consumer choice and the competitive environment in which retailers operate. A deeper knowledge of these issues is gained by looking at regularities across chains and by discovering exactly which other chains are patronised.

How do chains differ in these respects?

To a first order of approximation there is little difference from chain to chain in the average frequencies of buying at a chain or elsewhere. This is the overriding conclusion. Both observed and theoretical buying frequencies average about three times for a chain and about six times elsewhere. Not only is the correspondence between observed and theoretical values very close; in addition, deviations from the mean are slight. Buying frequencies at A & P are like those associated with Kroger, and Co-ops, and even the major groupings of chains.

Figure 11.2 presents this information graphically (see also the Appendix). For buyers at each chain (shown along the base) vertical bars are drawn; these are proportional to the annual number of purchases at the chain itself and at other chains. They are all roughly three or four times per year, irrespective of market share. Superimposed on the graph are asterisks to denote theoretical values and to highlight the accuracy of Dirichlet predictions. The few discrepancies that exist may be due to small sample sizes (only ninety panellists shop at Lucky in a year) or the effect of differential trade areas.

There is something of a systematic difference between big and small chains. Among big chains the ratio of buying at one chain and elsewhere is smaller; in fact the number of purchases is split evenly between both categories. This slight departure from the mean is normal and predictable. But the main conclusion is hardly affected – there remains little difference from chain to chain – but an interesting subsidiary issue is raised, to which we shall return.

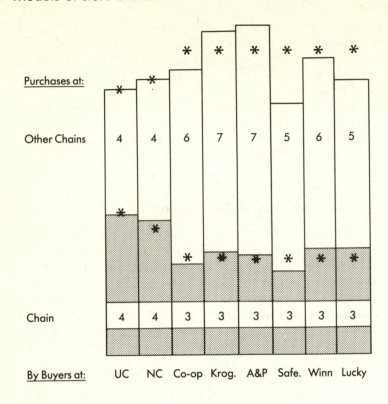

Figure 11.2 Average purchase frequency of instant coffee at stated chain and elsewhere in 48 weeks. Observed = bars, theoretical = *, both by market share.

To put the variations in Figure 11.2, in perspective we compare them against patronage. During a year just 3.2 million households shop at Lucky; by contrast 5.5 million patronise A & P, while 13 million shop at Co-ops. If chains are arranged in order of market share, a plot of patronage shows that the two measures parallel one another. Patronage varies with market share (Figure 11.3). A & P has a market share of 3.7 per cent and patronage lies at 5.5 million, whereas unnamed chains have a market share of 45 per cent and observed patronage is 49 million.

Superimposed on Figure 11.3 are the average purchase frequencies from the previous diagram. Patronage changes in line

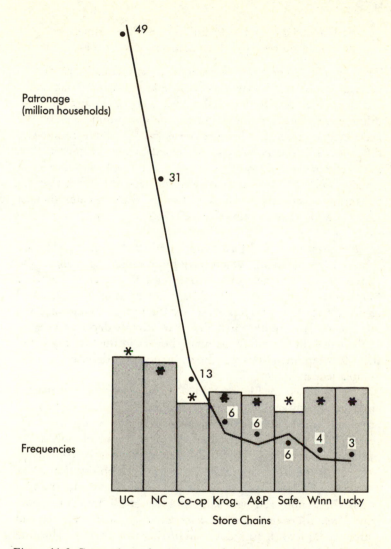

Figure 11.3 Comparison of patronage and average purchase frequency at chains selling instant coffee in 48 weeks. Observed = line, theoretical = *, both by market share.

with market shares, whereas the variation among frequencies is slight:

> At Unnamed Chains   49 million buy it 4.2 times.
> At Lucky Stores   3 million buy it 3.2 times.

Throughout, theoretical values convey an equally consistent message (these are shown as asterisks and dots on the diagram).

Sales matter most to the retailer, so it is critical to find that sales differ mainly because chains have different numbers of buyers (patronage), rather than because the average purchase frequencies differ much. Annual sales at unnamed chains amount to 206 million items, some twenty-one-fold more than volume sales at Lucky Stores. The major reason for this difference is that patronage at unnamed chains is sixteen times greater than at Lucky, rather than 1.3 times more frequent.

Double jeopardy   We have concluded that higher sales are achieved among chains which have more buyers (patronage and market share), rather than from variable average purchase frequencies. 'However, a subsidiary effect is observed; small chains attract fewer buyers who buy the product somewhat less often there. Apparently small chains are doubly deprived because of their inability to attract as many buyers in the first place and then to keep them buying there; hence the descriptive term 'double jeopardy'.

This is shown by Figure 11.3. Patronage depends on market share, as already stressed, but frequencies also decline slightly. At large unnamed and named chains over four purchases are recorded, whereas at individual chains a mean of only three purchases is achieved. This situation reflects double jeopardy.

Rarely is the effect dramatic, yet it has been observed in many situations. A related analysis of the US coffee market (for brands) shows that, compared with large brands, small brands not only have fewer users but they are somewhat less loyal (Uncles and Ehrenberg, 1986). British data add further confirmation, showing that purchase frequencies at independents are roughly two-thirds those at Cooperatives – the former, however, has one-fifth the number of instant coffee buyers and these are less committed, so it is doubly deprived (Kau, 1981; Kau and Ehrenberg, 1984).

The double jeopardy effect is also predicted very well from theory. Predictions of annual purchase frequencies fall from 4.3 for unnamed chains (4.2 observed) to 2.8 for Lucky (3.2 observed). Large chains have somewhat more committed users than smaller ones, but usually not that much.

A number of marketing implications stem from these observations. Maintenance of a chain's market share continues to be the dominant issue. If there are deviations from the pattern of double jeopardy then retailers might have some scope for movement – by reappraising their image, creating a higher profile, or building up good customer relations. But these strategic actions only apply where there are slight anomalies (see Jephcott, 1972; Jeuland *et al.*, 1980; Dunn and Wrigley, 1984). The main scope for retailers is to achieve more, or to defend, patronage.

What grouping of chains (partitioning) shows up?

Earlier we asked how often customers at a chain buy the product elsewhere. The answer was roughly twice as often in a year. Now we ask, at which chains do customers make these other purchases? The main idea in accounting for multi-store purchasing patterns is 'duplication'. A chain's duplication is the percentage of buyers of instant coffee who also buy it at another chain. By definition all A & P buyers purchase from A & P (100 per cent duplication). Over half these buyers also obtain the product from unnamed and named chains, while a negligible 2 per cent also patronise Lucky Stores, in line with its small market share.

The full set of duplication percentages for A & P is presented in Table 11.1. Appended to this table are patronage figures, i.e. the number of buyers attracted by the second chain (listed across the table). Excluding the 100 per cent entry, we see that patronage and duplication decline simultaneously. The correlation between these rows is 0.97. Experience from numerous such studies of brand choice accords with this newer evidence; duplication varies with patronage. This is the duplication law, which we have known empirically for many years (Ehrenberg, 1972) and which is also found to a very close approximation from the Dirichlet model (Goodhardt *et al.*, 1984).

The idea behind duplication is that some buyers at one chain

Table 11.1 Duplication of instant coffee buying at A & P

48 weeks	% who also bought at:									
	UC	*NC*	*Co-op*	*Misc.*	*Kroger*	*A&P*	*Safeway*	*Winn*	*Lucky*
Buyers at:									
A & P	65	57	14	14	5	(100)	5	8	2
Patronage, *b*	49	31	13	8	6	6	6	4	3

will probably buy elsewhere, and a complete duplication table shows the extent to which this is true (Table 11.2). Reading from the top left-hand corner, 40 per cent of buyers at unnamed chains also buy at named chains, 19 per cent buy at Co-ops, and so forth. All entries along the cross-diagonal are 100 per cent, and to preserve the visual image these are excluded.

Several patterns are discerned from Table 11.2. Within each column there is little variation, so the column average is a good summary. Irrespective of where consumers buy, roughly 63 per cent also buy at unnamed chains and only 4 per cent or so buy at Lucky. Secondly, duplication varies with patronage. We first encountered this relationship in Table 11.1 (where A & P declines in parallel with patronage); now we see that the relationship generalises to all stores. The correlation between average duplication and patronage is 0.99.

So regular are these patterns that average duplication is predictable using a single coefficient. The coefficient is derived from average duplication across all relevant chains (18 per cent) divided by average patronage across these chains (14 per cent), giving roughly 1.3. Coefficients in the range 1.2 to 1.4 are common, and show the extent of buying elsewhere. To the extent that patronage depends on market share, duplication is predictable from market share.

This well-defined structure helps us to identify regularities and then describe the salient features of store choice. Moreover, any deviations from the norm are noticed easily. Eyeballing the columns of Table 11.2, it is clear that most duplications are in line with the average. There are a couple of exceptions associated with Safeway and Lucky Stores. Of buyers at Lucky, 16 per cent also bought at Safeway, and of buyers at Safeway, 9 per cent bought at Lucky. These duplications are double what we expect from looking at the average.

Why? Many reasons – to do with retail competition, consumer choice and variety seeking – could be advanced. Knowledge of retail trading areas in the US provides a better explanation; quite simply the trading areas of Safeway and Lucky coincide more than usual. Safeway sells instant coffee in twenty-seven states, though 38 per cent of purchases occur in California alone; similarly Lucky, operates in seventeen states, yet 40 per cent of purchases are made in California. Along the Western Seaboard

Table 11.2 Duplication of instant coffee buying at chains in the USA

48 weeks	% who also bought at:								
	UC	NC	Co-op	Misc.	Kroger	A&P	Safeway	Winn	Lucky
Buyers at:									
Unnamed chains	—	40	19	13	9	7	7	5	4
Named chains	63	—	15	12	5	10	7	5	5
Co-ops	70	36	—	15	11	6	6	4	4
Miscellaneous	42	24	13	—	6	5	6	3	2
Kroger	73	26	23	14	—	5	6	5	4
A & P	65	57	14	14	5	—	5	8	2
Safeway	64	41	15	16	6	5	—	1	9
Winn Dixie	69	44	16	11	9	13	1	—	2
Lucky	60	45	16	7	7	4	16	2	—
Average duplication,	63	39	16	13	7	7	7	4	4
1.3 × b	63	40	17	10	8	7	7	5	4
Patronage, b	49	31	13	8	6	6	6	4	3

both chains enter the relevant choice sets of consumers, affecting levels of patronage.

Another exception – unexpectedly low duplication – is associated with Winn Dixie and Safeway. Again, the explanation might concern competitive strategies, or positioning in the market, or pricing regimens, etc. The crucial reason is that their trading areas hardly coincide. Winn Dixie doesn't make any sales of instant coffee in California; instead its regional strength is the Deep South. Only in Texas and around Indiana is there any overlap in store locations.

To emphasise the reason for these exceptions, the main trading areas of Safeway, Lucky Stores and Winn Dixie are mapped in Figure 11.4. Between South Eastern and West Coast chains duplication is low. And almost as a corollary, within these areas duplication between relevant chains is closer than average.

The regularities (and deviations) presented for American chains are not isolated instances of 'well behaved' duplication. Apart from store choice, the law has been observed across a wide range of product fields and brands. To reinforce this claim we

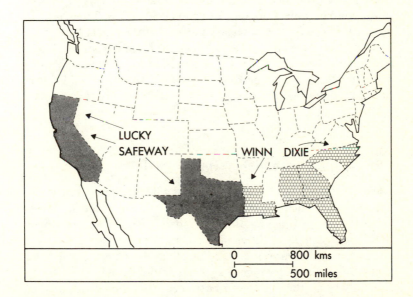

Figure 11.4 The main trading areas of Safeway, Lucky and Winn Dixie in the US, showing low duplication between East and West Coast chains.

take a sideways look at some UK evidence; this also provides a useful cross-cultural comparison.

Patterns of store duplication in Lancashire are depicted in Table 11.3 (Kau and Ehrenberg, 1984). Stores are classified into two blocks: collective groups of stores such as Co-ops and independent grocers; and major chains, including Kwiksave and Tesco. During a half year, for example, 32 per cent of buyers at miscellaneous stores also buy at Co-ops. As before, variation down each column is slight, and duplication largely varies with patronage; essentially British and American duplication patterns are alike.

The duplication coefficient of 1.2 differs by just 0.1 from the US, and the correlation of 0.98 between average duplication and patronage is equally convincing. The coincidence of trading areas in Lancashire is much closer than in our US example (for instance, at the time of the survey Sainsbury's was not trading in the county, so it was excluded). To some extent the pattern in Lancashire is closest to what occurs in North East and Mid-West US, where most national chains are in direct competition.

Evidence from the USA, therefore, shows that many aspects of multi-store patronage are regular and generalisable. There is little systematic partitioning of chains above what we expect from their market shares and the pattern of regional trading areas. Thus, two chains generally share the number of customers that their sheer market shares (or patronage) warrant. What is remarkable is not that there are exceptions, but that these are so few and relatively small.

What explanatory variables do we need?

Observation of how consumers buy at one chain and elsewhere enables us to identify several regularities: patronage increases steeply with lengthening time periods, whereas the growth of purchase frequencies is shallow; sales differ mainly because chains have different numbers of buyers, rather than because the average purchase frequencies differ much; and two chains generally share the number of customers that their sheer market shares (or patronage) warrant.

Underlying these regularities are hosts of potential influences,

Table 11.3 Duplication of instant coffee buying at chains in the UK

24 weeks (Lancashire)	% who also bought at:							
	Misc.	Co-op	Symbol	Independent	Kwiksave	Tesco	Asda	Fine Fare
Buyers at:								
Miscellaneous	—	32	16	15	25	29	13	8
Co-ops	38	—	12	13	21	22	19	4
Symbol	52	32	—	19	20	30	20	8
Independent	52	34	18	—	23	24	12	5
Kwiksave	37	26	9	11	—	22	9	7
Tesco	45	29	14	13	23	—	13	7
Asda	31	38	14	9	14	24	—	3
Fine Fare	50	23	16	11	29	27	9	—
Average duplication,	43	31	14	13	22	25	14	6
1.2 × b	46	34	12	13	26	25	17	6
Patronage, b	33	28	10	11	22	21	14	5

such as sales strategies, price promotions, retail stocks, trading hours and local competition. While these influences undoubtedly concern store managers, they are not central to a basic description of how consumers, in the aggregate, choose a store.

In practice very little information is required to predict the statistical patterns.

About the product class as a whole (here instant coffee) we need to know:

(a) size of market;

(b) number of buyers (patronage);

(c) average number of chains used;

where the last couple of measures are for some base period like a quarter or a year.

About the chains we need to know:

(d) relevant market share (within regional trading areas).

An understanding of observed patterns of behaviour does not rest on a detailed knowledge of pricing policies, promotions, number of outlets, image, standards of service, size of store, product variety, proportion of own-brands, etc. – in short, the marketing mix.

These conclusions are confirmed, explicitly, by thinking about how to calibrate the Dirichlet model. Predictions from this model have been accurate, and consistently so. Yet the only inputs are the fitted NBD frequency distributions of total purchases across all stores for the product field and just one chain-specific measure, like market share, which is independent of the time period. In practice we often use penetration since this refers specifically to the behaviour of people.

Discussion

The preceding account of how buyers choose a chain illustrates several important principles. These deepen our understanding of consumer behaviour and ought to assist in the practice of retail marketing. In this final section we discuss the utility of the results and remark upon some topics where active research is being pursued.

For stationary non-partitioned markets a set of general patterns is observed. Using Dirichlet theory, these patterns are predictable to an impressive degree of accuracy. The import of such generalisations is that they:

(a) facilitate comparisons of brands, stores, and products, as well as countries, methods, etc.;

(b) allow us to identify deviations;

(c) provide baselines for the study of marketing dynamics;

(d) require only market-shares as chain-specific inputs.

Description of the stationary state allows us to chart the basic dimensions of consumer behaviour (How many? How often? How regularly? Where else? etc.). This is done for numerous aspects of shopping activity, incuding choice of brands, patronage at stores, and purchasing from a product field. Replication across ·countries and alternative panel designs – scanner panels as well as conventional diaries (Barnard *et al.*, 1985) – confirms the robustness of these models and gives confidence in the results.

Once stationary norms are established, major deviations stand apart from the overall pattern and eyeballing is sufficient to identify all the major anomalies. Regularities also provide baselines for gauging the impact of perturbations in the market. Thus, non-stationarities and seasonal swings, and definite partitions within the market, emerge as deviations from the model, their full impact being noticeable and measurable. This is where we might look for additional variables (i.e. while market share accounts for most of the variation, some residual variation remains to be accounted for by other influences). At present, however, the quantitative effect is determined without having to probe too deeply into the mechanisms and nature of change.

Quite clearly much progress has been made already, but in taking stock of what has been achieved a number of areas needing more research come to light.

(a) Cross-cultural comparisons and intra-urban patterns.

(b) Combinations of product fields on shopping trips.

(c) Hierarchy of choice.

(d) Other independent variables.

(e) Determinants of market share and marketing dynamics.

Briefly we shall consider each of these topics in turn.

Cross-cultural comparisons and intra-urban patterns

Cross-national comparisons and scale are familiar geographical and marketing issues, and both have attracted attention from analysts and marketers. An early cross-national comparison of repeat-buying habits was published by Ehrenberg and Goodhardt (1968); they concluded that British and American habits are alike. While this chapter looked solely at the repeat-buying of brands, it covered a broad range of product fields (detergents, flour, etc.) and established the spatial transferability of NBD theory.

International comparison is now taken one stage further if we compare our results with those reported for the British retail coffee market (Kau, 1981; Kau and Ehrenberg, 1984); essentially patronage at US and UK chains is similar. This is despite differences in the comparative structures of retailing (for example, stricter local-authority planning controls in Britain, less marketing clout among US retailers, fewer dominant national chains in the States, etc.). The only other contrast is that US per capita consumption of instant coffee is half that in Britain.

Local comparisons are being undertaken too. Single-city studies are reported by Wrigley (1980) and Wrigley and Dunn (1984a; 1984b). The last of these papers shows how the duplication law holds for multi-store choice; their only proviso is that suburban stores draw upon a narrower catchment than city centre stores, and this must be taken into account when calibrating the Dirichlet model (just as we did for duplication between Safeway and Winn Dixie). Recently Halperin (1985) fitted the model to data from Santa Barbara; measures of store patronage and purchase frequency are consistent with previous experience, although his panel is too short (merely one month) to permit firm conclusions.

All these national and local comparisons confirm that the Dirichlet model transfers across space and scales (e.g. national or neighbourhood), giving the familiar measures of patronage and sales, store loyalty and repeat-patronage, and multi-store buying.

Combinations of product fields on shopping trips

We can successfully predict all patterns for one product without taking into account purchases of other products (for example $r = 0.99$ in the duplication table). Nevertheless experience shows that purchases are not isolated events even if we can treat them as such. Or are light buyers in one product-field also light buyers in another product-field? At a broader level, goods are bought on shopping trips, and we know that these are often multi-stage/multi-purpose events.

Retailers have to answer many related questions. What goods are bought in combination with each other? (Is there complementary purchasing? What does this imply about traffic building and loss leaders?) How does shopping fit into people's daily routines? (Does this mean more convenience shopping? Will the frequency of shop visits decline?) How are these trips structured? (One-stop visits or variety seeking?) Conceptually consumers might attempt to derive a bundle of benefits, rather than increase the utility from any single item (Bacon, 1984).

These are important questions which are unlikely to be answered from existing models alone; nevertheless regularities in trip making are worth identifying (Frisbie, 1980) as, too, are the links between several purchases on one trip.

Hierarchy of choice

The sequence of decisions giving rise to a purchase is of practical and theoretical interest. If selection of a shopping centre is the primary decision, then the success of a store depends on how the centre is perceived, its layout, ease of access, etc. If, by contrast, consumers choose a store knowing that they can obtain a desired brand there, then branding, promotion and advertising support are that much more important.

Thus far the Dirichlet model has been used to investigate brands within product fields and brands within stores. However, with modification, it should be possible to experiment with different configurations of the decision sequence and then isolate the most plausible hierarchy. Developments in the field of longitudinal discrete-choice analysis may assist, especially where elements of the sequence are nested or embedded within higher-level decisions (Broom, 1982).

Perhaps easier to study is the question of whether consumers place bounds on their choice sets, i.e. at each level of the decision hierarchy do they confine their selection to a limited portfolio of options? If so, how does this influence patterns of patronage, loyalty and duplication, and is it important for our understanding of buyer behaviour?

Other independent variables

Rather than partition stores (in terms of price, image, service, etc.), a growing number of researchers are looking at the influence of population segments – detailing the nature of demand rather than supply. Intuitively one expects small households to behave slightly differently from large ones; differences are expected between consumers with and without access to a car; and those who value time might behave differently from those who don't (Bowlby, 1984). The effect of household size on NBD predictions, for example, was studied many years ago (Ehrenberg, 1959). What we have are demand, or 'needs', segments.

Partial attempts to develop a longitudinal 'needs' model through the introduction of independent variables have been made over several years (Jones and Zufryden, 1980; Broom, 1982; Davies, R. B., 1984). The first operational approach, equally capable of dealing with binary and multiple-store choice cases, was proposed by Dunn and Wrigley (1985). In their study the extent to which store choice depends on income, household size, and the working status of shoppers was investigated. Their formulation rested on beta-logistic and multinomial-Dirichlet versions of what is, in essence, a Dirichlet model with independent variables. This has been replicated and tested in the context of binary and multiple travel choices on shopping trips (Uncles, 1985, 1987).

Determinants of market share and marketing dynamics

In answer to the question 'What explanatory variables do we need?' it was shown that only one variable is needed, typically market share, in order to obtain predictions of behaviour in stationary markets. A prediction of aggregate consumer behaviour does not rest on a detailed knowledge of the marketing mix.

In saying this we in no way claim that retailers should resignedly accept their current shares. An active policy is needed to maintain market share. If your competitor adopts an aggressive pricing policy and this begins to raise his market share, then you need to formulate a response. Do you cut prices too? Or do you enhance customer services, introducing delicatessen counters, packers at tills, and EFTPOS (electronic funds transfer at point of sale) facilities for in-store finance and credit? Whatever is done, the effect can be guided through market share, otherwise the desired response among customers may not happen. Implicitly retailers know this already; that is why stores begin to look alike.

To achieve a sales impact, therefore, market shares must alter. Because this issue is so central, greater thought is being given to marketing dynamics. What actually shapes market share? What happens when changes occur?

Work on dynamics proceeds on two fronts. Door-step and hall experiments with housewives are undertaken to assess price sensitivity and consumers' responsiveness to special offers and price (England and Ehrenberg, 1985; Ehrenberg, 1986). Secondly, conventional panels are used to monitor new product launches and to examine the effect of non-stationarities such as store promotions, deals and discounts (Wellan, 1985). A direct comparison between stationary norms and patterns arising out of changing market conditions enables us to assess, for example, whether increasing sales come from attracting more buyers or from existing buyers patronising more often.

Appendix

Theoretical predictions are derived from the Dirichlet model (Goodhardt *et al.*, 1984). Strictly speaking we are using a version known as the NBD-Dirichlet; this is more powerful than the alternative (empirical-Dirichlet) version. Predictions refer to all the basic measures of buyer behaviour at chains, such as patronage, purchase frequency, total purchases of the product, sole buying and repeat buying.

A stationary market is assumed by the theory; therefore any deviation from this condition might lead to poor predictions. For instance, a similar proportion of buyers is found to patronise a chain, week by week. If, however, there are irregular promotions, or seasonal effects, let alone systematic trends, the market shares become unpredictable.

By inspecting patronage each quarter (Table 11.A.1), we can assess the degree of stationarity. Average patronage at any chain is 45.6 per cent a quarter – somewhat higher in quarter I (3.9 per cent more) and lower during quarter III (3.7 per cent less). This suggests that patronage describes a U-shape across quarters, something that we see replicated across virtually all individual chains and groupings. Perhaps there is a summer lull and a winter peak (coffee is a hot beverage so this explanation is plausible). While the seasonal trend is systematic it is not substantial. None of the quarter-by-quarter variations is more significant than the within-quarter patterns, which show how patronage varies directly with market share.

A similar pattern is evident from the number of purchases per buyer (Table 11.A.2). Comparing across quarters, we see that frequencies dip slightly in quarter III, possibly owing to seasonal effects, but the change is not large. In general, frequencies hardly vary from the table average of 1.7 purchases per quarter – this is in marked contrast to the range of values associated with

Table 11.A.1 Patronage at chains selling instant coffee – percentage of households buying instant coffee, at least once, in each quarter (rounded)

	Market share (% annual)	Quarterly patronage (%)				Average (%)
		I	II	III	IV	
Any chain	100	50	46	42	45	46
Unnamed chains	45	30	26	24	26	27
Named chains	28	18	16	15	16	16
Co-ops	8	5	6	5	6	6
Kroger	4	3	3	2	3	3
A & P	4	3	3	2	2	2
Safeway	3	3	3	2	2	2
Miscellaneous	3	2	3	2	3	3
Winn Dixie	3	2	1	2	2	2
Lucky Stores	2	2	1	1	2	1
Average chain	11	8	7	6	7	7

Table 11.A.2   Average purchase frequency of instant coffee at chains – the average number of purchases per buyer in each quarter (rounded)

	Market share (% annual)	Quarterly patronage				Average
		I	II	II	IV	
Any chain	100	3	3	2	2	3
Unnamed chains	45	2	2	2	2	2
Named chains	28	2	2	2	2	2
Co-ops	8	2	2	2	2	2
Kroger	4	2	2	2	2	2
A & P	4	2	2	2	2	2
Safeway	3	2	1	2	2	2
Miscellaneous	3	2	1	1	1	1
Winn Dixie	3	2	2	2	2	2
Lucky Stores	2	2	2	2	2	2
Average chain	11	2	2	2	2	2

patronage. We have chosen to look at the two elements of the sales equation; equally we could have studied market shares or other measures of behaviour. The same conclusions about stationarity are reached in all circumstances.

The basic measures of buyer behaviour are brought together for an average quarter and a year in Tables 11.A.3 and 11.A.4 respectively. These tables summarise what we have described already in the text: patronage varies with market share; purchase frequencies hardly alter across chains; more buyers are attracted to chains as the length of analysis increases; these consumers buy somewhat more often there, but they buy more instant coffee from other chains. All these patterns are closely predicted by the Dirichlet model (correlations of 0.99 are recorded between observed and predicted patronage).

Acknowledgment

This chapter is part of an on-going programme of work at the Centre for Marketing and Communication. Studies of buyer behaviour are supported in part by CBS, Colgate Palmolive,

Table 11.A.3 Measures of buyer behaviour at chains: instant coffee, average quarter – observed measures and Dirichlet predictions in an average 12-week period

	Patronage (%)		Average purchase frequency		Total product purchases	
	O	D	O	D	O	D
*Any chain**	45.6	45.6	2.5	2.5	2.5	2.5
Unnamed chains	26.7	25.8	1.9	2.0	2.8	2.9
Named chains	16.3	18.0	2.0	1.8	2.9	3.0
Co-ops	5.5	5.4	1.6	1.6	2.9	3.2
Kroger	2.9	3.1	1.7	1.6	3.1	3.3
A & P	2.4	2.6	1.7	1.6	3.5	3.3
Safeway	2.4	2.3	1.5	1.6	2.7	3.3
Miscellaneous	2.5	2.2	1.4	1.6	3.8	3.3
Winn Dixie	1.6	1.8	1.8	1.6	3.1	3.3
Lucky Stores	1.4	1.6	1.8	1.6	2.8	3.3
Average chain	6.9	7.0	1.7	1.7	3.1	3.2

* Quarterly measures for any chain used in fitting Dirichlet model.
O = observed measures, D = Dirichlet predictions.

Table 11.A.4 Measures of buyer behaviour at chains: instant coffee, one year – observed measures and Dirichlet predictions in a 48-week period

	Patronage (%)		Average purchase frequency		Total product purchases	
	O	D	O	D	O	D
*Any chain**	67.6	69.9	6.7	6.5	6.7	6.5
Unnamed chains	48.7	47.4	4.2	4.3	7.9	7.7
Named chains	31.2	35.4	4.0	3.7	8.2	8.2
Co-ops	13.0	11.8	2.7	3.0	8.5	9.0
Kroger	6.3	6.9	3.1	2.9	9.7	9.1
A & P	5.5	5.8	3.0	2.9	9.8	9.2
Safeway	5.7	5.1	2.5	2.8	7.5	9.2
Miscellaneous	7.8	5.0	1.7	2.8	11.1	9.2
Winn Dixie	3.6	4.1	3.2	2.8	8.9	9.2
Lucky Stores	3.2	3.5	3.2	2.8	8.2	9.2
Average chain	13.9	13.9	3.1	3.1	8.9	8.9

* Quarterly measures for any chain used in fitting Dirichlet model.
O = observed measures, D = Dirichlet predictions.

General Foods, General Mills, Gillette, Mars, the Ogilvy Centre and Quaker Oats in the USA, and by over thirty leading companies in the UK. We are also indebted to MRCA for providing the data tapes.

PART 4 Retail analysis and forecasting – some wider themes

This final section of the book takes up one of the major themes of Chapter 1, and considers some of the implications of the introduction of computer-based information technology into retailing. EPOS (electronic point of sale) cash tills reading bar-coded products provide a base on which it is possible to build integrated management-information systems of considerable sophistication. In Chapter 12, Guy outlines the structure of such systems and considers their level of acceptance into British retailing. He notes that EPOS and EFTPOS (electronic funds transfer at point of sale) systems are currently in a period of intensive development and that retail management-information systems based on EPOS devices will provide on-line data which are of particular importance to the task of assessing store performance and market penetration.

In Chapter 13, Humby takes up several of the issues considered by Guy and presents some brief final observations on research priorities in retail analysis and forecasting. He stresses that EPOS systems are contributing to an information explosion for the retailer. If the retailer is not to be swamped by this information he must cut into it using the evolving techniques of market analysis to understand more about the discrete lifestyle or niche-segments of the market which his stores serve.

CHAPTER 12

Information technology and retailing: the implications for analysis and forecasting

Clifford M. Guy

Introduction

The interfaces between developments in information technology (IT), retailing strategies and consumer behaviour are attracting an increasing amount of attention in the marketing and geography literature. Most of this literature either summarises recent developments (e.g. Howard, 1985; Bennison, 1985; Davies, 1985) or speculates about future developments and their economic and social impacts (e.g. Rosenberg and Hirschman, 1980; Quelch and Takeuchi, 1981; Kirby, 1982; Dawson, 1983b; Taylor, 1984; Guy, 1985; Davies and Reynolds, 1986). This present chapter takes a somewhat different stance. The view is taken that the implications of IT in retailing and consumer behaviour should not be examined simply in the context of an abstracted discussion of social futures. Rather, a more positive view emphasising the opportunities that a more extensive use of IT would allow for market analysis and store-location strategy is presented.

IT and retailing: the current situation

The main uses of IT in retailing are summarised clearly in Distributive Trades EDC (1982). These include EPOS, EFTPOS, private viewdata systems and remote shopping (see Table 12.1). Experiments in these areas in Britain have generally proved fairly successful, but the overall impact of IT has so far been disappointing for most of its proponents. For example, EPOS systems involving scanners or laser wands are still exceptional among British grocery retailers, despite a history of experiments

Table 12.1 Applications of information technology in retailing

Acronym	Full name	Explanation
EPOS	Electronic point of sale	Ranges from electronic cash registers through tills linked to in-store micro- or mini-computers, to tills incorporating devices to read product details from bar codes, and providing fully itemised receipts for customers
EFTPOS	Electronic funds transfer at point of sale	An EPOS terminal is coupled with a device to identify the customer, from a plastic card, and charge the customer's bank or building society account for payment for the goods concerned
	Viewdata (also known as Videotex)	One- or two-way transmission of information along telephone or other cables, between users employing visual display units and keypads
	Private viewdata	Viewdata transmissions limited to users within one company or CLUG (closed user group)
	Prestel	Public viewdata system, run by British Telecom. Users have to pay subscription charges, plus telephone charges when using Prestel

stretching back well into the 1970s (Jones and Walman, 1979). EFTPOS systems have been discussed in detail since 1980 but until recently only one experiment known to the author has been carried out in the UK, involving petrol sales in Aberdeen, and retailers are clearly sceptical about its benefits (*Retail Business*, 1985a). Remote shopping using British Telecom's Prestel system has also progressed more slowly than expected; in November 1985 some 29,000 domestic users were registered, compared with original expectations of at least 200,000 users by the mid-1980s. Progress on remote shopping using cable TV has been virtually nil.

Despite this disappointing history, there are several indications that IT in retailing is beginning to emerge from this period into one of more intensive development of major schemes whose justification is financial as well as experimental. Similar conclusions have been drawn concerning North America (Howard, 1985). For example, J. Sainsbury PLC have recently placed a £20 million order with ICL for EPOS equipment using laser scanners (Bird, 1985). These tills will link to central IBM computers allowing exchange of up-to-date product-sales information throughout the company. This follows the successful development of a management communication network between 800 retail outlets owned by the Victoria Wine Co. Ltd (*Retail and Distribution Management*, 1984). Perhaps the most important communication network launched so far in Britain has been the Tradanet system which allows electronic exchange of information between manufacturers, distributors and retailers, thus cutting out vast quantities of paperwork (*Retail and Distribution Management*, 1985a; *Retail Business*, 1985b).

In the area of EFTPOS an important scheme has recently commenced in Northampton, involving investment of £2 million by ICL and the Anglia Building Society (Osman, 1985). Some eighty retailers, including major multiples, are taking part in this scheme and it was expected that around 50,000 Anglia Cards will have been issued to Anglia account-holders by the end of 1985. The scale of the experiment is such that both Anglia and ICL clearly expect to launch similar schemes elsewhere.

In the area of remote shopping, several important advances have been made recently. The Gateshead Shopping and Information Service, set up in 1980 to link elderly and disabled shoppers to a Tesco superstore and financed partly by the local borough council (Davies, 1985), has now been extended to five additional retailers, and a similar scheme has been launched in the Bradford area (Davies and Reynolds, 1986). British Telecom have recently added to their various Prestel shopping initiatives (for a review see Bennison, 1985) the Telecard Supershop scheme, making some 4,000 grocery lines available remotely to 8,000 domestic Prestel users in central and west London (Brooks, 1985; Davies and Reynolds, 1986).

These advances suggest that IT may soon be having important impacts on certain areas of retailing and consumer behaviour in Britain. It is noteworthy, however, that so far most of the major advances have been made through the efforts of hardware or software suppliers such as ICL and BT, and some 'second division' banks (Bank of Scotland), building societies (Nottingham,

Anglia), and retailers (for example the Lalani grocery firm involved in the Telecard scheme referred to above). To quote Brooks (1985), 'All these systems combine technology and entrepreneurial drive. But they still need one or more of the major stores groups to commit themselves. At present, the chains are playing a waiting game.' Involvement of major retail companies is vital if IT – especially EFTPOS and remote shopping – is to be of any real importance in this country. It is not the intention of this chapter to plead for such involvement; indeed it would be presumptuous to do so. Rather, the chapter examines the implications of IT for retail analysis and forecasting, assuming some major advances in the near future in the use of IT by major companies. These advances use technology which already exists in prototype form at least, but which may require substantial investment of capital and/or training resources to be used effectively.

The following diagnosis of the implications of IT for retail analysis and forecasting is in two parts. Firstly, the improvements in the analysis of store performance, market penetration, etc., which may result from increasing use of IT are examined. The potential of EFTPOS in this respect is discussed in particular. Secondly, possible changes in locational strategies, as well as market analysis, resulting from developments in remote shopping, are assessed. This discussion, which is inevitably more speculative than that of the first section, is preceded by a consideration of the most promising markets for promotion of remote shopping and the substitution effects of such activity.

IT, information networks and market analysis

Retail planning of any type requires information, whether on the performance of retail firms and stores, or consumer preferences, travel behaviour and purchasing habits, or contextual information such as local population trends or land-use planning policies. Obviously, advances in information technology should assist the provision and digestion of information as an aid to decision-making. The last few years have seen considerable advances in the manner in which certain types of detailed information can be made available to retail planners. Two examples may be given.

Firstly, the improvements in computer storage of and access to statistical information have enabled the creation of very large databases such as those held by CACI Market Analysis or Pinpoint Analysis Ltd, and the data on shopping-centre characteristics held by Chas. Goad Ltd and other agencies. More important than the sheer size of these databases is the ease with which special tabulations relating to any population group, geographical area or retail type can be retrieved and made available on-line to the prospective user.

A second example of important recent advances in IT lies in the development of private viewdata systems, as seen commonly, for example, in travel agents' premises. Accurate information on hotel room or flight availability is now cheaply and instantly available without recourse to the telephone. All these advances are now taken for granted but would have seemed remarkable fifteen years ago.

EPOS systems and market analysis

The linking of in-store EPOS systems (Figure 12.1) and microcomputers into an information network within a retail

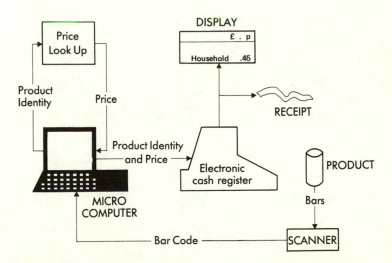

Figure 12.1 A typical EPOS system.

organisation represents a major advance in the use of IT in retailing at the present time. EPOS systems have been intended so far mainly as a means of improving stock control within the store, but increasingly their linking together (through private viewdata or some other system) is being seen as a major step towards the efficient management of resources over the whole firm, whether large (e.g. *Retail and Distribution Management*, 1984) or small (e.g. Sawers, 1984) – see Figure 12.2. A byproduct of this movement towards integrated retail management information networks will be the improvement in the internal information available to the analyst working within the retail firms. At present, only summary statistics of store-by-store sales of various product groups over (say) the previous week can be made available to the analyst, while information exchange is restricted to the telephone. On-line data on recent sales of much

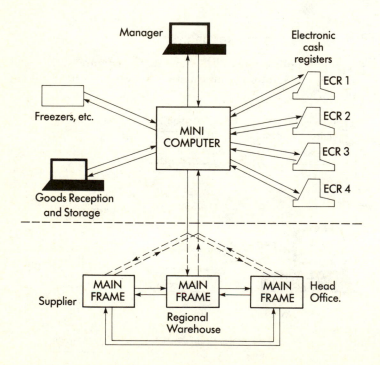

Figure 12.2 EPOS and management information systems.

more narrowly-defined products could be made available instantly from a fully-developed management information system, together with information on store-specific factors such as new-product launches or price cuts. Analysis of recent trends would thus be made easier.

Whether this potential flood of information is going to improve the tasks of assessing store performance and developing locational strategies depends of course less on the hardware and software and more on the capability of the retail analyst him(her)self.

It is not simply a question of purchasing the technology but more critical is the availability of manpower to analyse, interpret and distribute the relevant information to decision makers. It is the lack of this manpower, skilled in project evaluation techniques and in methods of information handling and interpretation, which promises to be the main stumbling block in the widespread exploitation of the benefits of IT in strategic decision making.
(Dawson, 1983b)

EFTPOS and market analysis

Of all the information required by retail analysts, that concerning consumer expenditure presents greatest problems. There is of course an excellent repertoire of population census data now available and this can be (approximately) translated into estimates of consumer expenditure over broad product categories (Wade, 1983). Most retail firms will also possess fairly reliable information on the socio-economic and demographic profiles of their typical customers, drawn from panel surveys and store-based interviews. Some information on typical expenditure patterns of socio-economic or demographic groups also exists from these sources and Family Expenditure Survey reports. However, any attempt to combine, say, demographic and geographical specificity is likely to pose problems. This is especially true when making estimates of turnover for various product groups in a proposed new store, for example.

The advent of EFTPOS systems (see Figure 12.3) in major store chains could in theory produce dramatic improvements in the quantity and quality of data available about the chain's

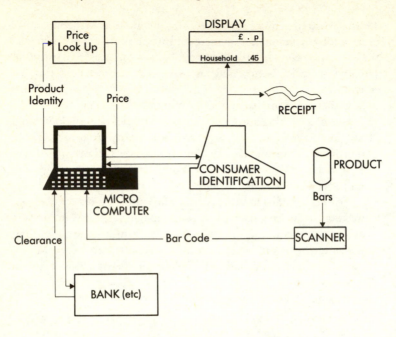

Figure 12.3 EPOS and EFTPOS systems.

customers and their expenditure patterns. The value of EFTPOS to the retailer lies not simply in simplifying purchasing transactions and speeding up cash flows. It also allows purchases made using this system to be related unambiguously to a specific customer – the owner of the plastic card in question. That customer's home address, and certain personal and household characteristics, will be known to the agency issuing the cards, whether it be retailer, bank, building society or some other body. A merging of expenditure information from the EPOS terminal with personal information from customer records is not an immediate prospect, but appears to be feasible in the long term. Given sufficiently high take-up of EFTPOS by both retailers and customers, a great deal of detailed analysis of consumer expenditure would be possible. This could considerably assist processes of market identification, product promotion and store performance examination, as well as analysis of regional or local expenditure patterns.

This type of information handling could however prove rather more controversial than the improvements discussed earlier in this chapter. The prospect of personal information collected, say, by a customer's bank, being used for commercial purposes unknown to the customer, would not be welcome to consumer organisations. Clearly it is not possible to preserve confidentiality by aggregating individual-level data, as is carried out for example with population census information. Safeguards against the identification of customers by third parties may have to be used. Further discussion of the implications of IT for consumer privacy may be found in Distributive Trades EDC (1982).

The impact of in-store and within-firm computerisation of information flows on market analysis may thus be important. While it has the potential to improve methods of sales forecasting and locational assessment, radical changes in store location strategies are unlikely to result. To investigate the possibilities of such changes occurring as a result of IT developments, it is necessary to turn to the topic of 'armchair' or 'remote' shopping (see Figure 12.4).

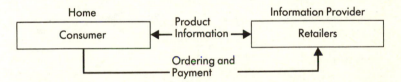

Figure 12.4 Armchair shopping.

Remote shopping and its impacts

Links between the development of remote shopping habits in the UK and future marketing or location strategies of retail firms are quite indirect. To investigate this question it is necessary: firstly to consider the likely characteristics of adopters of IT in consumer purchasing; secondly the ways in which such adopters may substitute remote shopping for conventional shopping trips; and finally the implications that such substitutions may have for both performance of existing stores and strategies for developing new outlets.

Adoption and substitution

In deciding whether to use IT in promotion or sales, an organisation must compare the characteristics of its potential customers with those of likely IT users. This is particularly important at present, since it is clear that remote purchasing has relatively little appeal generally for most shopping purchases (see Table 12.2). Remote shopping – whether involving simply promotion of goods over telecommunications networks, or purchase facilities as well – is most likely to succeed when a product suited to this process is aimed at a clearly-defined market receptive to using IT (Strauss, 1983).

Table 12.2   Attitudes towards shopping from home

Service	% of respondents expressing interest
Banking	36
Foreign holidays	29
Groceries (excluding fresh food)	18
Clothes and shoes	16
Books	16
TV, video or hifi	14
Cookers/fridges	12
Fresh food	12
Jewellery/fancy goods	7
No interest	32

Source: Henley Centre for Forecasting, reproduced in Davies and Reynolds, 1986.

The question posed was 'for which of these services can you imagine yourself 'armchair shopping'?'

Davies and Reynolds (1986) have suggested that three types of consumer may gain sufficient benefits from using IT in shopping to outweigh the capital and running costs involved. These types are shown in Table 12.3, together with speculative associations with socio-economic categories and ACORN neighbourhood categories. The first of these consumer types – high-income households with all members economically active – have been the main adopters so far in Britain and North America, and also the main targets for IT marketing experiments such as the Telecard scheme in West and Central London (Brooks, 1985). Their propensity to use remote shopping facilities is due mainly to lack of time available for conventional shopping trips, and a willingness to pay the extra initial capital costs involved. In addition, members of such households are likely to be well educated and are more likely than most to be familiar with computers and their peripheral equipment. This market is an attractive prospect both for marketers of the equipment concerned, and retailers interested in setting up remote shopping initiatives.

The second consumer type identified by Davies and Reynolds (1986) – the elderly, infirm and otherwise housebound – have been associated with remote shopping through considerations of social concern rather than examinations of lifestyle. Remote shopping has the potential here to create important benefits, releasing the elderly and disabled from difficulties of shopping travel and emancipating them from their 'disadvantaged consumer' status. Although it might be supposed that this type of consumer would be reluctant to experiment with the new technology, the experience of the Gateshead scheme (Davies, 1985) suggests that these difficulties have been exaggerated. Here, elderly people became adept at using keypads and visual display units, provided that skilled assistance was available initially. The problem in extending the use of remote shopping by this group lies more in a lack of commercial viability; expenditure

Table 12.3   Profiles of potential adopters of IT in shopping

Consumer type[1]	Socio-economic[2] group	ACORN category[3]
High-income households with little time to do shopping trips	1, 2, 3, 4	B04, B05, I30, I31
The elderly, infirm	Retired	D12, F21, K38
The fashion market	?	?
Remote rural dwellers	3, 14	A01, A02

Sources: 1 Davies and Reynolds (1986).
          2 Office of Population Censuses and Surveys, Census 1981 Reports, HMSO.
          3 Humby (1984).

per head tends to be low, and delivery of goods (the most expensive part of a remote shopping operation) is essential.

The third consumer type – the fashion market – consists of people interested in technological developments in their own right. Davies and Reynolds (1986) suggest that this group is more peripheral and is unlikely to remain stable in its behaviour in the medium term.

A fourth consumer type may be added to this list. This comprises households living in places geographically remote from large stores and major shopping centres. One of the most notable features of population change in the 1970s in Britain was growth, after decades of decline, in many remote rural areas (Champion, 1983). The 'wired society' may seem particularly attractive, or even essential, to educated ex-urbanites seeking a rural environment but nevertheless wishing to maintain contact with urban society (Garrett and Wright, 1980).

The major problem of course is that of delivering the goods ordered; similar transport problems, related to deliveries to retailers, already underlie the decline of conventional small shops in rural areas (Dawson and Kirby, 1979).

In order to examine the question of substitution of remote for conventional shopping, one needs to consider what types of product can confidently be ordered by the customer without visiting a retail outlet. Two main categories would seem to be: first, goods which are already familiar to the customer from everyday shopping experience, such as groceries; and second, goods which may not be familiar but which can be adequately described through promotional literature or, more appropriately, through teletext displays on an ordinary television receiver.

Armchair shopping for groceries

Use of armchair shopping for routine grocery purchases is now beginning to appear a serious commercial proposition. Public support is indicated by the finding that groceries were the most popular contender for remote shopping in a Henley Centre for Forecasting survey reported in ICL (1985) (Table 12.2). It may be argued that the British experiments in armchair shopping for groceries have so far had limited success; this may be due to diffident marketing and the reluctance of retailers to participate rather than consumer inhibitions or disinterest. If a major grocery multiple firm was to initiate a comprehensive and widely-available remote-shopping service, one would expect to see substantial improvements in both marketing of the service and its attractiveness to the shopper (Table 12.4).

Table 12.4   Remote shopping services: a hypothetical comparison

Service characteristic	Recent and current experiments	Hypothetical initiative by major multiple
Geographical coverage	Local	Regional/national
Initial publicity	Moderate	Intensive
Customer identification	Existing Prestel users	Existing shoppers
Initial costs to consumer	High/immediate	Moderate/deferred
Sorting and delivery – methods and costs	Manual/high	Automated/moderate

One may still object to such developments on grounds of the costs involved and the unproven nature of the benefits. It might seem that armchair shopping is worth promoting only if it allows growth in sales without the costs of having to develop new retail outlets. Major grocery firms have carried out, and are still pursuing, programmes of new store development, and these investments cannot be seen to be superfluous. In any case, most of the market would not be prepared to change to armchair shopping, and would want to continue using conventional stores.

This argument may however be inappropriate. Firstly, remote shopping, if carried out in substantial numbers by consumer type 1 (Table 12.3), could reduce the quantity of peak shopping trips, particularly on Thursday and Friday evenings, as these trips are associated with this type of shopper (Wrigley *et al.*, 1984). This could lead to staff savings and a more pleasant environment within the store at these times. Secondly, introduction of remote shopping for groceries might lead to an increase in market share, particularly if introduced by one company well ahead of its rivals.

Armchair shopping for other retail goods

Other areas where remote shopping appears to gain some support are clothes and shoes, books, and bulky electrical goods (Table 12.2). Of these, clothes, shoes and books have been prominent items in mail-order sales for many years, and the idea of purchasing them remotely is acceptable to many people. The poor-quality teletext displays available to viewdata users may have deterred developments in remote retailing of fashion goods, but in the near future displays of photographs will be possible within Prestel promotions. Bulky electrical goods can usually be described adequately in a remote manner, and are increasingly sold in retail warehouses where in-store assistance and advice are minimal (Guy, 1985). The advantages to the shopper of purchasing them remotely are, however, less clear than in the case of groceries, since shopping trips for comparison goods are less frequent and less likely to be regarded as time-wasting. This suggests that the advantages to the comparison-goods retailer of a major armchair-shopping promotion would initially be slight. In the longer term, the main purpose of such promotions would be to expand business without having to develop new retail outlets. While this may be the purpose of existing remote-shopping operations such as Comp-U-Card (*Retail and Distribution Management*, 1985b), they have been launched so far by firms acting as agents for manufacturers and distributors rather than by retailers operating in highly competitive markets such as clothing or electrical goods.

Impacts of armchair shopping upon trading performance

In a previous study of the possible medium-term impacts of viewdata shopping upon retail store performance (Guy, 1985), two types of impact were discussed. The first was the impact upon stores belonging to firms which decided to make armchair shopping available; the second type was a competitive impact upon those firms which decided against providing this service. In each case the impact was sub-divided further into a trading impact (cash flows) and a shopping impact (visits to stores). A similar approach is adopted below, although restricted to the types of products examined in the previous sections.

The basic objective of any firm introducing IT in selling its products to the consumer is to boost sales; a secondary objective may be to cut costs. This second objective is more problematic, since any savings in staff numbers within stores may be more than offset by the staff costs involved in assembling orders and delivering them to the customer's home. Certain conditions should be met. Firstly, there should be some possibility of new markets being opened to the firm as a result of the initiative. Secondly, any reductions in numbers of trips to the store, caused by substitution effects, should be identifiable with cost savings. Thirdly, the need for expensive new premises for storing and sorting goods destined for armchair customers should be avoided, at least initially.

In the case of grocery purchasing, there seems a reasonable chance that the three requirements could be met. The possibilities of increasing sales and reducing in-store costs at peak periods have already been suggested. Assembling remote customers' orders, although labour-intensive, could be carried out at 'quiet' periods. An additional major advantage is that the grocery superstore is already organised to carry a full range of goods and to combine storage and display functions. Remote shopping orders could therefore be met from the superstore and new distribution facilities would not be necessary. This means in turn that the impact upon store performance would be slight. Superstores would continue as the main type of outlet and the location of new stores would continue to be based on conventional criteria of catchment areas, competition from other stores, and development costs. The likely pattern of adoption of remote shopping, principally by affluent households with all adults working (Table 12.3), would not cause substantial changes in locational policy, since these households are already heavy users of superstores (Guy, 1984).

In the longer term, however, some changes in distribution methods might become worthwhile. Remote shopping orders could be fulfilled more efficiently at automated warehouses, where each record in the order would act as a signal for the appropriate item to be selected from storage (presumably through some form of bar coding), and moved to a point where the order was assembled. Technical limitations might mean that this facility was only available for very large sizes or batches of grocery items. Nevertheless, such warehouses could be considered for development after an initial period in which the demand for remote shopping was assessed. They might be initiated by existing grocery wholesalers or smaller multiple retail firms, rather than the existing major firms with their heavy commitment in superstores. An advantage of distributing from automated warehouses is that, so far as their location is concerned, customer accessibility and parking are of little importance; therefore cheap sites, formerly used for industrial purposes, would be suitable.

The competitive effects of armchair shopping for groceries upon other major firms which do not provide this service are unlikely to be sufficiently concentrated geographically to result in store closures or changes to locational strategies. The exception to this statement might occur where an exceptional concentration of consumer type 1 (see Table 12.3) existed within a store's catchment area and, because of the advantages of remote shopping, shifted their allegiances substantially. Otherwise, potential remote shoppers (the elderly, people in remote rural areas) would not generally be regular superstore shoppers at present. Some loss of trade for small grocery stores (where these remain) might occur however.

In other areas of retailing, the advantages of armchair shopping to established retail firms seem rather limited, and hence the effects on locational strategies could be minimal. More important would appear to be the progress made by existing mail order companies or other non-store retailers in setting up remote shopping systems using viewdata or cable TV. This might require new development of automated warehouses, especially for bulky electrical goods.

Some possible consequences in the longer term of widespread use of remote shopping have been suggested in a previous chapter (Guy, 1985). In clothing, shoes and other comparison goods, some replacement of conventional retail outlets by display showrooms might occur. The natural location for these would be either town centres or new out-of-town regional shopping centres, if town planning policies allow development of the latter. Showrooms displaying the latest fashions in a leisured atmosphere, devoid of sales pressure, would be an attractive part of the family-oriented environment which several writers have prognosticated for our major shopping centres.

In bulky electrical goods and possibly other 'retail warehouse' products, armchair shopping could affect further development of out-of-centre stores. It is not clear whether present stores of this type are sufficiently large to be efficient units for the purpose of handling remote orders. Partial replacement of these stores by very large automated warehouses, with regional catchment areas, might be more logical. Ultimately those firms not involved in remote shopping could suffer competitive effects. In the medium term at least, these would probably not be sufficient to cause closures, for reasons similar to those discussed in relation to grocery retailing.

Conclusions

In keeping with the theme of this volume, this chapter has concentrated on the impact of IT amongst the larger retail firms. This impact is peculiarly difficult to predict because progress in adoption of IT is likely to depend upon a small number of major investment decisions rather than a gradual assimilation of new methods. Thus the chapter assumes some major applications of existing IT methods by large firms, and examines some effects upon their market analysis methods and locational strategies.

Most of the other recent examinations of IT in retailing mentioned in this chapter have concluded that these effects are likely to be minor in the near future. This has partly been because of the reluctance of large retail firms to invest substantially in new methods of information handling while these are seen as being in an experimental phase. However, even if these methods (including remote shopping) were wholeheartedly adopted by several major firms, and marketed successfully to consumers, changes to firms' strategies might still be quite marginal. This is partly because retailers have enormous existing assets in their stores, warehouses, equipment and personnel, and wish to continue using them as efficiently as possible. Also, it appears that increasing use of IT will assist and accelerate trends which are already taking place in retailing, particularly the growing concern with market segmentation and targeting of selected consumers. IT will help firms to identify and reach their chosen market more efficiently – indeed this will probably be its most important impact in the near future.

Changes of any significance in locational strategies are likely to come about only through a major growth of use of IT by customers in their shopping behaviour. If (or when) this happens, most major retail firms would want to adapt remote shopping to their existing distribution network rather than vice versa. An extra factor which these firms need to be aware of, however, is the promotion of remote shopping by other agencies less committed to existing retailing patterns. These might include British Telecom and cable TV companies, banks and other institutions, wholesale distributors, mail-order firms, and small multiple retailers looking for a new way to expand their share of the market. These agencies will also target their products and services at carefully-selected market segments. Independent market research firms, especially those with access to EPOS and EFTPOS data, will no doubt be in demand for analyses of market potential (Rogers, 1985).

This raises a final issue. The position of academic researchers such as the author is not easy when factual material is hard to obtain. One of the ironies of the growing use of IT in retailing is that accurate information about this topic is restricted very much to those immediately and financially involved. This attitude has been justified by claims of the 'experimental' nature of the schemes so far. These claims are now becoming rather far-fetched when some schemes have been operating for two years or more and others involve investment of millions of pounds. It is to be hoped that some more complete and impartial assessments of retailers' and other agencies' experiences with IT can be made available to the general research community.

Two topics would be particularly relevant here: firstly, examination of the cost savings and other advantages or disadvantages of EPOS and management information networks; and secondly, examination of existing remote shopping schemes in terms of user characteristics and expenditure patterns. Until information of these types becomes readily available, impartial discussion of the prospects of IT in retailing will remain poorly informed and, hence, vague and speculative.

CHAPTER 13

Store choice, store location and market analysis: some final observations on future research priorities

Clive Humby

Introduction

In the last ten years or so the use of modelling techniques to understand how the retail environment functions have increased apace. This has been contributed to by the information explosion, the advent of cheaper computer resources, and the availability of well-researched methods. However, many of these techniques of retail analysis and forecasting have focused on the grocery/fast-moving consumer-goods market, and this has resulted in some severe limitations to the range of application of such methods.

In this short chapter some suggestions will be made concerning future research priorities in retail analysis and forecasting. However, to understand where research in this field might develop in the future we must first consider current trends and where existing methods are deficient.

Background

The information explosion

Today vast databases are available on the demographic, economic and social characteristics of Britain. These include most of the major factors which affect the retail market place. The 1981 Census, though ageing rapidly, is still a wealth of information, with over 500 million facts and figures on Britain, allocated to small areas of a few hundred houses. Through the efforts of commercial organisations like CACI, a vast wealth of other information has also been drawn together and comprehensive retail databases now exist covering the location, size and mix of retail and service outlets, the transport infrastructure, current workforce structures, local unemployment levels, rates of local population growth/decline, and market research information on over 4,000 product fields and 50,000 product lines. At CACI our total database runs to almost 9 gigabytes, and there are eight other agencies in Britain providing services in this area.

The price of technology and the implications for the retailer

Simultaneously with the explosion in information, computer hardware is falling in price rapidly. An IBM PC with 60 megabytes of storage can be obtained for less than £5,000. This means a retailer should be looking to have a comprehensive marketing database sitting on his desk in the next few years.

This shows us the way forward – the need for models and systems to allow the retailer to benefit from this revolution in computing. Tie this all back to the other information explosion – the arrival of EPOS (see Chapters 1 and 12 of this volume) and in a short amount of time the poor retailer will be buried by the range and complexity of his information resource.

However it should never be forgotten that retailers are not analysts of data. Their uses of computer systems are likely to be restricted to cost benefit problems such as stock control, ordering, pricing and other directly beneficial solutions. The retailer does not want to be swamped in a morass of information and his needs are simple – a clear understanding of how well his store will do if he makes a particular business decision.

The limitations of current retail analysis and forecasting techniques

The retail modelling research which has been dominant so far in British academia has a serious limitation. Almost without exception it has concentrated on the grocery market. One assumption that flows throughout the work is the concept of independence of choice; that is, that a person's choice (probability) of using retailer/product X is independent of his probability of using retailer/product Y. Whilst this is mostly true in the broad area of fast-moving consumer-goods and grocery retailing, it is not true of the durable, fashion goods and service retailing of the high street.

Moreover, it should not be forgotten that the market for these grocery-retailing forecasting techniques is rather small – with a dozen large grocery corporations accounting for virtually all the market. In these organisations teams of specialists have been built up over the last five years (see Chapter 4 of this volume) providing an in-house resource. The market for retail analysis and forecasting techniques amongst the much larger number and wider range of fashion goods and service retailers is potentially much larger, and there is much less in-house provision.

Future research priorities

Future research must pay more attention to the interrelationships of choice. The high street, the speciality retailer, the rapid change in lifestyles, are the fields where future efforts should be directed.

Products and choice

On the high street the choice of fashion outlet does *not* conform to the NBD and Dirichlet techniques applicable to the grocery market. There is much evidence that choice is an important factor in itself. After all the common title for such shopping is 'comparison'.

The fact that a young girl does *not* visit the Next chain probably *does* mean she is more likely to visit Chelsea Girl. Lifestyle is very important in these markets and all the work to date crumbles before the whim or fancy of our young shopper.

This is not to say, however, that her patterns cannot be predicted, but it does mean that attention must be focused on new techniques of research which take account of the overall attractiveness and internal layout of individual shopping centres, lifestyle or niche marketing, and so on. Certainly the work done in these areas to date, primarily in the commercial rather than academic sector, does show some of the ways forward for retailing research.

Moreover, it can be argued that these new fields of study are equally important to the traditional consumers of much academic research – the grocery giants. With recent moves out of town and the development of garden, fashion, clothing, durable, and now even car sales, by these organisations, we need to look afresh at their needs.

The same arguments imply that the independence-of-choice assumption is also no longer true in many areas of grocery retailing itself. With the rapid segmentation of product ranges, and high-mark-up speciality products like Perrier, French cheeses, and such like, retailers' profits are increasingly dependent on niche markets and the whims of those market segments.

Catchment areas

For the last fifteen years much research has been conducted on the interaction of stores and their consumers – who shops where. Models abound which are segmented by the transport infrastructure and the behavioural patterns of the shopper when he/she arrives by a particular mode. Certainly the car shopper uses the retail structure in a very different fashion to other segments of the market with differential access to public and private transport.

However, it is not an overstatement to suggest that the past couple of years have seen more progress than the last fifteen in understanding catchments. A retailer does not need to tailor a large piece of research to help him understand. The majority of retailers are sitting on, or have direct access to, a vast wealth of information on these patterns. Some is already collected in omnibus research; more importantly, there are over 15.5 million adults with credit cards in Britain. It is not difficult to analyse the relationship between their spending patterns at particular retail chains and the location of their homes. A pressing need now is to understand how to relate the patterns displayed in the credit-using society to the non-users. What interrelationships exist between these groups?

Lifestyle

The acid test of all the above work is lifestyle – the measurement and understanding, not of the whole population, but of discrete lifestyle or niche segments. We must set aside much of the existing research and look to the future; redraw our priorities and look again on how we will cope with the information revolution.

EPOS
Census
Lifestyle
Travel patterns
Market research

These are interrelated issues and we must learn to identify the wood from the trees if we are truly to understand store choice, store location and market analysis.

BIBLIOGRAPHY

The following list is intended to serve both as a reference list and research source. For this reason a number of items have been added which are not directly cited in the text.

Adler, T. J. and Ben Akiva, M. E. (1976), 'Joint choice model for frequency destination and travel mode for shopping trips', *Transportation Research Record*, 569, pp. 136–50.

Alty, R., Mackie, S., Moseley, J. and Rainford, P. (1979), *The South Yorkshire Shopping Model*, Reading, Unit for Retail Planning Information.

Applebaum, W. (1968), *Store Location Strategy*, Reading, Mass., Addison-Wesley.

Aske Research (1972), *Petrol*, London, Aske Research Ltd.

Bacon, R. W. (1971), 'An approach to the theory of consumer shopping behaviour', *Urban Studies*, 8, pp. 55–65.

Bacon R. W. (1984), *Consumer Spatial Behaviour: A Model of Purchasing Decisions over Space and Time*, Oxford, Clarendon Press.

Ballobar, B. and Stern, N. (1972), 'The optimal structure of market areas', *Journal of Economic Theory*, 4, pp. 174–9.

Barnard, N., Ehrenberg, A. S. C. and Goodhardt, G. J. (1985), *The NBD Model for Scanner Panel Data*, CMaC Working Paper, London Business School.

Bates, J. J. (1983), 'Stated preference techniques for the analysis of transport behaviour', Hamburg, World Conference on Transport Research.

Bates, J. J. (1984), 'Values of time from stated preference data', PTRC Summer Annual Meeting, Brighton, Paper H2.

Bates, J. J. and Roberts, M. (1983), 'Recent experience with models fitted to stated preference data', PTRC Summer Annual Meeting, Brighton.

Batsell, R. R. and Polking, J. C. (1985), 'A new class of market share models', *Marketing Science*, 4, pp. 177–98.

Batty, J. M. (1976), *Urban Modelling: Algorithms, Calibrations, Predictions*, Cambridge University Press.

Batty, J. M. (1978), 'Reilly's challenge: new laws of retail gravitation which define systems of central places', *Environment and Planning A*, 10, pp. 185–219.

Batty, J. M. and March, L. (1976), 'Method of residues in urban modelling', *Environment and Planning A*, 8, pp. 189–214.

Batty, J. M. and Saether, A. (1972), 'A note on the design of shopping models', *Journal of the Royal Town Planning Institute*, 58, pp. 303–6.

Baxter, R. S. (1976), *Computer and Statistical Techniques for Planners*, London, Methuen.

Beaumont, J. R. (1981), 'Location-allocation problems in a plane: a review of some models', *Socio-Economic Planning Sciences*, 15, pp. 217–29.

Beaumont, J. R. (1982), 'Mathematical programming in human geography', *Mathematical Social Sciences*, 2, pp. 213–43.

Beaumont, J. R. (1984), 'A description of structural change in a central place system: a speculation of using Q-analysis', *International Journal of Man-Machine Studies*, 20, pp. 567–94.

Beaumont, J. R. (1986a), 'Modelling should be more relevant: some personal reflections', Letter to the Editor, *Environment and Planning A*, 18, pp. 419–21.

Beaumont, J. R. (1986b), 'Location-allocation models and central place theory', in Ghosh, A., and Rushton, G. (eds), *Spatial Analysis and Location Allocation Models*, New York, Van Nostrand Reinhold, pp. 21–54.

Beaumont, J. R. and Beaumont, C. D. (1987), 'TELECOM: a business game', Coopers and Lybrand, London.

Beavon, K. S. O. and Hay, A. (1977), 'Consumer choice of shopping centre – hypergeometric model', *Environment and Planning A*, 9, pp. 1375–93.

Becker, G. S. (1965), 'A theory of the allocation of time', *Economic Journal*, 75, pp. 488–517.

Becker, G. S. (1976), *The Economic Approach to Human Behaviour*, University of Chicago Press.

Beggs, S., Cardell, N. S. and Hausman, J. (1981), 'Assessing the potential demand for electric cars', *Journal of Econometrics*, 16, pp. 1–9.

Bennison, D. J. (1985), 'Domestic viewdata services in Britain: past experience, present status, and future potential', *Environment and Planning B*, 12, pp. 151–64.

Bennison, D. J. and Davies, R. L. (1980), 'The impact of town centre shopping schemes in Britain: their impact on traditional retail environments', *Progress in Planning*, 14, pp. 1–104.

Berry, B. J. L. (1967), *Geography of Market Centres and Retail Distribution*, Englewood Cliffs, NJ, Prentice Hall.

Berry, B. J. L., Barnum, H. G. and Tennant, R. J. (1962), 'Retail location and consumer behaviour', *Papers of the Regional Science Association*, 9, pp. 65–106.

Bertuglia, C. and Leonardi, G. (1981), 'Heuristic algorithms for the normative location of retail activities systems', *Papers of the Regional Science Association*, 44, pp. 144–59.

Bird, J. (1985), 'ICL wins race to the till', *Sunday Times*, 14 July.

Birkin, M., Clarke, M. and Wilson, A. G. (1985), 'Theoretical properties of retail models', paper presented to a Colloquium on Retail Modelling, Erasmus University, Rotterdam, October.

Birkin, M. and Wilson, A. G. (1985), *Some Properties of Spatial-Structural-Economic-Dynamic Models*, Working Paper 440, School of Geography, University of Leeds.

Blommestein, H., Nijkamp, P. and Van Veenendaal, W. (1980), 'Shopping perceptions and preferences: a multi-dimensional attractiveness analysis of consumer and entrepreneurial attitudes', *Economic Geography*, 56, pp. 155–74.

Bowlby, S. (1984), 'Planning for women to shop in post-war Britain', *Society and Space*, 2, pp. 179–99.

Bowlby, S., Breheny, M. J. and Foot, D. (1984a), 'Problems and methods in store location, 1: Is locating a viable store becoming more difficult?', *Retail and Distribution Management*, 12, 5, pp. 31–3.

Bowlby, S., Breheny, M. J. and Foot, D. (1984b), 'Problems and methods in store location, 2: Expanding into new geographical areas', *Retail and Distribution Management*, 12, 6, pp. 42–6.

Bowlby, S., Breheny, M. J. and Foot, D. (1985a), 'Problems and methods in store location, 3: Choosing the right site', *Retail and Distribution Management*, 13, 1, pp. 44–8.

Bowlby, S., Breheny, M. J. and Foot, D. (1985b), 'Problems and methods in store location, 4: Local site and store evaluation issues', *Retail and Distribution Management*, 13, 2, pp. 40–4.

Breheny, M. J. (1978), 'The measurement of spatial opportunity in strategic planning', *Regional Studies*, 12, pp. 463–79.

Breheny, M. J. (1983a), 'The assessment of hypermarket and superstore impact; the manual model', in Wade, B. (ed.), *Assessing Hypermarket and Superstore Impact*, Paper 25, Reading, Unit for Retail Planning Information.

Breheny, M. J. (1983b), 'Modelling store location and performance; a review', *European Research*, 11, pp. 111–21.

Breheny, M. J., Green, J. and Roberts, A. J. (1981), 'A practical approach to the assessment of hypermarket impact', *Regional Studies*, 15, pp. 459–74.

Broadbent, T. A. (1971), 'A hierarchical interaction-allocation model for a two-level spatial system', *Regional Studies*, 5, pp. 23–7.

Brooks, R. (1985), 'Fingers do the shopping', *Sunday Times*, 22 December.

Broom, D. (1982), 'A two-stage model of shopping behaviour calibrated on diary data', paper presented at the Regional Science Association Conference (British Section), Reading.

Broom, D. and Wrigley, N. (1983), 'Incorporating explanatory variables into stochastic panel-data models of urban shopping behaviour', *Urban Geography*, 4, pp. 244–57.

Buck, S. F. (1982), 'Consumer panels in the UK: past, present and future', in *Proceedings of the Market Research Society Conference*, London, The Market Research Society.

Bucklin, L. P. (1971), 'Retail gravity models and consumer choice: a theoretical and empirical critique', *Economic Geography*, 47, pp. 489–97.

CACI (1981), *ACORN: A New Approach to Market Analysis*, London, CACI Ltd.

Cadwallader, M. (1975), 'A behavioural model of consumer spatial decision making', *Economic Geography*, 51, pp. 339–49.

Carmone, F. J. and Green, P. B. (1981), 'Model mis-specification in multi-attribute parameter estimation', *Journal of Marketing Research*, 18, pp. 87–9.

Cattin, P. and Wittink, D. R. (1982), 'Commercial use of conjoint analysis: a survey', *Journal of Marketing*, 46, pp. 44–53.

Champion, A. G. (1983), 'Population trends in the 1970s', in Goddard, J. B. and Champion, A. G. (eds), *The Urban and Regional Transformation of Britain*, London, Methuen, pp. 187–214.

Chapman, R. G. and Staelin, R. (1982), 'Exploiting rank ordered choice set data within the stochastic utility model', *Journal of Marketing Research*, 19, pp. 288–301.

Charlton, M., Openshaw, S. and Wymer, C. (1984), 'Some new classifications of census enumeration districts in Britain: a poor man's ACORN', paper presented at Conference on Census Analysis and Applications: Results of the 1981 Census, University of Sheffield.

Charlton, P. (1973), 'A review of store loyalty', *Journal of the Market Research Society*, 15, pp. 34–41.

Chatfield, C., Ehrenberg, A. S. C. and Goodhardt, G. J. (1966), 'Progress on a simplified model of stationary purchasing behaviour',

Journal of the Royal Statistical Society, Series A, 129, pp. 317–67.

Chatfield, C. and Goodhardt, G. J. (1975), 'Results concerning brand choice', *Journal of Marketing Research*, 12, pp. 110–13.

Christaller, W. (1933), *Die Centralen Orte in Sudddeutschland*, Jena, Gustav Fischer; English translation by Baskin, C. W., *Central Places in Southern Germany*, Englewood Cliffs, NJ, Prentice Hall.

Clark, D. (1975), 'Understanding canonical correlation analysis', *Concepts and Techniques in Modern Geography, No. 3*, Norwich, Geoabstracts.

Clarke, G. P. (1984a), *The Expansion of Service Outlets Across the City*, Working Paper 379, School of Geography, University of Leeds.

Clarke, G. P. (1984b), *The Changing Morphology of Urban Retailing in the Recession*, Working Paper 382, School of Geography, University of Leeds.

Clarke, G. P. (1985), *The Changing Expression of Small-Scale Retailing in the City, 1955–1983*, Working Paper 418, School of Geography, University of Leeds.

Clarke, G. P. (1986), *Retail Centre Usage and Structure: Empirical and Theoretical Explorations*, unpublished PhD thesis, School of Geography, University of Leeds.

Clarke, G. P. and Macgill, S. M. (1983), *The Changing Retail Structure in Leeds 1961–82: Initial Explorations with the Q-Analysis Algorithm*, Working Paper 368, School of Geography, University of Leeds.

Clarke, G. P. and Wilson, A. G. (1986), *Performance Indicators within a Model-Based Approach to Urban Planning*, Working Paper 446, School of Geography, University of Leeds.

Clarke, G. P., Clarke, M. and Wilson, A. G. (1985), 'Multiple bifurcation effects with a logistic attractiveness function in the supply side of a service system', *Sistemi Urbani*, 7, pp. 43–76.

Clarke, M. (1981), 'A note on the stability of equilibrium solutions in production-constrained spatial interaction models', *Environment and Planning A*, 13, pp. 601–4.

Clarke, M. (1984), *Integrating Dynamical Models of Urban Structure and Activities: An Application to Urban Retail Systems*, unpublished PhD thesis, School of Geography, University of Leeds.

Clarke, M. (1985), 'The role of attractiveness functions in the determination of equilibrium solutions to production-constrained spatial interaction models', *Environment and Planning A*, 17, pp.175–83.

Clarke, M. (1986), 'Demographic processes and household dynamics: a micro-simulation approach', in Woods, R. I. and Rees, P. H. (eds), *Population Structure and Models*, London, Allen & Unwin.

Clarke, M. and Williams, H. C. W. L. (1988), *Micro Analysis in Urban and Regional Systems*, Cambridge University Press.

Clarke, M. and Wilson, A. G. (1983), 'Dynamics of urban spatial structure: progress and problems', *Journal of Regional Science*, 23, pp. 1–18.

Clarke, M. and Wilson, A. G. (1984), *Models for Health Care Planning: The Case of the Piemonte Region*, Working Paper 36, IRES, Torino.

Clarke, M. and Wilson, A. G. (1985), *The Dynamics of Urban Spatial Structure: The Progress of a Research Program*, Working Paper 410, School of Geography, University of Leeds.

Clawson, C. J. (1974), 'Fitting branch locations, performance standards, and marketing strategies to local conditions', *Journal of Marketing*, 38, pp. 8–14.

Cochran, W. G. and Cox, G. M. (1957), *Experimental Designs*, 2nd edition, New York, John Wiley.

Coelho, J. D. and Williams, H. C. W. L. (1978), 'On the design of land use plans through locational surplus maximisation', *Papers of the Regional Science Association*, 40, pp. 71–86.

Coelho, J. D. and Wilson, A. G. (1976), 'The optimum location and size for shopping centres', *Regional Studies*, 10, pp. 413–21.

Coelho, J. D. and Wilson, A. G. (1977), 'Some equivalence theorems to integrate entropy maximising submodels within overall mathematical programming frameworks', *Geographical Analysis*, 9, pp. 160–73.

Coelho, J. D., Williams, H. C. W. L. and Wilson, A. G. (1978), 'Entropy maximising submodels within overall mathematical programming frameworks: a correction', *Geographical Analysis*, 10, pp. 195–201.

Collins, N. and Mughal, R. (1985), 'Why mega-money goes out of town', *Sunday Times*, 21 April.

Crask, M. R. (1979), 'A simulation model of patronage behaviour within shopping centres', *Decision Sciences*, 1, pp. 1–15.

Crouchley, R. and Wilson, A. G. (1983), *The Optimum Sizes and Locations of Schools*, Working Paper 369, School of Geography, University of Leeds.

Cunningham, R. M. (1961), 'Customer loyalty to store and brand', *Harvard Business Review*, 39, pp. 127–37.

Davies, K., Gilligan, C. T. and Sutton, C. J. (1986), 'The development of own label product strategies in grocery and DIY retailing in the United Kingdom', *International Journal of Retailing*, 1, pp. 6–19.

Davies, K. and Sparks, L. (1986), 'Asda-MFI: the superstore and the flat pack', *International Journal of Retailing*, 1, pp. 55–78.

Davies, R. B. (1984), 'A generalised beta-logistic model for longitudinal data with an application to residential mobility', *Environment and Planning A*, 16, pp. 1375–86.

Davies, R. L. (1969), 'Effects of consumer income differences on shopping movement behaviour', *Tijdschrift voor Economische en Social Geografie*, 60, pp. 111–21.

Davies, R. L. (1973), 'Evaluation of retail store attributes and sales performance', *European Journal of Marketing*, 7, pp. 89–102.

Davies, R. L. (1977a), *Marketing Geography*, London, Methuen.

Davies, R. L. (1977b), 'Store location and store assessment research: the integration of some new and traditional techniques', *Transactions of the Institute of British Geographers*, New Series 2, pp. 141–57.

Davies, R. L. (1984), *Retail and Commercial Planning*, London, Croom Helm.

Davies, R. L. (1985), 'The Gateshead Shopping and Information Service', *Environment and Planning B*, 12, pp. 209–20.

Davies, R. L. and Reynolds, J. (1986), 'Technological change in retailing: the long-term implications', paper presented at Annual Meeting of the Institute of British Geographers, Reading.

Davies, R. L. and Rogers, D. S. (eds) (1984), *Store Location and Store Assessment Research*, Chichester, John Wiley.

Dawson, J. A. (1983a), *Shopping Centre Development*, New York, Longman.

Dawson, J. A. (1983b), *IT and its Effects on the Distributive Trades*, Working Paper 8301, Department of Business Studies, University of Stirling.

Dawson, J. A. and Kirby, D. A. (1979), *Small Scale Retailing in the UK*, Farnborough, Saxon House.

Dawson, J. A. and Kirby, D. A. (1980), 'Urban retail provision and consumer behaviour: some examples from Western society', in Herbert, D. T. and Johnston, R. J. (eds), *Geography and the Urban Environment, Vol. 3*, Chichester, John Wiley, pp. 87–132.

Dawson, J. A. and Lord, J. D. (eds) (1985), *Shopping Centre Development: Policies and Prospects*, London, Croom Helm.

Distributive Trades Economic Development Council (1970), *Urban Models in Shopping Studies*, London, National Economic Development Office.

Distributive Trades Economic Development Council (1982), *Technology: The Issues for the Distributive Trades*, London, National Economic Development Office.

Drewett, R., Goddard, J. B. and Spence, N. (1975), 'What's happening to British cities?' *Town and Country Planning*, 43, pp. 523–30.

Drewett, R., Goddard, J. B. and Spence, N. (1976), 'What's Happening in British Cities?' *Town and Country Planning*, 44, pp. 14–24.

Drummey, G. (1984), 'Traditional methods of sales forecasting', in Davies, R. L. and Rogers, D. (eds), *Store Location and Store Assessment Research*, Chichester, John Wiley, pp. 279–300.

Dunn, E. S. (1956), 'The market potential concept and the analysis of location', *Papers of the Regional Science Association*, 2, pp. 183–94.

Dunn, R. and Wrigley, N. (1984), 'Store loyalty for grocery products; an empirical study', *Area*, 16, pp. 307–14.

Dunn, R. and Wrigley, N. (1985), 'Beta-logistic models of urban shopping centre choice', *Geographical Analysis*, 17, pp. 95–113.

Dunn, R., Reader, S. and Wrigley, N. (1983), 'An investigation of the assumptions of the NBD model as applied to purchasing at individual stores', *Applied Statistics*, 32, pp. 249–59.

Dunn, R., Reader, S. and Wrigley, N. (1987), 'A non-parametric approach to the incorporation of heterogeneity into repeated polytomous choice models of urban shopping behaviour', *Transportation Research A*, 21A, 4/5, pp. 327–43.

Eaton, B. C. and Lipsey, R. G. (1975), 'The principle of minimum differentiation reconsidered: some new developments in the theory of spatial competition', *Review of Economic Studies*, 42, pp. 27–49.

Eaton, B. C. and Lipsey, R. G. (1976), 'The non-uniqueness of equilibria in the Loschian location model', *American Economic Review*, 46, pp. 77–93.

Eaton, B. C. and Lipsey, R. G. (1979), 'Comparison shopping and the clustering of homogeneous firms', *Journal of Regional Science*, 19, pp. 421–35.

Eaton, B. C. and Lipsey, R. G. (1982), 'An economic theory of central places', *The Economic Journal*, 92, pp. 56–72.

Ehrenberg, A. S. C. (1959), 'The pattern of consumer purchases', *Applied Statistics*, 8, pp. 26–41.

Ehrenberg, A. S. C. (1972), *Repeat-Buying: Theory and Applications*, Amsterdam and New York, North-Holland Press. Second Edition (1988), Griffin, London; Oxford University Press, New York.

Ehrenberg, A. S. C. (1986), 'Pricing and brand differentiation', *Singapore International Marketing Review*, 1, pp. 5–15.

Ehrenberg, A. S. C. and Goodhardt, G. J. (1968), 'A comparison of American and British repeat-buying habits', *Journal of Marketing Research*, 5, pp. 29–33.

Ehrenberg, A. S. C. and Goodhardt, G. J. (1969a), 'A model of multi-brand buying', *Journal of Marketing Research*, 6, pp. 77–84.

Ehrenberg, A. S. C. and Goodhardt, G. J. (1969b), 'Duplication of television viewing between and within channels', *Journal of Marketing Research*, 6, pp. 169–78.

Ehrenberg, A. S. C. and Goodhardt, G. J. (1979), *Understanding Buyer Behaviour*, New York, J. Walter Thompson and MRCA.

Eilon, S., Watson-Gandy, C. D. T. and Christofides, N. (1971), *Distribution Management: Mathematical Modelling and Practical Analysis*, London, Griffin.

Engel, J. F., Blackwell, R. D. and Kollat, D. T. (1978), *Consumer Behaviour*, 3rd Edition, Hinsdale, Illinois, Dryden Press.

England, L. R. and Ehrenberg, A. S. C. (1985), *The 1984 Marketing Experiments*, CMaC Working Paper, London Business School.

Evans, A. W. (1972), 'On the theory of valuation and allocation of time', *Scottish Journal of Political Economics*, 19, pp. 1–17.

Fenwick, I. (1978), *Techniques in Store Location Research – A Review and Application*, Corbridge, Retail and Planning Associates.

Fotheringham, A. S. (1982), 'Multicollinearity and parameter estimates in a linear model', *Geographical Analysis*, 14, pp. 64–71.

Fotheringham, A. S. (1983a), 'A new set of spatial-interaction models: the theory of competing destinations', *Environment and Planning A*, 15, pp. 15–36.

Fotheringham, A. S. (1983b), 'Some theoretical aspects of destination choice and their relevance to production-constrained gravity models', *Environment and Planning A*, 15, pp. 1121–32.

Fotheringham, A. S. (1985), 'Spatial competition and agglomeration in urban modelling', *Environment and Planning A*, 17, pp. 213–30.

Fotheringham, A. S. (1986), 'Modelling hierarchical destination choice', *Environment and Planning A*, 18, pp. 401–18.

Frank, R. E., Massy, W. F. and Wind, Y. (1972), *Market Segmentation*, Englewood Cliffs, New Jersey, Prentice Hall.

Frisbie, G. A. (1980), 'Ehrenberg's negative binomial model applied to grocery store trips', *Journal of Marketing Research*, 17, pp. 385–90.

Garrett, J. and Wright, G. (1980), 'Micro is beautiful', in Forester, T. (ed.), *The Micro-electronics Revolution*, Oxford, Basil Blackwell, pp. 488–96.

Gautschi, D. A. (1981), 'Specification of patronage models for retail centre choice', *Journal of Marketing Research*, 18, pp. 162–81.

Getis, A. (1963), 'The determination of the location of retail activities with use of a map transformation', *Economic Geography*, 39, pp. 1–22.

Getis, A. (1984), 'Interaction modelling using second order analysis', *Environment and Planning A*, 16, pp. 173–84.

Goddard, J. B. and Champion, A. G. (eds) (1983), *The Urban and Regional Transformation of Britain*, London, Methuen.

Goodhardt, G. J., Ehrenberg, A. S. C. and Chatfield, C. (1984), 'The Dirichlet: a comprehensive model of buying behaviour', *Journal of the Royal Statistical Society A*, 147, pp. 621–55.

Goodhardt, G. J., Ehrenberg, A. S. C. and Collins, M. A. (1975), *The Television Audience*, Aldershot, Gower.

Green, P. E. and Srinivasan, V. (1978), 'Conjoint analysis in consumer research: issues and outlook', *Journal of Consumer Research*, 5, pp. 103–23.

Guy, C. M. (1975), *Consumer Behaviour and its Geographic Impact*, Geographical Paper 34, Department of Geography, University of Reading.

Guy, C. M. (1981), *Models and Simulation Methods in Hypermarket Impact Studies*, Papers in Planning Research 27, Department of Town Planning, University of Wales Institute of Science and Technology, Cardiff.

Guy, C. M. (1984), *Superstore Shopping in Cardiff*, Information Brief 84/5, Reading, Unit for Retail Planning Information.

Guy, C. M. (1985), 'Some speculations on the retailing and planning implications of "push-button shopping" in Britain', *Environment and Planning B*, 12, pp. 193–208.

Guy, C. M., Wrigley, N., O'Brien, L. G. and Hiscocks, G. (1983), *The Cardiff Consumer Panel: a report on the methodology*, Papers in Planning Research 68, Department of Town Planning, University of Wales Institute of Science and Technology, Cardiff.

Haag, G. and Wilson, A. G. (1986), *A Dynamic Service Sector Model: A Master Equations Approach with Prices and Land Rents*, Working Paper no. 447, School of Geography, University of Leeds.

Hall, B. F. (1982), 'Neighbourhood differences in retail food stores: income versus race and age of population', *Economic Geography*, 59, pp. 282–95.

Hall, P., Thomas, R., Gracey, H. and Drewett, R. (1973), *The Containment of Urban England*, London, Allen & Unwin.

Halperin, W. C. (1985), *Spatial Cognition and Consumer Behaviour*, unpublished PhD dissertation, Department of Geography, University of California, Santa Barbara.

Hansen, F. (1976), 'Psychological theories of consumer choice', *Journal of Consumer Research*, 3, pp. 117–42.

Hansen, W. G. (1959), 'How accessibility shapes land use', *Journal of the American Institute of Planning*, 25, pp. 73–6.

Hanson, S. (1977), 'Measuring the cognitive levels of urban residents', *Geografiska Annaler*, 59B, pp. 67–87.

Harris, B. (1964), *A Model of Locational Equilibrium for Retail Trade*, mimeo, Penn-Jersey Transportation Study, Philadelphia.

Harris, B. and Wilson, A. G. (1978), 'Equilibrium values and dynamics of attractiveness terms in production-constrained spatial-interaction models', *Environment and Planning A*, 10, pp. 371–88.

Harris, B., Choukroun, J. M. and Wilson, A. G. (1982), 'Economies of scale and the existence of supply-side equilibria in a production-constrained spatial-interaction model', *Environment and Planning A*, 14, pp. 823–37.

Harvard Business School (1982), *The US Retail Coffee Market (A)*,

Boston, Mass., Harvard Business School; International Case Clearing House, 9-582-087.

Harvey, D. (1985), *The Urbanization of Capital*, Oxford, Blackwell.

Haynes, K. E. and Fotheringham, A. S. (1984), *Gravity and Spatial Interaction Models*, Beverley Hills, Sage.

Hensher, D. A. (1984), 'Representativeness of the observable component of indirect utility functions: an empirical revelation', *Journal of Business*, 57, pp. 265–80.

Hillier Parker Research (1986), *Shopping Schemes in the Pipeline*, Research Department, Hillier Parker, London.

Hodgart, R. (1978), 'Optimising access to public services', *Progress in Human Geography*, 2, pp. 17–48.

Horton, F. E. and Reynolds, D. R. (1971), 'Effects of urban spatial structure on spatial behaviour', *Economic Geography*, 47, pp. 36–46.

Hotelling, H. (1929), 'Stability in competition', *Economic Journal*, 39, pp. 41–57.

Howard, E. B. (1985), 'Teleshopping in North America', *Environment and Planning B*, 12, pp. 141–50.

Hudson, R. (1974), 'Images of the retailing environment: an example of the use of the repertory grid methodology', *Environment and Behaviour*, 6, pp. 470–94.

Huff, D. L. (1964), 'Defining and estimating a trading area', *Journal of Marketing*, 28, pp. 34–8.

Huff, D. L. (1966), 'Optimal retail location', *Land Economics*, 42, pp. 293–303.

Humby, C. (1984), 'Shop location techniques: the options available, and how to choose', paper presented to RMDP Conference on Techniques for Shop Location, London, June.

ICL (1985), *Retailing Tomorrow: The Impact of Technology in Retailing*, London, ICL.

Institute of Fiscal Studies (1984), *The Regulation of Retail Trading Hours*, economic review conducted for the Home Office Committee of Inquiry into Proposals to Amend the Shops Acts, London, Institute for Fiscal Studies.

Jephcott, J. St G. (1972), 'Consumer loyalty – a fresh look', in *Proceedings of the 1972 Annual Conference*, London, Market Research Society.

Jeuland, A. P., Bass, F. M. and Wright, G. P. (1980), 'A multi-brand stochastic model compounding heterogeneous Erlang timing and multinomial choice processes', *Operations Research*, 28, pp. 255–77.

Jones, G. and Walman, B. (1979), 'The impact of mini and microcomputers in retailing', *Retail and Distribution Management*, 7, July/August, pp. 19–23.

Jones, J. M. and Zufryden, F. S. (1980), 'Adding explanatory variables to a consumer purchase behaviour model: an exploratory study', *Journal of Marketing Research*, 17, pp. 323–34.

Jones, K. and Mock, D. (1984), 'Evaluating retail trading performances', in Davies, R. L. and Rogers, D. (eds), *Store Location and Store Assessment Research*, Chichester, John Wiley, pp. 333–60.

Kaashoek, J. F. and Vorst, A. C. F. (1984), 'The cusp catastrophe in the urban retail model', *Environment and Planning A*, 16, pp. 851–62.

Katz, M. L. and Shapiro, C. (1984), *Consumer Shopping Behaviour in the Retail Coffee Market*, Working Paper, Princeton University.

Kau, Ah Keng (1981), *Patterns of Store Choice*, unpublished PhD dissertation, London Business School.

Kau, Ah Keng, and Ehrenberg, A. S. C. (1984), 'Patterns of store choice', *Journal of Marketing Research*, 21, pp. 399–409.

Kennett, S. and Spence, N. (1979), 'British population trends in the 1970s', *Town and Country Planning*, 48, pp. 221–4.

King, L. J. (1984), *Central Place Theory*, Beverley Hills, Sage.

Kirby, D. A. (1982), 'Retailing in the age of the chip', *Service Industries Review*, 2, pp. 9–21.

Kirby, D. A. (1986), 'Convenience stores: the polarisation of British retailing', *Retail and Distribution Management*, 13, March/April, pp. 7–12.

Koppelman, F. S. and Hauser, J. R. (1978), 'Destination choice behaviour for non-grocery shopping trips', *Transportation Research Record*, 673, pp. 157–65.

Kornblau, C. (ed.) (1968), *Guide to Store Location Research*, Reading, Mass., Addison-Wesley.

Lakshmanan, T. R. and Hansen, W. G. (1965), 'A retail market potential model', *Journal of the American Institute of Planning*, 31, pp. 134–43.

Landau, U., Prashker, J. N. and Alpern, B. (1982), 'Evaluation of activity constrained choice sets to shopping destination choice', *Transportation Research A*, 16A, pp. 199–207.

Leckenby, J. D. and Kishi, S. (1984), 'The Dirichlet multinomial distribution as a magazine exposure model', *Journal of Marketing Research*, 21, pp. 100–6.

Leonardi, G. (1978), 'Optimum facility location by accessibility maximising', *Environment and Planning A*, 10, pp. 1287–306.

Leonardi, G. (1981), 'A unifying framework for public location problems: Part 1: a critical overview and some unsolved problems; Part 2: some new models and extensions', *Environment and Planning A*, 13, pp. 1001–28 and 1085–108.

Leonardi, G. (1982), *Public Facility Location: Issues and Approaches*, PR-82–83, Laxenburg, International Institute for Applied Systems Analysis.

Lincoln, D. J. and Samli, A. C. (1979), 'Definitions, dimensions and measurement of store image: a literature summary and synthesis', in Franz, R., Hopkins, R. and Toma, A. (eds), *Proceedings of the Southern Marketing Association*, pp. 430–3.

Lloyd, R. and Jennings, D. (1978), 'Shopping behaviour and income: comparisons in an urban environment', *Economic Geography*, 54, pp. 157–67.

Lodish, L. M. and Reibstein, D. J. (1986), 'Keeping informed: new gold mines and minefields in market research', *Harvard Business Review*, 86, 1, pp. 168–82.

Lombardo, S. R. and Rabino, G. A. (1983), 'Non-linear dynamic models for spatial interaction: the results of some numerical experiments', paper presented to the 23rd European Congress, Regional Science Association, Poitiers, France.

Losch, A. (1940), *Die Raumliche Ordung Der Wirtschaft*, Jena, Gustav Fischer; English translation by Woglam, W. H. and Stolper, W. F. (1954), *The Economics of Location*, New Haven, Connecticut, Yale University Press.

Louviere, J. J. and Meyer, R. J. (1979), *Behavioural Analysis of Destination Choice: Theory and Empirical Evidence*, Technical Report 112, Institute of Urban and Regional Research, University of Iowa.

Louviere, J. J. and Meyer, R. J. (1981), 'A composite attitude–behaviour model of traveler decision making', *Transportation Research B*, 15B, pp. 411–20.

Luce, R. D. and Suppes, P. (1965), 'Preference utility and subjective probability', in Luce, R. D., Bush, R. and Galanter, E. C. (eds), *Handbook of Mathematical Psychology, Vol. 3*, New York, John Wiley.

McCarthy, P. S. (1980), 'A study of the importance of generalised attributes in shopping choice behaviour', *Environment and Planning A*, 12, pp. 1269–86.

McFadden, D. (1974), 'Conditional logit analysis of qualitative choice behaviour', in Zarembka, P. (ed.), *Frontiers in Econometrics*, New York, Academic Press, pp. 105–42.

Macgill, S. M. and Wilson, A. G. (1979), 'Equivalences and similarities between some alternative urban and regional models', *Sistemi Urbani*, 1, pp. 9–40.

Maddala, G. S. (1983), *Limited-Dependent and Qualitative Variables in Econometrics*, Cambridge University Press.

Mahajan, V., Jain, A. K. and Ratchford, B. T. (:1978), 'Use of binary attributes in the multiplicative competitive interactive choice model', *Journal of Consumer Research*, 5, pp. 210–15.

Mahmoud, E. (1984), 'Accuracy in forecasting: a survey', *Journal of Forecasting*, 3, pp. 139–48.

Management Horizons (1986), 'Siting for retail profit growth: gravity versus magnetism', paper presented at *Financial Times* Conference on 'Retailing to 1996', London, May.

Massam, B. (1975), *Location and Space in Social Administration*, London, Edward Arnold.

Massy, W. F., Montgomery, D. B. and Morrison, D. G. (1970), *Stochastic Models of Buyer Behaviour*, Cambridge, Mass., MIT Press.

May, R. M. (1976), 'Simple mathematical models with very complicated dynamics', *Nature*, 261, pp. 459–67.

Miller, E. J. and Lerman, S. R. (1981), 'Disaggregate modelling and decisions of retail firms: a case study of clothing retailers', *Environment and Planning A*, 13, pp. 729–46.

Miller, E. J. and O'Kelly, M. E. (1983), 'Estimating shopping destination choice models from travel diary data', *Professional Geographer*, 35, pp. 440–9.

Moore, L. A. R. (1985), *Stated Preference Analysis: A Critical Review*, unpublished working paper, Department of Geography, University of Bristol.

Nakanishi, M. and Cooper, L. G. (1974), 'Parameter estimation of a multiplicative interaction model: least squares approach', *Journal of Marketing Research*, 11, pp. 303–11.

Nelson, R. (1958), *The Selection of Retail Locations*, New York, Dodge.

Newman, L. (1980), 'A method of hypermarket catchment area definition using location-allocation techniques', paper presented to the Regional Science Association Workshop on Hypermarket Impact Assessment, Coventry, May.

Norkett, P. (1985), 'Stack 'em high, sell 'em fast: the key to supermarket success', *Accountancy*, 96, pp. 74–9.

Nystuen, J. D. and Dacey, M. F. (1961), 'A graph theory interpretation of nodal regions', *Papers of the Regional Science Association*, 7, pp. 25–42.

O'Brien, L. G. and Guy, C. M. (1985), 'Locational variability in retail grocery prices', *Environment and Planning A*, 17, pp. 953–62.

O'Kelly, M. E. (1981), 'A model of the demand for retail facilities incorporating multistop, multipurpose trips', *Geographical Analysis*, 13, pp. 134–48.

Openshaw, S. (1975), *Some Theoretical and Applied Aspects of Spatial Interaction Shopping Models*, Norwich, Geoabstracts.

Openshaw, S. (1978a), *Using Models in Planning: A Practical Guide*, Corbridge, Retail Planning Associates.

Openshaw, S. (1978b), 'An empirical study of some zone-design criteria', *Environment and Planning A*, 10, pp. 781–94.

Openshaw, S. (1979), 'A methodology for using models for planning purposes', *Environment and Planning A*, 11, pp. 879–96.

Openshaw, S. (1984), 'Ecological fallacies and the analysis of areal census data', *Environment and Planning A*, 16, pp. 17–31.

Openshaw, S. and Taylor, P. J. (1981), 'The modifiable areal unit problem', in Wrigley, N. and Bennett, R. J. (eds), *Quantitative Geography: A British View*, London, Routledge & Kegan Paul, pp. 60–9.

Orcutt, G., Caldwell, S. and Wertheimer, R. (1976), *Policy Exploration Through Micro-Analytic Simulation*, Washington, Urban Institute.

Osman, T. (1985), 'Pay without pain', *Sunday Times*, 3 November.

Pinch, S. and Williams, A. (1983), 'Social class change in British cities', in Goddard, J. B. and Champion, A. G. (eds), *The Urban and Regional Transformation of Britain*, London, Methuen, pp. 135–59.

Porter, M. E. and Miller, V. E. (1985), 'How information gives you competitive advantage', *Harvard Business Review*, 63, 4, pp. 149–60.

Poston, T. and Wilson, A. G. (1977), 'Facility size vs distance travelled: urban services and the fold catastrophe', *Environment and Planning A*, 9, pp. 681–6.

Potter, R. B. (1977), 'Spatial patterns of consumer behaviour and perception in relation to the social class variable', *Area*, 9, pp. 153–6.

Quelch, J. A. and Takeuchi, H. (1981), 'Non-store marketing: fast track or slow?', *Harvard Business Review*, 59, pp. 75–84.

Recker, W. W. and Kostyniuk, L. P. (1978), 'Factors influencing destination choice for the urban grocery trip', *Transportation*, 7, pp. 19–33.

Reilly, W. J. (1929), *Methods for the study of Retail Relationships*, Bulletin No. 2944, University of Texas.

Reilly, W. J. (1931), *The Law of Retail Gravitation*, New York, Putman & Sons.

Retail and Distribution Management (1984), 'Victoria Wine Company completes Thorn/EMI installation', *Retail and Distribution Management*, 12, May/June, pp. 33–45.

Retail and Distribution Management (1985a), 'Tradanet launched by ANA and ICL', *Retail and Distribution Management*, 13, May/June, pp. 42–3.

Retail and Distribution Management (1985b), 'Comp-U-Card's home shopping service', *Retail and Distribution Management*, 13, Nov/Dec, p. 47.

Retail Business (1985a), 'Attitudes to technology in the retail trade', *Retail Business*, no. 331, pp. 15–18.

Retail Business (1985b), 'Distribution technology', *Retail Business*, no. 334, pp. 17–18.

ReVelle, C., Marks, D. and Liebman, J. (1970), 'An analysis of private and public sector location models', *Management Science*, 16, pp. 692–707.

Richards, M. G. and Ben-Akiva, M. E. (1975), *A Disaggregate Travel Demand Model*, Farnborough, Saxon House.

Rijk, F. J. A. and Vorst, A. C. F. (1983), 'Equilibrium points in an urban retail model and their connection with dynamical systems', *Regional Science and Urban Economics*, 13, pp. 383–99.

RMDP (1984), *Techniques for Shop Location*, Seminar Proceedings, Brighton, Sussex, RMDP, 21 June.

RMDP (1985), *Shop Location Analysis*, Conference Proceedings, Brighton, Sussex, RMDP, 25 June.

Robertson, I. (1976), 'Accessibility to services in the Argyll District of Strathclyde: a locational model', *Regional Studies*, 10, pp. 89–95.

Rogers, D. (1984), 'Modern methods of sales forecasting, B: Regression analysis', in Davies, R. L. and Rogers, D. (eds), *Store Location and Store Assessment Research*, Chichester, John Wiley, pp. 319–32.

Rogers, D. (1985), 'Research tools for better merchandising', *Retail and Distribution Management*, 13, Nov/Dec, pp. 42–4.

Rogers, D. and Green, H. L. (1979), 'A new perspective on forecasting store sales – applying statistical models and techniques in the analog approach', *Geographical Review*, 69, 4, pp. 449–58.

Rosenberg, L. J. and Hirschman, E. C. (1980), 'Retailing without stores', *Harvard Business Review*, 58, pp. 103–12.

Rowley, G. (1986), *Let's Talk Shop: Relocational Trends in British Retailing*, Hatfield, Chas. E. Good.

Roy, J. R. and Johansson, B. (1984), 'On planning and forecasting the location of retail and service activity', *Regional Science and Urban Economics*, 14, pp. 433–52.

Rushton, G. (1969), 'Analysis of spatial behaviour by revealed space preferences', *Annals of the Association of American Geographers*, 59, pp. 391–400.

Sawers, L. (1984), 'Microcomputers in retailing: a case study', in Piercy, N. (ed.), *The Management Implications of New Information Technology*, Beckenham, Croom Helm.

Schiller, R. and Lambert, S. (1977), 'The quantity of major shopping development in Britain since 1965', *Estates Gazette*, 242, no. 5839, pp. 359–63.

Schuler, H. J. (1979), 'A disaggregate store-choice model of spatial decision-making', *Professional Geographer*, 31, pp. 146–56.

Shepherd, I. D. H. and Thomas, C. J. (1980), 'Urban consumer behaviour', in Dawson, J. A. (ed.), *Retail Geography*, London, Croom Helm.

Sherwood, D. (1983), *Financial Modelling: A Practical Guide*, London, Van Nostrand Reinhold.

Simmons, M. (1984), 'Store assessment procedures', in Davies, R. L. and Rogers, D. (eds), *Store Location and Store Assessment Research*, Chichester, John Wiley, pp. 263–78.

Sleight, P. (1983), 'The Pinpoint approach to location', paper presented to RMDP Conference on Shop Location Analysis, London, February.

Smith, G. C. (1976), 'The spatial information fields of urban consumers', *Transactions of the Institute of British Geographers*, New Series 1, pp. 175–89.

Smith, P. (1974), *The Use of the Potential Surface Technique in Sub-Regional Planning*, Geographical Paper 30, Department of Geography, University of Reading.

Sobel, K. L. (1980), 'Travel demand forecasting by using the nested multinomial logit model', *Transportation Research Record*, 775, pp. 48–55.

Sparks, L. (1986), 'The changing structure of distribution in retail companies: an example from the grocery trade', *Transactions of the Institute of British Geographers*, New Series 11, pp. 147–54.

Spence, N. and Goddard, J. B. (1976), 'Population and employment trends in the British urban system, 1951–71', paper presented at Conference of Institute of British Geographers Quantitative Methods Study Group, University of Sheffield, September.

Stanley, T. J. and Sewall, M. A. (1976), 'Image inputs to a probabilistic model: predicting retail potential', *Journal of Marketing*, 40, pp. 48–53.

Stouffer, S. A. (1940), 'Intervening opportunities: a theory relating mobility and distance', *American Sociology Review*, 5, pp. 845–67.

Stouffer, S. A. (1960), 'Intervening opportunities and competing migrants', *Journal of Regional Science*, 2, pp. 1–26.

Strauss, L. (1983), *Electronic Marketing: Emerging TV and Computer Channels for Interactive Home Shopping*, White Plains, New York, Knowledge Industry Publications.

Taylor, A. (1984), 'The planning implications of new technology in retailing and distribution', *Town Planning Review*, 55, pp. 161–76.

Taylor, P. J. (1977), *Quantitative Methods in Geography*, Boston, Houghton Mifflin.

Thomas, C. J. (1974), 'The effects of social class and car ownership on intra-urban shopping behaviour in Greater Swansea', *Cambria*, 2, pp. 98–126.

Timmermans, H. J. P. (1981), 'Multiattribute shopping models and ridge regression analysis', *Environment and Planning A*, 13, pp. 43–56.

Timmermans, H. J. P. (1983), 'Non-compensatory decision rules and consumer spatial choice behaviour: a test of predictive ability', *Professional Geographer*, 35, pp. 449–55.

Timmermans, H. J. P. (1984), 'Decompositional multiattribute preference models in spatial choice analysis: a review of some recent developments', *Progress in Human Geography*, 8, pp. 189–221.

Timmermans, H. J. P. (1986), 'Locational choice behaviour of entrepreneurs: an experimental analysis', *Regional studies*, 23, pp. 231–40.

Timmermans, H. J. P., van der Heijden, R. and Westerveld, H. (1982), 'The identification of factors influencing destination choice: an application of the repertory grid methodology', *Transportation*, 11, pp. 189–203.

Timmermans, H. J. P., van der Heijden, R. and Westerveld, H. (1984), 'Decision making between multiattribute alternatives: a model of spatial shopping behaviour using conjoint measurements', *Environment and Planning A*, 16, pp. 377–87.

Tounsey, S. (1964), *Self Service Retailing*, London, Iliffe.

Towsey, R. (1972), 'Finding the right site', *Marketing*, June, pp. 40–2.

Tversky, A. (1969), 'Intransitivity of preferences', *Psychological Review*, 76, pp. 31–48.

Tversky, A. (1972), 'Elimination by aspects: a theory of choice', *Psychological Review*, 79, pp. 281–99.

Tye, W. B., Sherman, L., Kinnucan, M., Nelson, D. and Tardiff, T. (1982), *Application of Disaggregate Travel Demand Models*, National Cooperative Highway Research Program, Report 253, Washington, DC, Transportation Research Board.

Uncles, M. D. (1985), *Models of Consumer Shopping Behaviour in Urban Areas: Analysis of the Cardiff Consumer Panel*, unpublished PhD dissertation, Department of Geography, University of Bristol.

Uncles, M. D. (1987), 'A beta-logistic model of mode choice: goodness of fit and intertemporal dependence', *Transportation Research B*, vol. 21B, 195–205.

Uncles, M. D. and Ehrenberg, A. S. C. (1986), *Buying Patterns in the US Coffee Market*, CMaC Working Paper, London Business School.

Unit for Retail Planning Information (1982), *List of UK Hypermarkets and Superstores*, Reading, Unit for Retail Planning Information.

Vorst, A. C. F. (1985), 'A stochastic version of the urban retail model', *Environment and Planning A*, 17, pp. 1569–80.

Wade, B. (1983), 'Retail planning without data', *Planner*, 69, Jan/Feb, pp. 26–8.

Walters, D. (1974), 'Retail site location, time for a new approach?', *Retail and Distribution Management*, 2, 6, pp. 28–31.

Wellan, D. (1985), *Repeat-Buying of a Successful New Brand*, unpublished PhD dissertation, London Business School.

White, R. W. (1977), 'Dynamic central place theory: results of a simulation approach', *Geographical Analysis*, 9, pp. 226–43.

Whitehead, J. (1983), 'CORA: CACI's new classification of retail centres', paper presented to RMDP Conference on Shop Location Analysis, London, February.

Williams, H. C. W. L. (1977), 'On the formation of travel demand models and economic evaluation measures of user benefit', *Environment and Planning A*, 9, pp. 285–344.

Williams, H. C. W. L. and Ortuzar, J. D. (1982), 'Behavioural theories of dispersion and the mis-specification of travel demand models', *Transportation Research B*, 16B, pp. 167–219.

Williams, P. A. and Fotheringham, A. S. (1984), *The Calibration of Spatial, Interaction Models by Maximum Likelihood Estimation with Program SIMODEL*, Geographic Monograph Series, Vol. 7, Department of Geography, Indiana University.

Wilson, A. G. (1967), 'A statistical theory of spatial distribution models', *Transportation Research*, 1, pp. 253–69.

Wilson, A. G. (1970), *Entropy in Urban and Regional Modelling*, London, Pion.

Wilson, A. G. (1971), 'A family of spatial interaction models and associated developments', *Environment and Planning*, 3, pp. 1–32.

Wilson, A. G. (1974), *Urban and Regional Models in Geography and Planning*, Chichester and New York, John Wiley.

Wilson, A. G . (1976), 'Retailers' profits and consumers' welfare in a spatial ineraction shopping model', in Masser, I. (ed.), *Theory and Practice in Regional Science*, London Papers in Regional Science, Vol. 6, London, Pion.

Wilson, A. G. (1978), 'Spatial interaction and settlement structure: towards an explicit central place theory', in Karlqvist, A, Lundqvist, L. Snickars, F. and Weibull, J. W. (eds), *Spatial Interaction Theory and Planning Models*, Amsterdam, North-Holland, pp. 137–56.

Wilson, A. G. (1981a), *Catastrophe Theory and Bifurcation: Applications in Urban and Regional Geography*, London, Croom Helm.

Wilson, A. G. (1981b), *Geography and the Environment: Systems Analytical Methods*, Chichester, John Wiley.

Wilson, A. G. (1981c), 'The evolution of urban spatial structure: the evolution of theory', in Bennett, R. J. (ed.), *European Progress in Spatial Analysis*, London, Pion, pp. 201–25.

Wilson, A. G. (1983), *A Generalised and Unified Approach to the*

Modelling of Service-Supply Structures, Working Paper 352, School of Geography, University of Leeds.

Wilson, A. G. (1985), *Structural Dynamics and Spatial Analysis: From Equilibrium Balancing Models to Extended Economic Models for Both Perfect and Imperfect Markets*, Working Paper 431, School of Geography, University of Leeds.

Wilson, A. G. and Bennett, R. J. (1985), *Mathematical Methods in Human Geography and Planning*, Chichester, John Wiley.

Wilson, A. G. and Clarke, M. (1979), 'Some illustrations of catastrophe theory applied to urban retailing structures', in Breheny, M. (ed.), *Developments in Urban and Regional Analysis*, London, Pion, pp. 5–27.

Wilson, A. G. and Macgill, S. M. (1979), 'A systems analytical framework for comprehensive urban and regional model building', *Geographical Polonica*, 42, pp. 9–25.

Wilson, A. G. and Oulton, M. J. (1983), 'The corner-shop to supermarket transition in retailing: the beginnings of empirical evidence', *Environment and Planning A*, 15, pp. 265–74.

Wilson, A. G., Coehlo, J. D., Macgill, S. M. and Williams, H. C.W. L. (1981), *Optimisation in Locational and Transport Analysis*, Chichester, John Wiley.

Wilson, B. (1984), 'Modern methods of sales forecasting, B: regression models' in Davies, R. L. and Rogers, D. (eds), *Store Location and Store Assessment Research*, Chichester, John Wiley, pp. 301–18.

Wood Mackenzie (1985), *Market Place*, issue 2, London, Wood Mackenzie Business Publications.

Wrigley, N. (1980), 'An approach to the modelling of shop-choice patterns: an exploratory analysis of purchasing patterns in a British city', in Herbert, D. T. and Johnston, R. J. (eds), *Geography and the Urban Environment*, vol. 3, Chichester, John Wiley, pp. 45–85.

Wrigley, N. (1985), *Categorical Data Analysis for Geographers and Environmental Scientists*, London, Longman.

Wrigley, N. and Dunn, R. (1984a), 'Stochastic panel-data models of urban shopping behaviour: 1. Purchasing at individual stores in a single city', *Environment and Planning A*, 16, pp. 629–50.

Wrigley, N. and Dunn, R. (1984b), 'Stochastic panel-data models of urban shopping behaviour: 2. Multistore purchasing patterns and the Dirichlet model', *Environment and Planning A*, 16, pp. 759–78.

Wrigley, N. and Dunn, R. (1984c), 'Stochastic panel-data models of urban shopping behaviour: 3. The interaction of store choice and brand choice', *Environment and Planning A*, 16, pp. 1221–36.

Wrigley, N. and Dunn, R. (1985), 'Stochastic panel-data models of urban shopping behaviour: 4. Incorporating independent variables into the NBD and Dirichlet models', *Environment and Planning A*, 17, pp. 319–31.

Wrigley, N., Guy, C. M. and Dunn, R. (1984), 'Sunday and late-night shopping in a British city: evidence from the Cardiff Consumer Panel', *Area*, 16, pp. 236–40.

Wrigley, N., Guy, C. M., Dunn, R. and O'Brien, L. G. (1985), 'The Cardiff Consumer Panel: methodological aspects of the conduct of the long-term panel survey', *Transactions of the Institute of British Geographers*, New Series 10, pp. 63–76.

AUTHOR INDEX

Kishi, S., 249, 339
Kollat, D. T., 226, 335
Koppelman, F. S., 137, 339
Kornblau, C., 112, 339
Kostyniuk, L. P., 131, 342

Lakshmanan, T. R., 165, 339
Lambert, S., 11, 343
Landau, V., 138, 339
Leckenby, J. D., 249, 339
Leonardi, G., 57, 58, 59, 330, 339
Lerman, S. R., 341
Liebman, J., 58, 343
Lincoln, D. J., 130, 340
Lipsey, R. J., 335
Lloyd, R., 132, 340
Lodish, L. M., 88, 340
Lombardo, S. R., 340
Lord, J. D., 334
Losch, A., 164, 340
Louviere, J. J., 130, 140, 207, 340
Luce, R. D., 214, 340

McCarthy, P. S., 137, 204, 340
McFadden, D., 127, 340
Macgill, S. M., 99, 100, 177, 332, 340, 347
Mackie, S., 328
Maddala, G. S., 190, 340
Mahajan, V., 340
Mahmoud, E., 96, 341
Management Horizons, 13, 23, 341
March, L., 329
Marks, D., 58, 343
Massam, B., 59, 341
Massy, W. F., 216, 226, 336, 341
May, R. M., 176, 341
Meyer, R. J., 130, 140, 207, 340
Miller, E. J., 127, 341
Miller, V. E., 91, 342
Mock, D., 64, 339
Montgomery, D. B., 226, 341
Moore, L. A. R., 38, 203, 205, 341
Morrison, D. G., 227, 341
Moseley, J., 328
Mughal, R., 23, 333

Nakanishi, M., 140, 341
Nelson, D., 158n, 345
Nelson, R., 341
Newman, L., 59, 341
Nijkamp, P., 207, 330
Norkett, P., 18, 20–1, 341

Nystuen, J. D., 184–5, 341

O'Brien, L. G., 254, 337, 341, 348
O'Kelly, M. E., 127, 341
Openshaw, S., 92, 93, 96, 127, 138, 149, 331, 341, 342
Orcutt, G., 95, 342
Ortuzar, J. D., 127, 346
Osman, T., 307, 342
Oulton, M. J., 102, 170, 175, 347

Penny, N. J., 31, 33, 37, 41, 106
Pinch, S., 10, 342
Polking, J. C., 158n, 328
Porter, M. E., 91, 342
Poston, T., 342
Potter, R. B., 139, 342
Prashker, J. N., 138, 339

Quelch, J. A., 305, 342

Rabino, G. A., 340
Rainford, P., 328
Ratchford, B. T., 340
Reader, S., 226, 227, 228, 257, 335
Recker, W. W., 131, 342
Reibstein, D. J., 88, 340
Reilly, W. J., 165, 342
Retail and Distribution Management, 19, 307, 310, 318, 342
Retail Business, 306, 307, 343
ReVelle, C., 58, 343
Reynolds, D. R., 139, 338
Reynolds, J., 305, 307, 314, 315, 316, 334
Richards, M. G., 204, 343
Rijk, F. J. A., 343
RMDP, 343
Roberts, A. J., 53, 330
Roberts, M., 215, 328
Robertson, I., 59, 343
Rogers, D., 66, 67, 73, 76, 77, 96, 106, 322, 334, 343
Rosenberg, L. J., 305, 343
Rowley, G., 12, 343
Roy, J. R., 343
Ruston, G., 343

Saether, A., 329
Samli, A. C., 130, 340
Sawers, L., 310, 343
Schiller, R., 11, 343
Schuler, H. J., 130, 207, 343

SUBJECT INDEX